ESSAYS ON THE MAKING OF THE CONSTITUTION

ESSAYS ON THE MAKING OF THE CONSTITUTION

EDITED BY
Leonard W. Levy

SECOND EDITION

NEW YORK OXFORD

OXFORD UNIVERSITY PRESS

1987

OXFORD UNIVERSITY PRESS

Oxford   New York   Toronto
Delhi   Bombay   Calcutta   Madras   Karachi
Petaling Jaya   Singapore   Hong Kong   Tokyo
Nairobi   Dar es Salaam   Cape Town
Melbourne   Auckland

and associated companies in
Beirut   Berlin   Ibadan   Nicosia

Published by Oxford University Press, Inc.,
200 Madison Avenue, New York, New York 10016

Oxford is a registered trademark of Oxford University Press

Library of Congress Cataloging-in-Publication Data
Essays on the making of the Constitution.
  Bibliography: p.
  1. United States—Constitutional history.
I. Levy, Leonard Williams, 1923–
KF4541.E88   1987   342.73'029   86–16255
                         347.30229
ISBN 0–19–504902–0 (alk. paper)

9 8 7 6 5 4 3 2 1

Printed in the United States of America
on acid-free paper

To my Grandchildren
   Aaron
   Adam
   Natalie

CONTENTS

INTRODUCTION: THE MAKING
OF THE CONSTITUTION, 1776-1789

On July 4, 1776, King George III wrote in his diary, "Nothing of importance this day." When the news of the Declaration of Independence reached him, he still could not know how wrong he had been. The political philosophy of social compact, natural rights, and limited government that generated the Declaration of Independence also spurred the most important, creative, and dynamic constitutional achievements in history; the Declaration itself was merely the beginning. Within a mere thirteen years Americans invented or first institutionalized a bill of rights against all branches of government, the written constitution, the constitutional convention, federalism, judicial review, and a solution to the colonial problem (admitting territories to the Union as states fully equal to the original thirteen). Religious liberty, the separation of church and state, political parties, separation of powers, an acceptance of the principle of equality, and the conscious creation of a new nation were also among American institutional "firsts," although not all these initially appeared between 1776 and 1789. In that brief span of time, Americans created what are today the oldest major republic, political democracy, state constitution, and national constitution. These unparalleled American achievements derived not from originality in speculative theory but from the constructive application of old ideas, which Americans took so seriously that they constitutionally based their institutions of government on them.

From thirteen separate colonies the Second Continental Congress "brought forth a new nation," as Abraham Lincoln

From *Encyclopedia of the American Constitution*, ed. Leonard W. Levy (New York: Macmillan, 1986), under the title "Constitutional History, 1776–1789."

said. In May 1776, Congress urged all the colonies to suppress royal authority and adopt permanent governments. On that advice and in the midst of a war the colonies began to frame the world's first written constitutions. When Congress triggered the drafting of those constitutions, Virginia instructed its delegates to Congress to propose that Congress should declare "the United Colonies free and independent states." Neither Virginia nor Congress advocated state sovereignty. Congress's advice implied the erection of state governments with sovereign powers over domestic matters or "internal police."

On June 7, 1776, Congressman Richard Henry Lee of Virginia introduced the resolution as instructed, and Congress appointed two committees, one to frame the document that became the Declaration of Independence and the other to frame a plan of confederation—a constitution for a continental government. When Lincoln declared, "The Union is older than the States, and in fact created them as States," he meant that the Union (Congress) preexisted the states. The Declaration of Independence, which stated that the colonies had become states, asserted the authority of the "United States of America, in General Congress, Assembled."

The "spirit of '76" tended to be strongly nationalistic. The members of Congress represented the states, of course, and acted on their instructions, but they acted for the new nation, and the form of government they thought proper in 1776 was a centralized one. As a matter of fact Benjamin Franklin had proposed such a government on July 21, 1775, when he presented to Congress "Articles of Confederation and perpetual Union." Franklin urged a congressional government with an executive committee that would manage "general continental Business and Interests," conduct diplomacy, and administer finances. His plan empowered Congress to determine war and peace, exchange ambassadors, make foreign alliances, settle all disputes between the colonies, plant new colonies, and, in a sweeping omnibus clause, make laws for "the General Welfare" concerning matters on which individual colonies "cannot be competent," such as "our general Commerce," "general Currency," the establishment of a post office, and governance of "our Common Forces." Costs were to be paid from a common treasury supplied by each colony in proportion to its male inhabitants, but each colony would raise its share by taxing its inhabitants. Franklin provided for an easy amendment process: Congress recommended amendments that would become part of the Articles when approved by a majority of colonial assemblies. Franklin's plan of union seemed much too radical in July 1775, when independence was a year away and reconciliation with Britain on American terms was the object of the war. Congress simply tabled the Franklin plan.

As the war continued into 1776, nationalist sentiment strengthened. Thomas Paine's *Common Sense* called for American independence and "a Continental form of Government." Nationalism and centralism were twin causes. John Langdon of New Hampshire favored independence and "an American Constitution" that provided for appeals from every colony to a national congress "in everything of moment relative to governmental matters." Proposals for a centralized union became common by the spring of 1776, and those proposals, as the following representative samples suggest, tended to show democratic impulses. Nationalism and mitigated democracy, not nationalism and conservatism, were related. A New York newspaper urged the popular election of a national congress with a "superintending power" over the individual colonies as to "all commercial and Continental affairs," leaving to each colony control over its "internal policy." A populistic plan in a Connecticut newspaper recommended that the congress be empowered to govern "all matters of general concernment" and "every other thing proper and necessary" for the benefit of the whole, allowing the individual colonies only that which fell "within the territorial jurisdiction of a particular assembly." The "Spartacus" essays, which newspapers in New York,

Philadelphia, and Portsmouth printed, left the state "cantons" their own legislatures but united all in a national congress with powers similar to those enumerated by Franklin, including a paramount power to "interfere" with a colony's "provincial affairs" whenever required by "the good of the continent." "Essex" reminded his readers that "the strength and happiness of America must be Continental, not Provincial, and that whatever appears to be for the good of the whole, must be submitted to by every Part." He advocated dividing the colonies into many smaller equal parts that would have equal representation in a powerful national congress chosen directly by the people, including taxpaying widows. Carter Braxton, a conservative Virginian, favored aristocratic controls over a congress that could not "interfere with the internal police or domestic concerns of any Colony . . ."

Given the prevalence of such views in the first half of 1776, a representative committee of the Continental Congress probably mirrored public opinion when it framed a nationalist plan for confederation. On July 12, one month after the appointment of a thirteen-member committee (one from each state) to write a draft, John Dickinson of Pennsylvania, the committee chairman, presented to Congress a plan that borrowed heavily from Franklin's. The Committee of the Whole of Congress debated the Dickinson draft and adopted it on August 20 with few changes. Only one was significant. Dickinson had proposed that Congress be empowered to fix the western boundaries of states claiming territory to the Pacific coast and to form new states in the west. The Committee of the Whole, bending to the wishes of eight states with extensive western claims, omitted that provision from its revision of the Dickinson draft. That omission became a stumbling block.

On August 20 the Committee of the Whole reported the revised plan of union to Congress. The plan was similar to Franklin's, except that Congress had no power over "general commerce." But Congress, acting for the United States, was clearly paramount to the individual states. They were not even referred to as "states." Collectively they were "the United States of America"; otherwise they were styled "colonies" or "colony," terms not compatible with sovereignty, to which no reference was made. Indeed, the draft merely reserved to each colony "sole and exclusive Regulation and Government of its internal police, in all matters that shall not interfere with the Articles of this Confederation." That crucial provision, Article III, making even "internal police" subordinate to congressional powers, highlighted the nationalist character of the proposed confederation.

The array of congressional powers included exclusive authority over war and peace, land and naval forces, treaties and alliances, prize cases, crimes on the high seas and navigable rivers, all disputes between states, coining money, borrowing on national credit, Indian affairs, post offices, weights and measures, and "the Defence and Welfare" of the United States. Congress also had power to appoint a Council of State and civil officers "necessary for managing the general Affairs of the United States." The Council of State, consisting of one member from each of the thirteen, was empowered to administer the United States government and execute its measures. Notwithstanding this embryonic executive branch, the government of the United States was congressional in character, consisting of a single house whose members were to be elected annually by the legislatures of the colonies. Each colony cast one vote, making each politically equal in Congress. On all important matters, the approval of nine colonies was required to pass legislation. Amendments to the Articles needed the unanimous approval of the legislatures of the various colonies, a provision that later proved to be crippling.

The Articles reported by the Committee of the Whole provoked dissension. States without western land claims opposed the omission of the provision in the Dickinson draft that gave Congress control over western lands. Large states opposed the principle of one vote for each state, preferring instead proportionate representation with each delegate voting. Sharp differences also emerged concerning the rule by which each state was to pay its quota to defray common expenses. Finally some congressmen feared the centralizing nature of the new government. As Edward Rutledge of South Carolina said, "The Idea of destroying all Provincial Distinctions and making every thing of the most minute kind bend to what they call the good of the whole. . . ." Rutledge resolved "to vest the Congress with no more Power than what is absolutely necessary." James Wilson of Pennsylvania could declare that Congress represented "all the individuals of the states" rather than the states, but Roger Sherman of Connecticut answered, "We are representatives of states, not individuals." That attitude would undo the nationalist "spirit of '76."

Because of disagreements and the urgency of prosecuting the war, Congress was unable to settle on a plan of union in 1776. By the spring of 1777 the nationalist momentum was spent. By then most of the states had adopted constitutions and had legitimate governments. Previously, provisional governments of local "congresses," "conventions," and committees had controlled the states and looked to the Continental Congress for leadership and approval. But the creation of legitimate state governments reinvigorated old provincial loyalties. Local politicians, whose careers were provincially oriented, feared a strong central government as a rival institution. Loyalists no longer participated in politics, local or national, depleting support for central control. By late April of 1777, when state sovereignty triumphed, only seventeen of the forty-eight congressmen who had been members of the Committee of the Whole that adopted the Dickinson draft remained in Congress. Most of the new congressmen opposed centralized government.

James Wilson, who was a congressman in 1776 and 1777, recalled what happened when he addressed the Constitutional Convention on June 8, 1787:

Among the first sentiments expressed in the first Congs. one was that Virga. is no more. That Massts. is no more, that Pa. is no more &c. We are now one nation of brethren. We must bury all local interests and distinctions. This language continued for some time. The tables at length began to turn. No sooner were the State Govts. formed than their jealousy & ambition began to display themselves. Each endeavored to cut a slice from the common loaf, to add to its own morsel, till at length the confederation became frittered down to the impotent condition in which it now stands. Review the progress of the articles of Confederation thro' Congress & compare the first and last draught of it. [Farrand, ed., *Records*, I, 166–67]

The turning point occurred in late April 1777, when Thomas Burke of North Carolina turned his formidable localist opinions against the report of the Committee of the Whole. Its Article III, in his words, "expressed only a reservation (to the states) of the power of regulating the internal police, and consequently resigned every other power (to Congress)." Congress, he declared, sought even to interfere with the states' internal police and make its own powers "unlimited." Burke accordingly moved the following substitute for Article III, which became Article II of the Articles as finally adopted: "Each State retains its sovereignty, freedom and independence, and every power, jurisdiction and right, which is not by this confederation expressly delegated to the United States in Congress assembled." Burke's motion carried by the votes of eleven states, vitiating the powers of the national government recommended by the Committee of the Whole.

In the autumn of 1777 a Congress dominated by state-sovereignty advocates completed the plan of confederation. Those who favored proportionate representation in Congress with every member entitled to vote lost badly to those who favored voting by states with each state having one vote. Thereafter the populous wealthy states had no stake in supporting a strong national government that could be controlled by the votes of lesser states. The power of Congress to negotiate commercial treaties effectively died when Congress agreed that under the Articles no treaty should violate the power of the states to impose tariff duties or prohibit imports and exports. The power of Congress to settle all disputes between states became merely a power to make recommendations. The permanent executive branch became a temporary committee with no powers except as delegated by the votes of nine states, the number required to adopt any major measure. Congress also agreed that it should not have power to fix the western boundaries of states claiming lands to the Pacific.

After the nationalist spurt of 1776 proved insufficient to produce the Articles, the states made the Confederation feckless. Even as colonies the states had been particularistic, jealous, and uncooperative. Centrifugal forces originating in diversity— of economics, geography, religion, class structure, and race— produced sectional, provincial, and local loyalties that could not be overcome during a war against the centralized powers claimed by Parliament. The controversy with Britain had produced passions and principles that made the Franklin and Dickinson drafts unviable. Not even those nationalist drafts empowered Congress to tax, although the principle of no taxation without representation had become irrelevant as to Congress. Similarly, Congress as late as 1774 had "cheerfully" acknowledged Parliament's legitimate "regulation of our external commerce," but in 1776 Congress denied that Parliament had any authority over America, and by 1777 Americans were unwilling to grant their own central legislatures powers they preferred their provincial assemblies to wield. Above all, most states refused to repose their trust in any central authority that a few large states might dominate, absent a constitutionally based principle of state equality.

Unanimous consent for amendments to the Articles proved to be too high a price to pay for acknowledging the "sovereignty" of each state, although that acknowledgement made Maryland capable of winning for the United States the creation of a national domain held in common for the benefit of all. Maryland also won the promise that new states would be admitted to the union on a principle of state equality. That prevented the development of a colonial problem from Atlantic to Pacific and with the Northwest Ordinance of 1787 was the Confederation's finest and most enduring achievement.

The Constitution of 1787 was unthinkable in 1776, impossible in 1781 or at any time before it was framed. The Articles were an indispensable transitional stage in the development of the Constitution. Not even the Constitution would have been ratified if its framers had submitted it for approval to the state legislatures that kept Congress paralyzed in the 1780s. Congress, representing the United States, authorized the creation of the states and ended up, as it had begun, as their creature. It possessed expressly delegated powers with no means of enforcing them. That Congress lacked commerce and tax powers was a serious deficiency, but not nearly so crippling as its lack of sanctions and the failure of the states to abide by the Articles. Congress simply could not make anyone, except soldiers, do anything. It acted on the states, not on people. Only a national government that could execute its laws independently of the states could have survived.

The states flouted their constitutional obligations. The Articles obliged the states to "abide by the determinations of the United States, in Congress assembled," but there was no way to force the states to comply. The states were not sovereign, except as to their internal police and tax powers; rather, they behaved unconstitutionally. No foreign nation recognized the states as sovereign, because Congress possessed the external attributes of sovereignty especially as to foreign affairs and war powers.

One of the extraordinary achievements of the Articles was the creation of a rudimentary federal system. It failed because its central government did not operate directly on individuals within its sphere of authority. The Confederation had no independent executive and judicial branches, because the need for them scarcely existed when Congress addressed its acts mainly to the states. The framers of the Articles distributed the powers of government with remarkable acumen, committing to Congress about all that belonged to a central government except, of course, taxation and commercial regulation, the two powers that Americans of the Revolutionary War believed to be part of state sovereignty. Even Alexander Hamilton, who in 1780 advocated that Congress should have "complete sovereignty," excepted "raising money by internal taxes."

Congress could requisition money from the states, but they did not pay their quotas. In 1781 Congress requisitioned $8,000,000 for the next year, but the states paid less than half a million. While the Articles lasted the cumulative amount paid by all the states hardly exceeded what was required to pay the interest on the public debt for just one year.

Nationalists vainly sought to make the Articles more effective by both interpretation and amendment. Madison devised a theory of implied powers by which he squeezed out of the Articles congressional authority to use force if necessary against states that failed to fulfill their obligations. Congress refused to attempt coercion just as it refused to recommend an amendment authorizing its use. Congress did, however, charter a bank to control currency, but the opposition to the exercise of a power not expressly delegated remained so intense that the bank had to be rechartered by a state. Congress vainly sought unanimous state consent for various amendments that would empower it to raise money from customs duties and to regulate commerce, foreign and domestic. In 1781 every state but Rhode Island approved an amendment empowering Congress to impose a five percent duty on all foreign imports; never again did an amendment to the Articles come so close to adoption. Only four states ratified an amendment authorizing a congressional embargo against the vessels of any nation with whom the United States had no treaty of commerce. Congress simply had no power to negotiate commercial treaties with nations such as Britain that discriminated against American shipping. Nor had Congress the power to prevent states from violating treaties with foreign nations. In 1786 John Jay, Congress's Secretary of Foreign Affairs, declared that not a day had passed since ratification of the 1783 treaty of peace without its violation by at least one state. Some states also discriminated against the trade of others. Madison likened New Jersey, caught between the ports of Philadelphia and New York, "to a cask tapped at both ends." More important, Congress failed even to recommend needed amendments. As early as 1784 Congress was so divided it defeated an amendment that would enable it to regulate commerce, foreign and domestic, and to levy duties on imports and exports. Often Congress could not function for lack of a quorum. The requisite number of states was present for only three days between October 1785 and April 1786. In 1786 Congress was unable to agree on any amendments for submission to the states.

The political condition of the United States during the 1780s stagnated partly because of the constitutional impotence of Congress and the unconstitutional conduct of the states. The controversy with Britain had taught that liberty and localism were congruent. The 1780s taught that excessive localism was incompatible with nationhood. The Confederation was a necessary point of midpassage. It bequeathed to the United States the fundamentals of a federal system, a national domain, and a solution to the colonial problem. Moreover the Articles contained several provisions that were antecedents of their counterparts in the Constitution of 1787: a free speech clause for congressmen and legislative immunity, a privileges and immunities clause, a clause on the extradition of fugitives from justice, a full faith and credit clause, and a clause validating United States debts. The Confederation also started an effective government bureaucracy when the Congress in 1781 created secretaries for foreign affairs, war, marine, and finance—precursors of an executive branch. When the new departments of that branch began to function in 1789, a corps of experienced administrators, trained under the Articles, staffed them. The courts established by Congress to decide prize and admiralty cases as well as boundary disputes foreshadowed a national judiciary. Except for enactment of the great Northwest Ordinance, however, the Congress of the Confederation was moribund by 1787. It had successfully prosecuted the war, made foreign alliances, established the national credit, framed the first constitution of the United States, negotiated a favorable treaty of peace, and created a national domain. Congress's accomplishments were monumental, especially during wartime, yet in the end it failed.

By contrast, state government flourished. Excepting Rhode Island and Connecticut, all the states adopted written constitutions during the war, eight in 1776. Madison exultantly wrote, "Nothing has excited more admiration in the world than the manner in which free governments have been established in America, for it was the first instance, from the creation of the world that free inhabitants have been seen deliberating on a form of government, and selection of such of their citizens as possessed their confidence to determine upon and give effect to it."

The Virginia Constitution of 1776, the first permanent state constitution, began with a Declaration of Rights adopted three weeks before the Declaration of Independence. No previous bill of rights had restrained all branches of government. Virginia's reflected the widespread belief that Americans had been thrown back into a state of nature from which they emerged by framing a social compact for their governance, reserving to themselves certain inherent or natural rights, including life, liberty, the enjoyment of property, and the pursuit of happiness. Virginia's declaration explicitly declared that as all power derived from the people, for whose benefit government existed, the people could reform or abolish government when it failed them. On the basis of this philosophy Virginia framed a constitution providing for a bicameral legislature, a governor, and a judicial system. The legislature elected a governor, who held office for one year, had no veto power, and was encumbered by an executive council. The legislature chose many important officials, including judges.

Some states followed the more democratic model of the Pennsylvania Constitution of 1776, others the ultraconservative one of Maryland, but all state constitutions prior to the Massachusetts Constitution of 1780 were framed by legislatures, which in some states called themselves "conventions" or assemblies. Massachusetts deserves credit for having originated a new institution of government, a specially elected constitutional convention whose sole function was to frame the constitution and submit it for popular ratification. That procedure became the standard. Massachusetts's constitution, which is still operative, became the model American state constitution. The democratic procedure for making it fit the emerging theory that the sovereign people should be the source of the constitution and authorize its framing by a constitutional convention, rather than the legislature to which the constitution is paramount. Massachusetts was also the first state to give more than lip service to the principle of separation of powers. Everywhere else, excepting perhaps New York, unbalanced government and legislative supremacy prevailed. Massachusetts established the precedent for a strong, popularly elected executive with a veto power; elsewhere the governor tended to be a ceremonial head who depended for his existence on the legislature.

The first state constitutions and related legislation introduced significant reforms. Most states expanded voting rights by reducing property qualifications, and a few, including Vermont (an independent state from 1777 to 1791), experimented with universal manhood suffrage. Many state constitutions provided for fairer apportionment of representation in the legislature. Every southern state either abolished its establishment of religion or took major steps to achieve separation of church and state. Northern states either abolished slavery or provided for its gradual ending. Criminal codes were made more humane. The confiscation of Loyalist estates and of crown lands, like the opening of a national domain westward to the Mississippi, led to a democratization of land holding, as did the abolition of feudal relics like the law of primogeniture and entail. The pace of democratic change varied from state to state, and in some states was nearly imperceptible, but the Revolution without doubt occasioned constitutional and political developments that had long been dammed up under the colonial system.

The theory that a constitution is supreme law encouraged the development of judicial review. Written constitutions with bills of rights and the emerging principle of separation of powers contributed to the same end. Before the Revolution appellate judges tended to be dependents of the executive branch; the Revolution promoted judicial independence. Most state constitutions provided for judicial tenure during good behavior rather than for a fixed term or the pleasure of the appointing power. Inevitably when Americans believed that a legislature had exceeded its authority they argued that it had acted unconstitutionally, and they turned to courts to enforce the supreme law as law. The dominant view, however, was that for a court to hold a statute unconstitutional insulted the sovereignty of the legislature, as the reactions to *Holmes v. Walton* (1780) and *Trevett v. Weeden* (1786) showed. *Commonwealth v. Caton* (1782) was probably the first case in which a state judge declared that a court had power to hold a statute unconstitutional, though the court in the case sustained the act before it. In *Rutgers v. Waddington* (1784), Hamilton as counsel argued that a state act violating a treaty was unconstitutional, but the court declared that the judicial power advocated by counsel was "subversive of all government." Counsel in *Trevett* also contended that the court should void a state act. Arguments of counsel do not create precedents but can reveal the emergence of a new idea. Any American would have agreed that an act against a constitution was void; although few would have agreed that courts have the final powers to decide matters of constitutionality, that idea was spreading. The *Ten Pound Act Cases* (1786) were the first in which an American court held a state enactment void, and that New Hampshire precedent was succeeded by a similar decision in the North Carolina case of *Bayard v. Singleton* (1787). The principle of *Marbury v. Madison* (1803) thus originated at a state level before the framing of the federal Constitution.

The Constitution originated in the drive for a strong national government that preceded the framing of the Articles of Confederation. The "critical period" of 1781–87 intensified that drive, but it began well before the defects of the Articles expanded the ranks of the nationalists. The weaknesses of the United States in international affairs, its inability to enforce the peace treaty, its financial crisis, its helplessness during Shays's Rebellion, and its general incapacity to govern resulted in many proposals—in Congress, in the press, and even in some states—for national powers to negotiate commercial treaties, regulate the nation's commerce, and check state policies that adversely affected creditor interests and impeded economic growth. Five states met at the Annapolis Convention in 1786, ostensibly to discuss a "uniform system" of regulating commerce, but those who masterminded the meeting had a much larger agenda in mind—as Madison put it, a "plenipotentiary Convention for amending the Confederation."

Hamilton had called for a "convention of all the states" as early as 1780, before the Articles were ratified, to form a government worthy of the nation. Even men who defended state sovereignty conceded the necessity of a convention by 1787. William Grayson admitted the "the present Confederation is utterly inefficient and that if it remains much longer in its present State of imbecility we shall be one of the most contemptible Nations on the face of the earth. . . ." Luther Martin admitted that Congress was "weak, contemptibly weak," and Richard Henry Lee believed that no government "short of force, will answer." "Do you not think," he asked George Mason, "that it ought to be declared . . . that any State act of legislation that shall contravene, or oppose, the authorized acts of Congress, or interfere with the expressed rights of that body, shall be *ipso facto* void, and of no force whatsoever?" Many leaders, like Thomas Jefferson, advocated executive and judicial branches for the national government with "an appeal from state judicatures to a federal court in all cases where the act of Confederation controlled the question. . . ." Rufus King, who also promoted a "vigorous Executive," thought that the needed power of Congress to regulate all commerce "can never be well exercised without a Federal Judicial." A consensus was developing.

The Annapolis Convention exploited and nurtured that consensus when it recommended to all the states and to Congress that a constitutional convention "meet at Philadelphia on the second Monday in May next (1787), to take into consideration the situation of the United States, to devise such further provisions as shall appear to them necessary to render the constitution of the federal government adequate to the exigencies of the Union. . . ." Several states, including powerful Virginia and Pennsylvania, chose delegates for the Philadelphia convention, forcing Congress to save face on February 21, 1787, by adopting a motion in accord with the Annapolis recommendation, although Congress declared that the "sole and express purpose" of the convention was "revising the articles of confederation."

The Constitutional Convention of 1787, which formally organized itself on May 25, lasted almost four months, yet reached its most crucial decision almost at the outset. The first order of business was the nationalistic Virginia Plan (May 29), and the first vote of the Convention, acting as a Committee of the Whole, was the adoption of a resolution "that a *national* Government ought to be established consisting of a *supreme* legislative, Executive and Judiciary" (May 30). Thus the Convention immediately agreed on abandoning, rather than amending, the Articles; on writing a new Constitution; on creating a national government that would be supreme; and on having it consist of three branches.

The radical character of this early decision may be best understood by comparing it with the Articles. The Articles failed mainly because there was no way to force the states to fulfill their obligations or to obey the exercise of such powers as Congress did possess. "The great and radical vice in the construction of the existing Confederation," said Alexander Hamilton, "is the principle of legislation for states or governments, in their corporate capacities, and as contradistinguished from the individuals of which they consist." The Convention remedied that vital defect in the Article, as George Mason pointed out (May 30), by agreeing on a government that "could directly operate on individuals." Thus the framers solved the critical problem of sanctions by establishing a national government that was independent of the states.

On the next day, May 31, the Committee of the Whole made other crucial decisions with little or no debate. One, reflecting the nationalist bias of the Convention, was the decision to establish a bicameral system whose larger house was to be elected directly by the people rather than by the state legislatures. Mason, no less, explained, "Under the existing confederacy, Congress represent the States not the people of the States; their acts operate on the States, not on the individuals. The case will be changed in the new plan of Government. The people will be represented; they ought therefore to choose the

Representatives." Another decision of May 31 was to vest in the Congress the sweeping and undefined power, recommended by the Virginia Plan, "to legislate in all cases to which the separate States are incompetent; or in which the harmony of the U.S. may be interrupted by the exercise of individual (state) legislation; to negative all laws passed by the several States contravening in the opinion of the National Legislature the articles of Union, or any treaties subsisting under the authority of the Union." Not a state voted "nay" to this exceptionally nationalistic proposition. Nor did any state oppose the decision of the next day to create a national executive with similarly broad, undefined powers.

After deliberating for two weeks, the Committee of the Whole presented the Convention with its recommendations, essentially the adoption of the Virginia Plan. Not surprisingly, several of the delegates had second thoughts about the hasty decisions that had been made. Gerry reiterated "that it was necessary to consider what the people would approve." Scrapping the Articles contrary to instructions and failing to provide for state equality in the system of representation provoked a reconsideration along lines described by William Paterson of New Jersey as "federal" in contradistinction to "national." Yet injured state pride was a greater cause of dissension than were the powers proposed for the national government. Some delegates were alarmed, not because of an excessive centralization of powers in the national government, but because of the excessive advantages given to the largest states at the expense of the others. Three states—Virginia, Massachusetts, and Pennsylvania—had forty-five percent of the white population in the country. Under the proposed scheme of proportionate representation, the small states feared that the large ones would dominate the others by controlling the national government.

On June 15, therefore, Paterson of New Jersey submitted for the Convention's consideration a substitute plan. It was a small states plan rather than a states' rights one, for it too had a strong nationalist orientation. Contemplating a revision, rather than a scrapping, of the Articles, it retained the unicameral Congress with its equality of state representation, thus appeasing the small states. But the plan vested in Congress one of the two critical powers previously lacking: "to pass Acts for the regulation of trade and commerce," foreign and interstate. The other, the power of taxation, appeared only in a stunted form; Congress was to be authorized to levy duties on imports and to pass stamp tax acts. Except for its failure to grant full tax powers, the Paterson Plan proposed the same powers for the national legislature as the finished Constitution. The Plan also contained the germ of the national supremacy clause of the Constitution, Article Six, by providing that acts of Congress and United States treaties "shall be the supreme law of the respective States . . . and that the Judiciary of the several States shall be bound thereby in their decisions, any thing in the respective laws of the Individual States to the contrary notwithstanding." The clause also provided for a federal judiciary with extensive jurisdiction and for an executive who could muster the military of the states to compel state obedience to the supreme law. Compulsion of states was unrealistic and unnecessary. Paterson himself declared that the creation of a distinct executive and judiciary meant that the government of the Union could "be exerted on individuals."

Despite its nationalist features, the Paterson Plan retained a unicameral legislature, in which the states remained equal, and the requisition system of rising a revenue, which had failed. "You see the consequence of pushing things too far," said John Dickinson of Delaware to Madison. "Some of the members from the small States wish for two branches in the General Legislature and are friends to a good National Government; but we would sooner submit to a foreign power than submit to be deprived of an equality of suffrage in both branches of the Legislature, and thereby be thrown under the domination of the large states." Only a very few dissidents were irreconcilably opposed to "a good National Government." Most of the disidents were men like Dickinson and Paterson, "friends to a good National Government" if it preserved a wider scope for small state authority and influence.

When Paterson submitted his plan on June 15, the Convention agreed that to give it "a fair deliberation," it should be referred to the Committee of the Whole and that "in order to place the two plans in due comparison, the other should be recommitted." After debating the two plans, the Committee of the Whole voted in favor of reaffirming the original recommendations based on the Virginia Plan "as preferable to those of Mr. Paterson." Only three weeks after their deliberations, had begun the framers decisively agreed, for the second time, on a strong, independent national government that would operate directly on individuals without the involvement of states.

But the objections of the small states had not yet been satisfied. On the next day, Connecticut, which had voted against the Paterson Plan, proposed the famous Great Compromise: proportionate representation in one house, "provided each State had an equal voice in the other." On that latter point the Convention nearly broke up, so intense was the conflict and deep the division. The irreconcilables in this instance were the leaders of the large-state nationalist faction, otherwise the most constructive and influential members of the Convention: Madison and James Wilson. After several weeks of debate and deadlock, on July 16 the Convention narrowly voted for the compromise. With ten states present, five supported the compromise, four opposed (including Virginia and Pennsylvania), and Massachusetts was divided. The compromise saved small-state prestige and saved the Convention from failure.

Thereafter consensus on fundamentals was restored, with Connecticut, New Jersey, and Delaware becoming fervent supporters of Madison and Wilson. A week later, for example, there was a motion that each state should be represented by two senators who would "vote per capita," that is, as individuals. Luther Martin of Maryland protested that per capita voting conflicted with the very idea of "the States being represented," yet the motion carried, with no further debate, 9–1.

On many matters of structure, mechanics, and detail there were angry disagreements, but agreement prevailed on the essentials. The office of the presidency is a good illustration. That there should be a powerful chief executive provoked no great debate, but the Convention almost broke up, for the second time, on the method of electing him. Some matters of detail occasioned practically no disagreement and revealed the nationalist consensus. Mason, of all people, made the motion that one qualification of Congressmen should be "citizenship of the United States," and no one disagreed. Under the Articles of Confederation, there was only state citizenship; that there should be a concept of national citizenship seemed natural to men framing a constitution for a nation. Even more a revelation of the nationalist consensus was the fact that three of the most crucial provisions of the Constitution—the taxing power, the necessary-and-proper clause, and the supremacy clause—were casually and unanimously accepted without debate.

Until midway during its sessions, the Convention did not take the trouble to define with care the distribution of power between the national government and the states, although the very nature of the "federal" system depended on that distribution. Consensus on fundamentals once again provides the explanation. There would be no difficulty in making that distribution; and, the framers had taken out insurance, because at the very outset, they had endorsed the provision of the Virginia Plan vesting broad, undefined powers in a national legislature that would act on individuals. Some byplay of July 17 is illuminating. Roger Sherman of Connecticut thought that the line drawn between the powers of Congress and those left to the states was so vague that national legislation might "interfere . . . in any matters of internal police which respect the Government of such States only, and wherein the general welfare of the United States is not concerned." His motion to protect the "internal police" of the states brought no debaters to his side and was summarily defeated; only Maryland supported Connecticut. Immediately after, another small-state delegate, Gunning Bedford of Delaware, shocked even Edmund Randolph of Virginia, who had presented the Virginia Plan, by a motion to extend the powers of Congress by vesting authority "to legislate in all cases for the general interest of the Union." Randolph observed, "This is a formidable idea indeed. It involves the power of violating all the laws and constitution of the States, of intermeddling with their police." Yet the motion passed.

On July 26 the Convention adjourned until August 6 to allow a Committee on Detail to frame a "constitution conformable to the Resolutions passed by the Convention." Generously construing its charge, the committee acted as a miniature convention and introduced a number of significant changes. One was the explicit enumeration of the powers of Congress to replace the vague, omnibus provisions adopted previously by the Convention. Although enumerated, those powers were liberally expressed and formidable in their array. The committee made specific the spirit and intent of the Convention. Significantly the first enumerated power was that of taxation and the second that of regulating commerce among the states and with foreign nations: the two principal powers that had been withheld from Congress by the Articles. When the Convention voted on the provision that Congress "shall have the power to lay and collect taxes, duties, imposts and excises," the states were unanimous and only one delegate, Gerry, was opposed. When the Convention next turned to the commerce power, there was no discussion and even Gerry voted affirmatively.

Notwithstanding its enumeration of the legislative powers, all of which the Convention accepted, the Committee on Detail added an omnibus clause that has served as an ever-expanding source of national authority: "And to make all laws that shall be necessary and proper for carrying into execution the foregoing powers." The Convention agreed to that clause without a single dissenting vote by any state or delegate. The history of the great supremacy clause, Article Six, shows a similar consensus. Without debate the Convention adopted the supremacy clause, and not a single state or delegate voted nay. Finally, Article One, Section 10, imposing restrictions on the economic powers of the states with respect to paper money, *ex post facto* laws, bills of credit, and contracts, also reflected a consensus in the Convention. In sum, consensus, rather than compromise, was the most significant feature of the convention, outweighing in importance the various compromises that occupied most of the time of the delegates.

But why was there such a consensus? There have been many interpretations of the framing and ratification of the Constitution, and Charles Beard managed to endorse most of them, at one point or another in his career, as well as dominate any discussion of them. In *The Supreme Court and the Constitution* (1912), he wrote, "It is not merely patriotic pride that compels one to assert that never in the history of assemblies has there been a convention of men richer in political experience and in practical knowledge, or endowed with a profounder insight into the springs of human action and the intimate essence of government." This estimate, which brings to mind Jefferson's more succinct judgment of the Constitutional Convention as "an assembly of demigods," is not necessarily inconsistent with Beard's most famous book, *An Economic Interpretation of the Constitution* (1913), but the tone is altogether different. The *Economic Interpretation* is written in the same spirit that would describe the performances of a great violin virtuoso as the scraping of horse hair on dried cats' guts. Beard explained the consensus by construing the Constitution as a conservative economic document framed by an unrepresentative minority employing undemocratic means to protect personal property interests by establishing a central government responsive to their needs and able to thwart populistic majorities in the states. He viewed the Constitution as the work of personalty interests, that is, of personal property interests as opposed to realty interests, in short, as Beard put it, "capital as opposed to land." Minority business groups—manufacturers, merchants, shippers, speculators in land values, and above all, public securities holders—manipulated the call for the Convention in the hope of obtaining what Beard called "the adoption of a revolutionary program." They dominated the Convention in whose outcome they had a direct, immediate, personal stake. They wrote what is essentially an economic document consisting of two basic parts. The first or positive part comprised four great powers to be vested in the new national government: war, taxation, commerce, and control of western lands. Thus the government could protect business against foreign competition and from internal disruption on the part of desperate debtors like the Shaysites, and with its ample revenues could pay the claims of public creditors. The second basic part of the Constitution was negative in character, comprising the restrictions on the economic powers of the states. The same groups that wrote the Constitution also dominated the state conventions that ratified it, their opposition deriving mainly from small farmers and debtors.

Another prong of the Beard thesis was that the Constitution was an undemocratic document, indeed that it was the work of a conspiratorial, reactionary group, operating in an undemocratic society and utilizing undemocratic methods for the purpose of hamstringing democratic majorities by an elaborate system of checks and balances. There was no popular vote on the calling of the convention; and, property qualifications for voting and officeholding excluded both the propertyless masses and the small farmer, debtor interests from participating in the framing and ratification of the Constitution. The scrapping of the Articles and the submission of the Constitution for ratification by nine specially elected state conventions, contrary to the requirements in the Articles for unanimous approval by the state legislatures, were, said Beard, revolutionary acts which if performed by a Napoleon would be pronounced a coup d'état. About three-fourths of the adult men failed to vote on the Constitution; it was ratified by probably not more than one-sixth of the adult men, and in five states there is doubt whether a majority of those voting actually approved of ratification despite the action of their respective conventions.

Since the *Economic Interpretation*, historians have engaged in a prolonged debate on questions raised by Board either directly or indirectly. Were the framers enlightened, disinterested statesmen seeking to rescue—indeed to create—a nation then dangerously drifting toward anarchy? Were they conspiratorial representatives of a rising financial and industrial capitalism? Were they the leaders of a Thermidorian reaction to the Articles of Confederation which embodied the democratic principles of the Declaration of Independence? Was the Constitution mainly an economic or a political document? If its chief significance was political, was it the product of a clash and compromise between large and small states, or between town and tidewater against farm and frontier, or between conflicting north-south sectionalisms? Or, was the political conflict between men of nationalist principles and those devoted to states' rights, or between an aristocratic elite and the localist forces of democratic majoritarianism? In short was the Constitution an undemocratic document framed and ratified by an undemocratic minority for an undemocratic society? Or, were the framers practical, though masterly, politicians keenly conscious of the need for popular approval if their work was to be accepted? Did they substantially and even necessarily play the great game of politics according to the prevailing rules when radically reconstructing the American governmental system? These are among the questions to which the historians represented in this anthology address themselves.

The answers to the question, why did the extraordinary consensus at the Constitutional Convention exist, are the obvious ones. In the first place, opponents either did not get elected or, if elected, stayed away or walked out. In the second place, experience had proved that the nationalist constitutional position was right. If the United States was to survive and flourish, a strong national government had to be established. The framers of the Constitution were accountable to public opinion; the Convention was a representative body. That its members were prosperous, well-educated political leaders made them no less representative than Congress. The state legislatures, which elected the members of the Convention, were the most unlikely instruments for thwarting the popular will. The Framers, far from being able to do as they pleased, were not free to promulgate the Constitution. Although they adroitly arranged for its ratification by nine state ratifying conventions rather than by all state legislatures, they could not present a plan that the people of the states would not tolerate. They could not control the membership of those state ratifying conventions. They could not even be sure that the existing Congress would submit the Constitution to the states for ratification, let alone for ratification by state conventions that had to be specially elected. If the Framers got too far astray from public opinion, their work would have been wasted. The consensus in the Convention coincided with an emerging consensus in the country that recaptured the nationalist spirit of '76. That the Union had to be strengthened was an almost universal American belief.

For its time the Constitution was a remarkably democratic document framed by comparatively democratic methods. The procedure of the Articles of Confederation for constitutional amendment was not democratic, because it allowed Rhode Island, with one-sixtieth of the nation's population, to exercise a veto power. The Convention sent its Constitution to the lawfully existing government, the Congress of the Confederation, for submission to the states, and Congress, which could have censured the Convention for exceeding its authority, freely complied—and thereby exceeded its own authority under the Articles! A coup d'etat ordinarily lacks the deliberation and consent that marked the making of the Constitution and is characterized by a military element that was wholly lacking in 1787. A Convention elected by the state legislatures and consisting of many of the foremost leaders of their time deliberated for almost four months. Its members included many opponents of the finished scheme. The nation knew the Convention was considering changes in the government. The proposed Constitution was made public, and voters in every state were asked to choose delegates to vote for or against it after open debate. The use of state ratifying conventions fit the theory that a new fundamental law was being adopted and, therefore, conventions were proper for the task.

The Constitution guaranteed to each state a republican or representative form of government and fixed no property or religious qualifications on the right to vote or hold office, at a time when such qualifications were common in the states. The Convention, like the Albany Congress of 1754, the Stamp Act Congress, the Continental Congresses, and the Congresses of the Confederation, had been chosen by state (or colonial) legislatures, but the Constitution created a Congress whose lower house was popularly elected. When only three states directly elected their chief executive officer, the Constitution provided for the indirect election of the President by an Electoral College that originated in the people and is still operative. The Constitution's system of separation of powers and elaborate checks and balances was not intended to refine out popular influence on government but to protect liberty; the framers divided, distributed, and limited powers to prevent one branch, faction, interest, or section from becoming too powerful. Checks and balances were not undemocratic, and the Federalists were hard pressed not to apologize for checks and balances but to convince the Anti-Federalists, who wanted far more checks and balances, that the Constitution had enough. Although the Framers were not democrats in a modern sense, their opponents were even less democratic. Those opponents sought to capitalize on the lack of a Bill of Rights, and ratification of the Constitution became possible only because leading Federalists committed themselves to amendments as soon as the new government went into operation. At that time, however, Anti-Federalists opposed a Bill of Rights, because it would allay popular fears of the new government, ending the chance for state sovereignty amendments.

Although the Framers self-consciously refrained from referring to slavery in the Constitution, it recognized slavery, the most undemocratic of all institutions. That recognition was a grudging but necessary price of Union. The three-fifths clause of Article I provided for counting three-fifths of the total number of slaves as part of the population of a state in the apportionment of representation and direct taxation. Article IV, section 2, provided for rendition of fugitive slaves to the slaveholder upon his claim. On the other hand, Article I, section 9, permitted Congress to abolish the slave trade in twenty years. Most delegates, including many from slaveholding states, would have preferred a Constitution untainted by slavery; but Southern votes for ratification required recognition of slavery. By choosing a Union with slavery, the Convention deferred the day of reckoning and made ratification possible.

The Constitution is basically a political document. Modern scholarship has discredited the once popular view, associated with Charles Beard, that the Constitution was undemocratically made to advance the economic interests of personalty groups, chiefly creditors. The largest public creditor at the Convention was Elbridge Gerry, who refused to sign the Constitution and opposed its ratification, and the largest private creditor was George Mason who did likewise. Indeed seven men who either quit the Convention in disgust or refused to sign the Constitution seem to have held public securities that were worth over twice the holdings of the thirty-nine men who signed the Constitution. The most influential framers, among them Madison, Wilson, Paterson, Dickinson, and Gouverneur Morris, owned no securities. Others, like Washington, who acted out of patriotism, not profit, held trifling amounts. Eighteen members of the Convention were either debtors or held property that depreciated after the new government became operative. On crucial issues at the Convention, as in the state ratifying conventions, the dividing line between groups for and against the Constitution was not economic, not between realty and personalty, or debtors and creditors, or town and frontier. The restrictions of Article I, section 10 on the economic powers of the states were calculated to protect creditor interests and promote business stability, but those restrictions were not undemocratic; if impairing the obligations of contracts or emitting bills of credit and paper money were democratic hallmarks, the Constitution left Congress free to be democratic. The interest groups for and against the Constitution were substantially similar. Economic interests did influence the voting on ratification, but no simple explanation that ignores differences between states and even within states will suffice, and many noneconomic influences were also at work. In the end the Constitution was framed and ratified because most voters came to share the vision held by Franklin in 1775 and Dickinson in 1776; those two, although antagonists in Pennsylvania politics, understood for quite different reasons that a strong central government was indispensable for nationhood.

The members of the Constitutional Convention of 1787 had seemingly belied their reputations as tough-minded realists on the most crucial of all issues. They had behaved, rather, like innocent idealists for whom politics is the art of the impossible, because they framed a constitutional blueprint for the kind of government that history and political theory had proved to be not only unprecedented but impossible. It was to be "one grand federal republic," rhapsodized a supporter, for which "the world was too young to furnish a parallel." That indeed was precisely what made the proposed Constitution so different and frightening, for as the same writer acknowledged, "It is generally agreed, that a great extended nation can long continue under no single form of government, except a despotism. . . ."

Men did not then take for granted that a national government for all of the states could survive and preserve liberty. Opponents of the Constitution shared Patrick Henry's conviction that a continent-wide republican form of government "contradicts all the experience of the world." A fellow Virginian, Richard Henry Lee, argued that "a free elective government cannot be extended over large territories," a proposition that Elbridge Gerry of Massachusetts, a member of the Constitutional Convention who refused to sign its handiwork, converted into "an insuperable objection to the adoption of the new system." Robert Yates of New York, who walked out of the Convention in disgust, contended that liberty would be "swallowed up," because thirteen states were too big for a republican government. James Winthrop of Massachusetts invoked the opinion of past sages to prove that the idea of a large republic was a dangerous absurdity unless "made up of a confederacy of smaller states." George Clinton of New York explained that the immensity and complexity of the United States—it had so large a population and such dissimilar climates, economies, morals, politics, and peoples—proved the "intuitive truth" that a "consolidated republican form of government" could not possibly achieve any of the great objectives stated in the preamble to the Constitution. In sum, the minority members of the Pennsylvania ratifying convention epitomized the nearly universal view among Anti-Federalists when they declared, "We dissent, first, because it is the opinion of the most celebrated writers on government, and confirmed by uniform experience, that a very extensive territory cannot be governed on the principles of freedom, otherwise than by a confederation of republics."

Although these proved to be the views of a minority, the dangers to which they referred were real enough, increasing the natural difficulties attending the American experiment with a national union. The federal system was a novelty; the centralization of powers in the national government was awesome; and the lack of a national bill of rights was intimidating. No other republic had, in fact, been so vast, and no nation had ever begun its political existence without first achieving a cultural nationalism. The extraordinary diversity of the United States was commonly regarded as a handicap; it was composed of too many governments, local traditions, religions, races, national stocks, and economic interests to be a good bet for survival. In the face of so many centrifugal forces, there was no king, no national church, no army, and few centripetal loyalties to provide unity. Unique political forms only seemed to compound the problem and make even more "impracticable" and "visionary," in Gerry's words, the national enterprise designed by the framers of the Constitution.

If, seemingly, their politics was the art of the impossible, the most influential artist among them was James Madison of Virginia. He argued persuasively that opponents of the Constitution had confused a republic with a direct democracy. The latter alone was limited by geographic distance and population so that the citizens might meet together and exercise the government in person; but in a republic the citizens governed through elected representatives, and if they could meet as needed in some central place, size and numbers did not matter. As for America's great diversity, it was the very safeguard of liberty, an insurance that no one class, or religion, or section, or interest, or faction could become too powerful, jepardizing the liberty of others. Diversity constituted a natural system of checks and balances, making for an equilibrium of powers that ensured liberty. Moreover, Madison explained, the Constitution contained an elaborate scheme of checks and balances contributing to the same end, and chief among these was the distribution of powers between the national government and the states. Had the Constitution concentrated all government authority in the national government, the worst fears of its misinterpreters who spoke of "consolidation" would be justified. But the government's jurisdiction extended only to specific, enumerated objects; its powers were expressly delegated, leaving all others to the states.

But the Constitutional Convention had blundered. It had provided for a strong new national government that would operate directly on individuals, yet the Founders had omitted a bill of rights. They had compounded the blunder by explicitly protecting a few selected rights (see final essay in this volume), thereby provoking the legitimate fear that all the remaining rights that had been omitted stood in jeopardy. The blunder jeopardized ratification and made politically indispensable the ten amendments that collectively are cherished as the Bill of Rights, without which the Constitution would have been incomplete—and would have failed to secure popular commitment to the new system.

ESSAYS ON THE MAKING OF THE CONSTITUTION

AN ECONOMIC INTERPRETATION OF
THE CONSTITUTION
Charles A. Beard

EDITOR'S NOTE To opponents of reform in the
years before World War I, the Constitution as judi-
cially construed was an implacable and unimpeach-
able bulwark of the status quo. In 1913, however,
Charles A. Beard of Columbia University appeared
to demonstrate irrefutably and with all the para-
phernalia of scientific scholarship that the venerated
Constitution was itself the product of economic interests rather than of ultimate juristic truths. The
book, *An Economic Interpretation of the Constitution of the United States*, immediately became
one of the weapons in the reformers' armory. When
the celebrated volume was republished in 1935,
Beard denied that it had been written to support
or oppose the Progressives of 1913. He professed
to be bewildered why conservatives should have
condemned the book and reformers should have
praised it with equal fervor. He was but an impartial scholar, he claimed, and, by implication, a
humble one, for he had not said that his was "the"
history of the making of the Constitution, not even
that it was "the" economic interpretation, only that
it was "an" economic interpretation. The framers
themselves, he wrote, had emphasized the impor-

tance of economic interests on political forces and on the making of the Constitution, and he had simply followed their lead. He had merely balanced the conventional view of the Constitution as a victory of disinterested national patriots over their narrow, localistic opponents. From a scholarly standpoint, he pointed out, there was nothing partisan about using an economic interpretation; it was a neutral instrument of analysis. He had not, he added heatedly, condemned men on either side of the struggle of 1787–88 and certainly had not accused the framers of seeking to line their own pockets. He argued, too, that he had distinguished an economic interpretation from economic determinism.

That an economic interpretation of history was a two-edged sword which cut the Jeffersonians more deeply than the Hamiltonians Beard himself revealed in his *Economic Origins of Jeffersonian Democracy* (1915). Indeed, careful readers of the earlier work should have observed that Beard admired the framers, Hamilton even more than Madison. Buried in a footnote is the statement that "the present writer believes that the success of the national government could not have been secured under any other policy than that pursued by Hamilton." At one point in the text, Beard said of the framers that "as practical men they were able to build the new government upon the only foundations which could be stable: fundamental economic interests." In his preface to the 1935 edition, he wrote that the framers were "among the great practicing statesmen of all ages." If the book showed the Constitution to be a product of its time, thereby aiding the reformers of 1913, his preceding book, *The Supreme Court and the Constitution*, published just the year before in 1912, damaged their cause. Reform-minded scholars, jurists, politicians, and journalists, seeking to discredit conservative judicial decisions purportedly based on the Constitution, attacked the courts, spoke of judicial review as a usurpation of power unintended by the framers, and demanded either the recall of judges or of their decisions. Yet the thesis of *The Supreme Court and the Constitution* was that the framers had intended judicial review.

That earlier and less known book was, in fact, a dress rehearsal of its celebrated successor. In 1912 Beard had already depicted the framers as representatives of "the solid, conservative, commercial and financial interests of the country," who, having been "made desperate by the imbecilities of the Confederation and harried by state legislatures . . . drew together in a mighty effort to establish a government that would be strong enough to pay the national debt, regulate interstate and foreign commerce, provide for the national defence, prevent fluctuations in the currency created by paper emissions, and control the propensities of legislative majorities to attack private rights." The principle of judicial control, he added, harmonized with the purpose of the Constitution. Its opponents were "radicals" who viewed government, especially if highly centralized, as an evil. The system of checks and balances imposed by the Constitution safeguarded property interests against the radical majority. Chapter four, in particular, contained the essence of the 1913 volume except for one major difference: the 1913 one relied heavily on Treasury Department records to "prove" that the "dynamic element" among the conservative nationalists was the holder of public securities.

Ironically Beard himself abandoned the "Beard thesis" in later books. He maintained it in his general history, *The Rise of American Civilization* (1927), but in the 1940's, in three books (*The Re-*

public, the *Basic History of the United States*, and *The Enduring Federalist*), he adopted a conventional political interpretation, cast along lines of conservative nationalism that recalled the nineteenth-century works of filiopietism that the early Beard had so forcefully repudiated and ridiculed.

○   ○   ○   ○

A SURVEY of the economic interests of the members of the Convention presents certain conclusions:

A majority of the members were lawyers by profession.

Most of the members came from towns, on or near the coast, that is, from the regions in which personalty was largely concentrated.

Not one member represented in his immediate personal economic interests the small farming or mechanic classes.

The overwhelming majority of members, at least five-sixths, were immediately, directly, and personally interested in the outcome of their labors at Philadelphia, and were to a greater or less extent economic beneficiaries from the adoption of the Constitution.

1. Public security interests were extensively represented in the Convention. Of the fifty-five members who attended no less than forty appear on the Records of the Treasury Department for sums varying from a few dollars up to more than one hundred thousand dollars. Among the minor holders were Bassett, Blount, Brearley, Broom, Butler, Carroll, Few, Hamilton, L. Martin, Mason, Mercer, Mifflin, Read, Spaight, Wilson, and Wythe. Among the larger holders (taking the sum of about $5000 as the criterion) were Baldwin, Blair, Clymer, Dayton, Ellsworth, Fitzsimons, Gilman, Gerry, Gorham, Jenifer, Johnson, King, Langdon, Lansing, Livingston, McClurg, R. Morris, C. C. Pinckney, C. Pinckney, Randolph, Sherman, Strong, Washington, and Williamson.

It is interesting to note that, with the exception of New York, and possibly Delaware, each state had one or more prominent representatives in the Convention who held more than a negligible amount of securities, and who could therefore speak with feeling and authority on the question of providing in the new Constitution for the full discharge of the public debt:

Langdon and Gilman, of New Hampshire.

Gerry, Strong, and King, of Massachusetts.

Ellsworth, Sherman, and Johnson, of Connecticut.

Hamilton, of New York. Although he held no large amount personally, he was the special pleader for the holders of public securities and the maintenance of public faith.

Dayton, of New Jersey.

Robert Morris, Clymer, and Fitzsimons, of Pennsylvania.

Mercer and Carroll, of Maryland.

Blair, McClurg, and Randolph, of Virginia.

Williamson, of North Carolina.

The two Pinckneys, of South Carolina.

Few and Baldwin, of Georgia.

2. Personalty invested in lands for speculation was represented by at least fourteen members: Blount, Dayton, Few, Fitzsimons, Franklin, Gilman, Gerry, Gorham, Hamilton, Mason, R. Morris, Washington, Williamson, and Wilson.

3. Personalty in the form of money loaned at interest was represented by at least twenty-four members: Bassett, Broom, Butler, Carroll, Clymer, Davie, Dickinson, Ellsworth, Few, Fitzsimons, Franklin, Gilman, Ingersoll, Johnson, King, Langdon, Mason, McHenry, C. C. Pinckney, C. Pinckney, Randolph, Read, Washington, and Williamson.

4. Personalty in mercantile, manufacturing, and shipping lines was represented by at least eleven members: Broom, Clymer, Ellsworth, Fitzsimons, Gerry, King, Langdon, McHenry, Mifflin, G. Morris, and R. Morris.

5. Personalty in slaves was represented by at least fifteen

members: Butler, Davie, Jenifer, A. Martin, L. Martin, Mason, Mercer, C. C. Pinckney, C. Pinckney, Randolph, Read, Rutledge, Spaight, Washington, and Wythe.

It cannot be said, therefore, that the members of the Convention were "disinterested." On the contrary, we are forced to accept the profoundly significant conclusion that they knew through their personal experiences in economic affairs the precise results which the new government that they were setting up was designed to attain. As a group of doctrinaires, like the Frankfort assembly of 1848, they would have failed miserably; but as practical men they were able to build the new government upon the only foundations which could be stable: fundamental economic interests.

The Underlying Political Science of the Constitution

Before taking up the economic implications of the structure of the federal government, it is important to ascertain what, in the opinion of *The Federalist*, is the basis of all government. The most philosophical examination of the foundations of political science is made by Madison in the tenth number. Here he lays down, in no uncertain language, the principle that the first and elemental concern of every government is economic.

1. "The first object of government," he declares, is the protection of "the diversity in the faculties of men, from which the rights of property originate." The chief business of government, from which, perforce, its essential nature must be derived, consists in the control and adjustment of conflicting economic interests. After enumerating the various forms of propertied interests which spring up inevitably in modern society, he adds: "The regulation of these various and interfering interests forms the principal task of modern legislation, and involves the spirit of party and faction in the ordinary operations of the government."

2. What are the chief causes of these conflicting political forces with which the government must concern itself? Madison answers. Of course fanciful and frivolous distinctions have sometimes been the cause of violent conflicts; "but the most common and durable source of factions has been the various and unequal distribution of property. Those who hold and those who are without property have ever formed distinct interests in society. Those who are creditors, and those who are debtors, fall under a like discrimination. A landed interest, a manufacturing interest, a mercantile interest, a moneyed interest, with many lesser interests grow up of necessity in civilized nations, and divide them into different classes actuated by different sentiments and views."

3. The theories of government which men entertain are emotional reactions to their property interests. "From the protection of different and unequal faculties of acquiring property, the possession of different degrees and kinds of property immediately results; *and from the influence of these on the sentiments and views of the respective proprietors, ensues a division of society into different interests and parties.*" Legislatures reflect these interests. "What," he asks, "are the different classes of legislators but advocates and parties to the causes which they determine." There is no help for it. "The causes of faction cannot be removed," and "we well know that neither moral nor religious motives can be relied on as an adequate control."

4. Unequal distribution of property is inevitable, and from it contending factions will rise in the state. The government will reflect them, for they will have their separate principles and "sentiments"; but the supreme danger will arise from the fusion of certain interests into an overbearing majority, which Madison, in another place, prophesied would be the landless proletariat,—an overbearing majority which will make its "rights" paramount, and sacrifice the "rights" of the minority. "To secure the public good," he declares, "and private rights

against the danger of such a faction and at the same time preserve the spirit and the form of popular government is then the great object to which our inquiries are directed."

5. How is this to be done? Since the contending classes cannot be eliminated and their interests are bound to be reflected in politics, the only way out lies in making it difficult for enough contending interests to fuse into a majority, and in balancing one over against another. The machinery for doing this is created by the new Constitution and by the Union. (*a*) Public views are to be refined and enlarged "by passing them through the medium of a chosen body of citizens." (*b*) The very size of the Union will enable the inclusion of more interests so that the danger of an overbearing majority is not so great. "The smaller the society, the fewer probably will be the distinct parties and interests composing it; the fewer the distinct parties and interests, the more frequently will a majority be found of the same party. . . . Extend the sphere, and you take in a greater variety of parties and interests; you make it less probable that a majority of the whole will have a common motive to invade the rights of other citizens; or if such a common motive exists, it will be more difficult for all who feel it to discover their strength and to act in unison with each other."

Q.E.D., "in the extent and proper structure of the Union, therefore, we behold a republican remedy for the diseases most incident to republican government.". . .

[Beard then explained how the Constitution provided for a balance of powers that prevented the rise of overbearing majorities which might threaten private rights. The House was elected directly by the people, though only for two-year terms. The Senate, however, was elected for by the state legislatures for six years and with staggered terms, while the President was chosen by electors elected in turn by the people every four years, and the Supreme Court was appointed for life by the President with the concurrence of the Senate, both of which were removed from the direct popular control and held longer terms than the House. No two branches were chosen by the same source or held office for the same period. Thus it was improbable that any interest group or combination of them could dominate the government by forming an alliance of the three branches. "The keystone of the whole structure," Beard added, was judicial review, "the most unique contribution to the science of government which has been made by American political genius." The framers intended that the Supreme Court should pass upon the constitutionality of acts of Congress, thereby insuring that its great powers would not go unchecked if abused.]

Nevertheless, it may be asked why, if the protection of property rights lay at the basis of the new system, there is in the Constitution no provision for property qualifications for voters or for elected officials and representatives. This is, indeed, peculiar when it is recalled that the constitutional history of England is in a large part a record of conflict over the weight in the government to be enjoyed by definite economic groups, and over the removal of the property qualifications early imposed on members of the House of Commons and on the voters at large. But the explanation of the absence of property qualifications from the Constitution is not difficult.

The members of the Convention were, in general, not opposed to property qualifications as such, either for officers or voters. "Several propositions," says Mr. S. H. Miller, "were made in the federal Convention in regard to property qualifications. A motion was carried instructing the committee to fix upon such qualifications for members of Congress. The committee could not agree upon the amount and reported in favor of leaving the matter to the legislature. Charley Pinckney objected to this plan as giving too much power to the first legislature. . . . Ellsworth objected to a property qualification on account of the difficulty of fixing the amount. If it was made high enough for the South, it would not be applicable to the Eastern States. Franklin was the only speaker who opposed the proposition to require property on principle, saying that 'some of the greatest rogues he was ever acquainted with were the richest rogues.' A resolution was also carried to require a property qualification for the Presidency. Hence it was evident that the lack of all property requirements for office in the United States Constitution was not owing to any opposition of the convention to such qualifications per se."

Propositions to establish property restrictions were defeated, not because they were believed to be inherently opposed to the genius of American government, but for economic reasons —strange as it may seem. These economic reasons were clearly set forth by Madison in the debate over landed qualifications for legislators in July, when he showed, first, that slight property qualifications would not keep out the small farmers whose paper money schemes had been so disastrous to personalty; and, secondly, that landed property qualifications would exclude from Congress the representatives of "those classes of citizens who were not landholders," i.e. the personalty interests. This was true, he thought, because the mercantile and manufacturing classes would hardly be willing to turn their personalty into sufficient quantities of landed property to make them eligible for a seat in Congress.

The other members also knew that they had most to fear from the very electors who would be enfranchised under a slight freehold restriction, for the paper money party was everywhere bottomed on the small farming class. As Gorham remarked, the elections at Philadelphia, New York, and Boston, "where the merchants and mechanics vote, are at least as good as those made by freeholders only." The fact emerges, therefore, that the personalty interests reflected in the Convention could, in truth, see no safeguard at all in a freehold qualification against the assaults on vested personalty rights which had been made by the agrarians in every state. And it was obviously impossible to establish a personalty test, had they so desired, for there would have been no chance of securing a ratification of the Constitution at the hands of legislatures chosen by freeholders, or at the hands of conventions selected by them. . . .

Indeed, there was little risk to personalty in thus allowing the Constitution to go to the states for approval without any property qualifications on voters other than those which the state might see fit to impose. Only one branch of new government, the House of Representatives, was required to be elected by popular vote; and, in case popular choice of presidential electors might be established, a safeguard was secured by the indirect process. Two controlling bodies, the Senate and Supreme Court, were removed altogether from the possibility of popular election except by constitutional amendment. Finally, the conservative members of the Convention were doubly fortified in the fact that nearly all of the state constitutions then in force provided real or personal property qualifications for voters anyway, and radical democratic changes did not seem perilously near.

The Powers Conferred upon the Federal Government

1. The powers for positive action conferred upon the new government were few, but they were adequate to the purposes of the framers. They included, first, the power to lay and collect taxes; but here the rural interests were conciliated by the provision that direct taxes must be apportioned among the states according to population, counting three-fifths of the slaves. This, in the opinion of contemporaries eminently qualified to speak, was designed to prevent the populations of the manufacturing states from shifting the burdens of taxation to the sparsely settled agricultural regions.

In a letter to the governor of their state, three delegates from North Carolina, Blount, Spaight, and Williamson, explained the advantage of this safeguard on taxation to the southern planters and farmers: "We had many things to hope from a National Government and the chief thing we had to fear from such a Government was the risque of unequal or heavy Taxation, but we hope you will believe as we do that the Southern states in general and North Carolina in particular are well secured on that head by the proposed system. It is provided in the 9th section of article the first that no Capitation or direct Tax shall be laid except in proportion to the number of inhabitants, in which number five blacks are only counted as three. If a land tax is laid, we are to pay the same rate; for example, fifty citizens of North Carolina can be taxed no more for all their Lands than fifty Citizens in one of the Eastern States. This must be greatly in our favour, for as most of their farms are small and many of them live in Towns we certainly have, one with another, land of twice the value that they possess. When it is also considered that five Negroes are only to be charged the same Poll Tax as three whites, the advantage must be considerably increased under the proposed Form of Government. The Southern states have also a better security for the return of slaves who might endeavour to escape than they had under the original Confederation."

The taxing power was the basis of all other positive powers, and it afforded the revenues that were to discharge the public debt in full. Provision was made for this discharge in Article VI to the effect that "All debts contracted and engagements entered into before the adoption of this Constitution shall be valid against the United States under this Constitution as under the Confederation."

But the cautious student of public economy, remembering the difficulties which Congress encountered under the Articles of Confederation in its attempts to raise the money to meet the interest on the debt, may ask how the framers of the Constitution could expect to overcome the hostile economic forces which had hitherto blocked the payment of the requisitions.

The answer is short. Under the Articles, Congress had no power to lay and collect taxes immediately; it could only make requisitions on the state legislatures. Inasmuch as most of the states relied largely on direct taxes for their revenues, the demands of Congress were keenly felt and stoutly resisted. Under the new system, however, Congress is authorized to lay taxes on its own account, but it is evident that the framers contemplated placing practically all of the national burden on the consumer. The provision requiring the apportionment of direct taxes on a basis of population obviously implied that such taxes were to be viewed as a last resort when indirect taxes failed to provide the required revenue.

With his usual acumen, Hamilton conciliates the freeholders and property owners in general by pointing out that they will not be called upon to support the national government by payments proportioned to their wealth. Experience has demonstrated that it is impracticable to raise any considerable sums by direct taxation. Even where the government is strong, as in Great Britain, resort must be had chiefly to indirect taxation. The pockets of the farmers "will reluctantly yield but scanty supplies, in the unwelcome shape of impositions on their houses and lands; and personal property is too precarious and invisible a fund to be laid hold of in any other way than by the imperceptible agency of taxes on consumption." Real and personal property are thus assured a generous immunity from such burdens as Congress had attempted to impose under the Articles; taxes under the new system will, therefore, be less troublesome than under the old.

2. Congress was given, in the second place, plenary power to raise and support military and naval forces, for the defence of the country against foreign and domestic foes. These forces were to be at the disposal of the President in the execution of national laws; and to guard the states against renewed attempts of "desperate debtors" like Shays, the United States

15

guaranteed to every commonwealth a republican form of government and promised to aid in quelling internal disorder on call of the proper authorities.

The army and navy are considered by the authors of *The Federalist* as genuine economic instrumentalities. As will be pointed out below, they regarded trade and commerce as the fundamental cause of wars between nations; and the source of domestic insurrection they traced to class conflicts within society. "Nations in general," says Jay, "will make war whenever they have a prospect of getting anything by it"; and it is obvious that the United States dissevered and discordant will be the easy prey to the commercial ambitions of their neighbors and rivals.

The material gains to be made by other nations at the expense of the United States are so apparent that the former cannot restrain themselves from aggression. France and Great Britain feel the pressure of our rivalry in the fisheries; they and other European nations are our competitors in navigation and the carrying trade; our independent voyages to China interfere with the monopolies enjoyed by other countries there; Spain would like to shut the Mississippi against us on one side and Great Britain fain would close the St. Lawrence on the other. The cheapness and excellence of our productions will excite their jealousy, and the enterprise and address of our merchants will not be consistent with the wishes or policy of the sovereigns of Europe. But, adds the commentator, by way of clinching the argument, "if they see that our national government is efficient and well administered, our trade prudently regulated, our militia properly organized and disciplined, our resources and finances discreetly managed, our credit re-established, our people free, contented, and united, they will be much more disposed to cultivate our friendship than provoke our resentment."

All the powers of Europe could not prevail against us. "Under a vigorous national government the natural strength and resources of the country, directed to a common interest, would baffle all the combinations of European jealousy to restrain our growth. . . . An active commerce, an extensive navigation, and a flourishing marine would then be the off-spring of moral and physical necessity. We might defy the little arts of the little politicians to control or vary the irre-sistible and unchangeable course of nature." In the present state of disunion the profits of trade are snatched from us; our commerce languishes; and poverty threatens to overspread a country which might outrival the world in riches.

The army and navy are to be not only instruments of de-fence in protecting the United States against the commercial and territorial ambitions of other countries; but they may be used also in forcing open foreign markets. What discrimina-tory tariffs and navigation laws may not accomplish the sword may achieve. The authors of *The Federalist* do not contem-plate that policy of mild and innocuous isolation which was later made famous by Washington's farewell address. On the contrary—they do not expect the United States to change human nature and make our commercial classes less ambitious than those of other countries to extend their spheres of trade. A strong navy will command the respect of European states. "There can be no doubt that the continuance of the Union under an efficient government would put it within our power, at a period not very distant, to create a navy which, if it could not vie with those of the great maritime powers, would at least be of respectable weight if thrown into the scale of either of two contending parties. . . . A few ships of the line sent op-portunely to the reinforcement of either side, would often be sufficient to decide the fate of a campaign, on the event of which interests of the greatest magnitude were suspended. Our position is, in this respect, a most commanding one. And if to this consideration we add that of the usefulness of sup-plies from this country, in the prosecution of military opera-tions in the West Indies, it will be readily perceived that a situation so favorable would enable us to bargain with great advantage for commercial privileges. A price would be set not only upon our friendship, but upon our neutrality. By a steady adherence to the Union, we may hope, ere long, to become the arbiter of Europe in America, and to be able to incline the balance of European competitions in this part of the world as our interest may dictate."

As to dangers from class wars within particular states, the authors of *The Federalist* did not deem it necessary to make extended remarks: the recent events in New England were only too vividly impressed upon the public mind. "The tempestuous situation from which Massachusetts has scarcely emerged," says Hamilton, "evinces that dangers of this kind are not merely speculative. Who can determine what might have been the issue of her late convulsions, if the malcontents had been headed by a Caesar or by a Cromwell." The strong arm of the Union must be available in such crises.

In considering the importance of defence against domestic insurrection, the authors of *The Federalist* do not overlook an appeal to the slave-holders' instinctive fear of a servile revolt. Naturally, it is Madison whose interest catches this point and drives it home, by appearing to discount it. In dealing with the dangers of insurrection, he says: "I take no notice of any unhappy species of population abounding in some of the states who, during the calm of regular government are sunk below the level of men; but who, in the tempestuous scenes of civil violence, may emerge into human character and give a superiority of strength to any party with which they may associate themselves."

3. In addition to the power to lay and collect taxes and raise and maintain armed forces on land and sea, the Constitution vests in Congress plenary control over foreign and interstate commerce, and thus authorizes it to institute protective and discriminatory laws in favor of American interests, and to create a wide sweep for free trade throughout the whole

American empire. A single clause thus reflects the strong impulse of economic forces in the towns and young manufacturing centres. In a few simple words the mercantile and manufacturing interests wrote their *Zweck im Recht*; and they paid for their victory by large concessions to the slave-owning planters of the south.

While dealing with commerce in *The Federalist* Hamilton does not neglect the subject of interstate traffic and intercourse. He shows how free trade over a wide range will be to reciprocal advantage, will give great diversity to commercial enterprise, and will render stagnation less liable by offering more distant markets when local demands fall off. "The speculative trader," he concludes, "will at once perceive the force of these observations and will acknowledge that the aggregate balance of the commerce of the United States would bid fair to be much more favorable than that of the thirteen states without union or with partial unions."

4. Another great economic antagonism found its expression in the clause conferring upon Congress the power to dispose of the territories and make rules and regulations for their government and admission to the Union. In this contest, the interests of the states which held territories came prominently to the front; and the ambiguity of the language used in the Constitution on this point may be attributed to the inability of the contestants to reach precise conclusions. The leaders were willing to risk the proper management of the land problem after the new government was safely launched; and they were correct in their estimate of their future political prowess.

These are the great powers conferred on the new government: taxation, war, commercial control, and disposition of western lands. Through them public creditors may be paid in full, domestic peace maintained, advantages obtained in dealing with foreign nations, manufactures protected, and the development of the territories go forward with full swing. The remaining powers are minor and need not be examined here. What implied powers lay in the minds of the framers likewise need not be inquired into; they have long been the subject of juridical speculation.

None of the powers conferred by the Constitution on Congress permits a direct attack on property. The federal government is given no general authority to define property. It may tax, but indirect taxes must be uniform, and these are to fall upon consumers. Direct taxes may be laid, but resort to this form of taxation is rendered practically impossible, save on extraordinary occasions, by the provision that they must be apportioned according to population—so that numbers cannot transfer the burden to accumulated wealth. The slave trade may be destroyed, it is true, after the lapse of a few years; but slavery as a domestic institution is better safeguarded than before.

Restrictions Laid Upon State Legislatures

Equally important to personalty as the positive powers conferred upon Congress to tax, support armies, and regulate commerce were the restrictions imposed on the states. Indeed, we have the high authority of Madison for the statement that of the forces which created the Constitution, those property interests seeking protection against omnipotent legislatures were the most active.

In a letter to Jefferson, written in October, 1787, Madison elaborates the principle of federal judicial control over state legislation, and explains the importance of this new institution in connection with the restrictions laid down in the Constitution on laws affecting private rights. "The mutability of the laws of the States," he says, "is found to be serious evil. The injustice of them has been so frequent and so flagrant as to alarm the most steadfast friends of Republicanism. I am persuaded I do not err in saying that the evils issuing from these sources contributed more to that uneasiness which produced the Convention, and prepared the public mind for a general reform, than those which accrued to our national character and interest from the inadequacy of the Confederation to its immediate objects. A reform, therefore, which does not make provision for private rights must be materially defective."

Two small clauses embody the chief demands of personalty against agrarianism: the emission of paper money is prohibited and the states are forbidden to impair the obligation of contract. The first of these means a return to a specie basis—when coupled with the requirement that the gold and silver coin of the United States shall be the legal tender. The Shays and their paper money legions, who assaulted the vested rights of personalty by the process of legislative depreciation, are now subdued forever, and money lenders and security holders may be sure of their operations. Contracts are to be safe, and whoever engages in a financial operation, public or private, may know that state legislatures cannot destroy overnight the rules by which the game is played.

A principle of deep significance is written in these two brief sentences. The economic history of the states between the Revolution and the adoption of the Constitution is compressed in them. They appealed to every money lender, to every holder of public paper, to every man who had any personalty at stake. The intensity of the economic interests reflected in these two prohibitions can only be felt by one who has spent months in the study of American agrarianism after the Revolution. In them personalty won a significant battle in the conflict of 1787–1788.

The authors of *The Federalist* advance in support of these two clauses very substantial arguments which bear out the view here expressed. "The loss which America has sustained since the peace, from the pestilential effects of paper money on the necessary confidence between man and man, on the necessary confidence in the public councils, on the industry and morals of the people, and on the character of republican government, constitutes an enormous debt against the States chargeable with this unadvised measure, which must long remain unsatisfied; or rather an accumulation of guilt which can be expiated no otherwise than by a voluntary sacrifice on the altar of justice of the power which has been the instrument of it." Speaking on the contract clause—that "additional bulwark in favor of personal security and private rights"— Madison is sure that the "sober people of America are weary of the fluctuating policy which has directed the public councils," and will welcome a reform that will "inspire a general prudence and industry and give a regular course to the business of society."

Hamilton on several occasions laid great stress on the contract clause as one of the features of the Constitution which had warmly commended it to its supporters. In a communication to Washington, dated May 29, 1790, he wrote: "This, to the more enlightened part of the community, was not one of the least recommendations of that Constitution. The too frequent intermeddlings of the state legislatures in relation to private contracts were extensively felt and seriously lamented; and a Constitution which promised a preventative was, by those who felt and thought in that manner, eagerly embraced."

There was not a little discussion of the obligation of contract clause in the contemporary press during the period of ratification, and there can be no doubt that it was favorably viewed by the supporters of the Constitution as an added safeguard against paper money and stay laws. A writer in the New Hampshire Spy, on November 3, 1787, in commending the new frame of government to his fellow citizens, calls particular attention to this provision: "It also expressly prohibits those destructive laws in the several states which alter or impair the obligation of contracts; so that in future anyone may be certain of an exact fulfilment of any contract that may be entered into or the penalty that may be stipulated for in case of failure."

Another writer of the period approves the same principle with more vigor. "My countrymen, the devil is among you. Make paper as much as you please. Make it a tender in all *future* contracts, or let it rest on its own credit—but remember that *past* contracts are sacred things—and that legislatures have no right to interfere with them—they have no right to say, a debt shall be paid at a discount, or in any manner which the parties never intended. . . . To pay *bona fide* contracts for cash, in paper of little value, or in old horses, would be a dishonest attempt in an individual: but for legislatures to frame laws to support and encourage such detestable villainy, is like a judge who should inscribe the arms of a rogue over the seat of justice."

The full import of the obligation of contract clause was doubtless better understood by Chief Justice Marshall than by any man of that generation. He had taken an active part in the adoption of the Constitution in his state, and he had studied long and arduously the history of the period for his classic defence of Federalism, *The Life of Washington*. In more than one decision he applied the clause with great effect, and voiced the views of his Federalist contemporaries on this point, explaining the deep-seated social antagonism which is reflected in it. And when at length, in his declining years, he saw it attacked in the legislatures by Jacksonian democracy, and beheld the Supreme Court itself surrendering the position which he had earlier taken, he spread on record in a dissenting opinion a warning and a protest which for cogency and vigor equals any of his great dissertations delivered in the name of the Court.

In the case of Ogden *v.* Saunders, decided in the January term of 1827, the Supreme Court was compelled to pass upon the issue: "Does a bankrupt law which applies to contracts made *after* its passage impair the obligation of those contracts?" The newer school on the bench, Washington, Johnson, Trimble, and Thompson were of opinion that such a law did not impair the obligation of contract and was valid. Marshall, Duvall, and Story dissented. The Chief Justice took the high ground that the obligation of a contract inhered in the contract itself, and could not be changed by any external legislation whatever. Therefore, obviously, legislation affecting adversely the obligation of future contracts was just as unconstitutional as legislation attacking contracts already made. In other words, Marshall, who ought to have known what the framers of the Constitution intended better than any man on the supreme bench, believed that it was designed to bring under the ban substantially all legislation which affected personalty adversely—in other words that it was similar in character to the due process clause of the Fourteenth Amendment.

Speaking on the contract clause he said with great solemnity: "We cannot look back to the history of the times when the august spectacle was exhibited of the assemblage of the whole people by their representatives in convention, in order to unite thirteen independent sovereignties under one government, so far as might be necessary for the purposes of union, without being sensible of the great importance attached to the tenth section of the first article. The power of changing the relative situation of debtor and creditor, of interfering with contracts, a power which comes home to every man, touches the interest of all, and controls the conduct of every individual in those things which he supposes to be proper for his own exclusive management, had been used to such an excess by the state legislatures as to break in upon the ordinary intercourse of society, and destroy all confidence between man and man. The mischief had become so great, so alarming as not only to impair commercial intercourse, and threaten the existence of credit, but to sap the morals of the people, and destroy the sanctity of private faith. To guard against the continuance of the evil was an object of deep interest with all the truly wise, as well as virtuous, of this great community, and was one of the important benefits expected from a reform of the government.". . .

[Beard concluded this chapter by stating that the Constitution was "an economic document" drawn with great skill by men "whose property interests were immediately at stake" and who appealed to identical interests in the country. The following extract introduces his discussion of the ratification controversy and gives his conclusions about it.]

The Progress of Ratification

On the 17th day of September, 1787, the Convention at Philadelphia finished its work and transmitted the new Constitution to Congress, with the suggestion that "it should afterwards be submitted to a convention of delegates chosen in each state by the people thereof, under the recommendation of its legislature for their assent and ratification; and that each convention assenting to and ratifying the same should give notice thereof to the United States in Congress assembled." The Philadelphia Convention further proposed that when nine states had ratified the new instrument, it should go into effect as between the states ratifying the same. Eleven days later, on September 28, the Congress, then sitting in New York, resolved to accept the advice of the Convention, and sent the Constitution to the state legislatures to be transmitted by them to conventions chosen by the voters of the respective commonwealths.

This whole process was a departure from the provisions of the then fundamental law of the land—the Articles of Confederation—which provided that all alterations and amendments should be made by Congress and receive the approval of the legislature of every state. If to-day the Congress of the United States should call a national convention to "revise" the Constitution, and such a convention should throw away the existing instrument of government entirely and submit a new frame of government to a popular referendum, disregarding altogether the process of amendment now provided, we should have something analogous to the great political transformation of 1787–89. The revolutionary nature of the work of the Philadelphia Convention is correctly characterized by Professor John W. Burgess when he states that had such acts been performed by Julius or Napoleon, they would have been pronounced *coups d'état.*

This revolutionary plan of procedure was foreshadowed in the Virginia proposals at the opening of the Convention, and was, therefore, contemplated by some of the leaders from the beginning. . . .

A survey of the facts here presented yields several important generalizations:

Two states, Rhode Island and North Carolina refused to ratify the Constitution until after the establishment of the new government which set in train powerful economic forces against them in their isolation.

In three states, New Hampshire, New York, and Massachusetts, the popular vote as measured by the election of delegates to the conventions was adverse to the Constitution; and ratification was secured by the conversion of opponents and often the repudiation of their tacit (and in some cases express) instructions.

In Virginia the popular vote was doubtful.

In the four states which ratified the constitution with facility, Connecticut, New Jersey, Georgia, and Delaware, only four or five weeks were allowed to elapse before the legislatures acted, and four or five weeks more before the elections to the conventions were called; and about an equal period between the elections and the meeting of the conventions. This facility of action may have been due to the general sentiment in favor of the Constitution; or the rapidity of action may account for the slight development of the opposition.

In two commonwealths, Maryland and South Carolina, deliberation and delays in the election and the assembling of the conventions resulted in an undoubted majority in favor of the new instrument; but for the latter state the popular vote has never been figured out.

In one of the states, Pennsylvania, the proceedings connected with the ratification of the Constitution were conducted with unseemly haste.

THE POPULAR VOTE ON THE CONSTITUTION

WHILE one hesitates to generalize about the vote cast in favor of the Constitution on the basis of the fragmentary evidence available, it seems worth while, nevertheless, to put together several related facts bearing on the matter.

In addition to the conclusion, brought out by Dr. Jameson, that about 5 per cent of the population voted in Massachusetts in the period under consideration, we have other valuable data. Dr. Paullin has shown that the electoral vote in the presidential election of 1788 in New Hampshire was 2.8 per cent of the free population; that the vote in Madison's electoral district in Virginia in the same election was 2.7 per cent of the white population; that the vote in the first congressional election in Maryland was 3.6 per cent of the white population and that the vote in the same congressional election in Massachusetts was 3 per cent. Speaking of the exercise of the franchise as a whole in the period, Dr. Paullin says, "The voting was done chiefly by a small minority of interested property holders, a disproportionate share of whom in the northern states resided in the towns, and the wealthier and more talented of whom like a closed corporation controlled politics."

In view of these figures, in view of the data given above on the election of delegates (to the ratifying conventions) in the cities of Boston, Philadelphia, and Baltimore, in view of the fact that the percentage participating in the country was smaller than in the towns, and in view of the fact that only

3 per cent of the population resided in cities of over 8000, it seems a safe guess to say that not more than 5 per cent of the population in general, or in round numbers, 160,000 voters, expressed an opinion one way or another on the Constitution. In other words, it is highly probable that not more than one-fourth or one-fifth of the adult white males took part in the election of delegates to the state conventions. If anything, this estimate is high.

Now in four of the states, New Hampshire, Massachusetts, New York, and Virginia, the conventions at the time of their election were either opposed to the ratification of the Constitution or so closely divided that it was hard to tell which way the final vote would go. These four states, with Rhode Island and North Carolina, which were at first against ratification, possessed about three-fifths of the population—in round numbers 1,900,000 out of 3,200,000 free persons. Of the 1,900,000 population in these states we may, with justice it seems, set off at least 900,000, that is, 45,000 voters as representing the opposition. Add to these the voters in Pennsylvania who opposed the ratification of the Constitution, approximately 6000, and we have 51,000 dissenting voters, against ratification. Adding the dissenters in Maryland, South Carolina, and Connecticut, and taking the other states as unanimous, we may reasonably conjecture that of the estimated 160,000 who voted in the election of delegates, not more than 100,000 men favored the adoption of the Constitution at the time it was put into effect—about one in six of the adult males.

Admitting that these figures are rough guesses, it appears, nevertheless, that the Constitution was not "an expression of the clear and deliberate will of the whole people," nor of a majority of the adult males, nor at the outside of one-fifth of them.

Indeed, it may very well be that a majority of those who voted were against the adoption of the Constitution as it then stood. Such a conjecture can be based on the frank statement of no less an authority than the great Chief Justice Marshall who took a prominent part in the movement which led to the formation and ratification of the new instrument of government.

At all events, the disfranchisement of the masses through property qualifications and ignorance and apathy contributed largely to the facility with which the personality-interest representatives carried the day. The latter were alert everywhere, for they knew, not as a matter of theory, but as a practical matter of dollars and cents, the value of the new Constitution. They were well informed. They were conscious of the identity of their interests. They were well organized. They knew for weeks in advance, even before the Constitution was sent to the states for ratification, what the real nature of the contest was. They resided for the most part in the towns, or the more thickly populated areas, and they could marshall their forces quickly and effectively. They had also the advantage of appealing to all discontented persons who exist in large numbers in every society and are ever anxious for betterment through some change in political machinery.

Talent, wealth, and professional abilities were, generally speaking, on the side of the Constitutionalists. The money to be spent in the campaign of education was on their side also; and it was spent in considerable sums for pamphleteering, organizing parades and demonstrations, and engaging the interest of the press. A small percentage of the enormous gain to come through the appreciation of securities alone would have financed no mean campaign for those days.

The opposition on the other hand suffered from the difficulties connected with getting a backwoods vote out to the town and county elections. This involved sometimes long journeys in bad weather, for it will be remembered that the elections were held in the late fall and winter. There were no such immediate personal gains to be made through the defeat of the Constitution, as were to be made by the security holders on the other side. It was true the debtors knew that they would probably have to settle their accounts in full and the small farmers were aware that taxes would have to be paid to discharge the national debt if the Constitution was adopted; and the debtors everywhere waged war against the Constitution—of this there is plenty of evidence. But they had no money to carry on their campaign; they were poor and uninfluential—the strongest battalions were not on their side. The wonder is that they came so near defeating the Constitution at the polls.

Economics of the Vote on the Constitution

Three conclusions seem warranted by the data presented in this chapter:

Inasmuch as the movement for the ratification of the Constitution centred particularly in the regions in which mercantile, manufacturing, security, and personalty interests generally had their greatest strength, it is impossible to escape the conclusion that holders of personalty saw in the new government a strength and defence to their advantage.

Inasmuch as so many leaders in the movement for ratification were large security holders, and inasmuch as securities constituted such a large proportion of personalty, this economic interest must have formed a very considerable dynamic element, if not the preponderating element, in bringing about the adoption of the new system.

The state conventions do not seem to have been more "disinterested" than the Philadelphia convention; but in fact the leading champions of the new government appear to have been, for the most part, men of the same practical type, with actual economic advantages at stake.

The opposition to the Constitution almost uniformly came from the agricultural regions, and from the areas in which debtors had been formulating paper money and other depreciatory schemes.

[Final] Conclusions

AT THE close of this long and arid survey—partaking of the nature of catalogue—it seems worth while to bring together the important conclusions for political science which the data presented appear to warrant.

The movement for the Constitution of the United States was originated and carried through principally by four groups of personalty interests which had been adversely affected under the Articles of Confederation: money, public securities, manufactures, and trade and shipping.

The first firm steps toward the formation of the Constitution were taken by a small and active group of men immediately interested through their personal possessions in the outcome of their labors.

No popular vote was taken directly or indirectly on the proposition to call the Convention which drafted the Constitution.

A large propertyless mass was, under the prevailing suffrage qualifications, excluded at the outset from participation (through representatives) in the work of framing the Constitution.

The members of the Philadelphia Convention which drafted the Constitution were, with a few exceptions, immediately, directly, and personally interested in, and derived economic advantages from, the establishment of the new system.

The Constitution was essentially an economic document based upon the concept that the fundamental private rights of property are anterior to government and morally beyond the reach of popular majorities.

The major portion of the members of the Convention are on record as recognizing the claim of property to a special and defensive position in the Constitution.

In the ratification of the Constitution, about three-fourths of the adult males failed to vote on the question, having abstained from the elections at which delegates to the state conventions were chosen, either on account of their indifference or their disfranchisement by property qualifications.

The Constitution was ratified by a vote of probably not more than one-sixth of the adult males.

It is questionable whether a majority of the voters participating in the elections for the state conventions in New York, Massachusetts, New Hampshire, Virginia, and South Carolina, actually approved the ratification of the Constitution.

The leaders who supported the Constitution in the ratifying conventions represented the same economic groups as the members of the Philadelphia Convention; and in a large number of instances they were also directly and personally interested in the outcome of their efforts.

In the ratification, it became manifest that the line of cleavage for and against the Constitution was between substantial personalty interests on the one hand and the small farming and debtor interests on the other.

The Constitution was not created by "the whole people" as the jurists have said; neither was it created by "the states" as Southern nullifiers long contended; but it was the work of a consolidated group whose interests knew no state boundaries and were truly national in their scope.

FEARS OF DISUNION

Charles Warren

EDITOR'S NOTE   Charles Warren was a Boston
patrician, a practicing lawyer, Assistant Attorney
General of the United States, a frequent university
lecturer, and a prolific historian of distinction.
Among his many books are A *History of the American Bar* (1911), *The Supreme Court in United
States History* (1923)—a three volume work that
won the Pulitzer Prize—and *Congress, the Constitution, and the Supreme Court* (1925). The following selection is taken from his *Making of the Constitution* (1928), still the best detailed history of
the subject. Completely rejecting Beard's *Economic
Interpretation* to which he did not even allude,
Warren adhered to a straightforward political interpretation. Although his research surpassed in
depth and richness the classic works of Richard
Hildreth, George Ticknor Curtis, and George Bancroft, Warren represented the grand tradition of
the old school of conservative nationalist historians.
Unlike them, however, he understood that the
framers shared the occupational disease of professional politicians who invariably identify the national interest with their own views on desirable
public policy. But Warren also believed that the
framers were able to give their loyalty to a concept
of national interest that transcended purse and
status without compromising republican principles.

From Charles Warren, *The Making of the Constitution*, pp. 1–14. Copy-
right 1928, 1937 by Charles Warren; renewed 1965 by Annie Louise
Bliss Warren. Reprinted without footnotes by permission of the Harvard
University Press.

He would have endorsed the dictum of Justice Oliver Wendell Holmes that high-mindedness is not impossible in man. "I don't readily give up the belief," said Holmes, "that Washington and the rest had for their dominant motive a patriotic desire to see a powerful nation take the place of squabbling states." In his introduction Warren explained that what people think to be true is often more important than the actual truth; history, therefore, was founded on belief as much as on fact. The economic and political conditions leading to the making of the Constitution may not in reality, Warren admitted, have been as black or disastrous as they seemed to the framers, but they "at least believed them to be so, and acted on that belief." He sought to picture the *necessity* of the Constitution as understood by the framers, and concluded that the principal motive that impelled them in their great task was the conviction that without the new Constitution, the Union would dissolve and republican government would disappear.

o   o   o   o

IN RECENT YEARS there has been a tendency to interpret all history in terms of economics and sociology and geography—of soil, of debased currency, of land monopoly, of taxation, of class antagonism, of frontier against seacoast, and the like—and to attribute the actions of peoples to such general materialistic causes. This may be a wise reaction from the old manner of writing history almost exclusively in terms of wars, politics, dynasties, and religions. But its fundamental defect is, that it ignores the circumstance that the actions of men are frequently based quite as much on sentiment and belief as on facts and conditions. It leaves out the souls of men and their response to the inspiration of great leaders. It forgets that there are such motives as patriotism, pride in country, unselfish devotion to the public welfare, desire for independence, inherited sentiments, and convictions of right and justice. The historian who omits to take these facts into consideration is a poor observer of human nature. No one can write true history who leaves out of account the fact that a man may have an inner zeal for principles, beliefs, and ideals. "It seems to me a great truth," wrote Thomas Carlyle, "that human things cannot stand on selfishness, mechanical utilities, economics, and law courts." Those who contend, for instance, that economic causes brought about the War of the Revolution will always find it difficult to explain away the fact that the men who did the fighting thought, themselves, that they were fighting for a belief—a principle. Sixty-two years after the battle of Concord and Lexington, an able American historian had an interview with one of the men who had been in that battle, and asked him the reasons which impelled him, a plain, simple working man, to take arms. And this was the colloquy between the historian and the man who fought:

"Why did you? . . . My histories tell me that you men of the Revolution took up arms against intolerable oppressions."

"What were they? Oppressions? I didn't feel them."

"What, were you not oppressed by the Stamp Act?"

"I never saw one of those stamps. . . . I am certain I never paid a penny for one of them."

"Well, what about the tea tax?"

"Tea tax, I never drank a drop of the stuff. The boys threw it all overboard."

"Then, I suppose, you had been reading Harrington, or Sidney and Locke, about the eternal principles of liberty?"

"Never heard of 'em."

"Well, then, what was the matter, what did you mean in going into the fight?"

"Young man, what we meant in going for those red-coats, was this: we always had governed ourselves and we always meant to. They didn't mean we should."

In other words, it was an idea, a principle—belief in self-government—for which this New England yeoman and his fellow-countrymen were fighting.

In the same manner, the men who urged and framed and advocated the Constitution were striving for an idea, an ideal —belief in a National Union, and a determination to maintain it, and the men who opposed the Constitution were also fighting for the preservation of an idea—self-rule as opposed to control by a central government which they feared would destroy their local governments. Historians who leave these factors out of account and who contend that these men were moved chiefly by economic conditions utterly fail to interpret their character and their acts. To appreciate the patriotic sincerity of the motives which inspired the framing of the Constitution, it is necessary to read the hopes and fears of the leading American statesmen prior to 1787, as expressed in their own words. Thomas Jefferson wrote, one hundred years ago, that "the opening scenes of our present government" would not be "seen in their true aspect until the letters of the day, now held in private hoards, shall be broken up and laid open to public use." Within the last thirty-five years, these letters have been very fully published; and unless their authors, in writing to intimate personal friends, were expressing one reason for desiring a change in the form of government, while in fact moved by other and more selfish reasons, then these letters must portray, with accuracy, the motives which led the writers to advocate a new Constitution. These letters, moreover, embody the principles on which the new Government was to be built—principles which were distinctively American and little connected with economics.

The actual evils which led to the Federal Convention of 1787 are familiar to every reader of history and need no detailed description here. As is well known, they arose, in general, first, from lack of power in the Government of the Confederation to legislate and enforce at home such authority as it possessed, or to maintain abroad its credit or position as a sovereign Nation; second, from State legislation unjust to citizens and productive of dissensions with neighboring States—the State laws particularly complained of being those staying process of the Courts, making property a tender in payment of debts, issuing paper money, interfering with foreclosure of mortgages, setting aside judgments of the Courts, interfering with private concerns, imposing commercial restrictions on goods and citizens of other States. The Articles of Confederation as agreed upon by the Continental Congress on November 15, 1777, had provided for a Government consisting simply of a Congress with a single House, in which each State had equal representation—a Government having no Executive and no adequate Court—a Government in which Congress had no power to tax, to raise troops, to regulate commerce, or to execute or enforce its own laws and treaties—a Government in which each of the various States had power to tax, to make its own money, to impose its own import and export duties, and to conform or not, as it chose, to the acts or treaties of Congress, or to its requisitions for money or troops. Congress could only supplicate; it could not enforce.

> *Glendower.* "I can call spirits from the vasty deep."
> *Hotspur.* "Why, so can I, or so can any man.
> But will they come when you do call for them?"

Such a Government could not operate successfully for any length of time and there could be no real Union of the States, except in time of war when need of mutual protection would prevent undue dissensions. From the very outset, and long before economic disturbances had arisen in the States, the voices of American statesmen were heard urging upon the people the necessity of a change. Even before the whole thirteen States had decided to ratify the Articles, Alexander Hamilton formulated the additional authority which Congress ought to possess; and in this comprehensive document, written in 1780 (when he was only twenty-three years old), he anticipated most of the powers which were granted, seven years later, by the Constitution. The ink was scarcely dry on the signatures of the delegates from Maryland—the last of the thirteen States to sign the Articles (on March 1, 1781)—when James Madison, James Duane of New York, and James M. Varnum of Rhode Island were appointed a Committee to report on needful changes. This Committee recommended vesting power in Congress to employ the Continental army and navy "to compel any delinquent State to fulfill its Federal engagement, by restraining its vessels, merchandise, and trade." Another Committee, consisting of Edmund Randolph of Virginia, Oliver Ellsworth of Connecticut and James M. Varnum, five months later, in August, 1781, reported a long list of additional powers for Congress, as necessary in order to make the Government efficient, among which was the important suggestion that Congress be authorized "to distrain the property of a State delinquent in its assigned proportion of men and money." No action was ever taken on this Report. A year later a strong appeal made by Robert Morris, Superintendent of Finance, that Congress be granted power to levy excise, land, and poll taxes, to discharge the Government debts was adversely reported on by a Congressional Committee. In 1783, Congress rejected a motion by Alexander Hamilton and James Wilson that that body should be given power to levy a land tax; but, a month later, Congress voted to ask the States to grant to it the power to levy import duties.

It is also to be noted that the idea of a Convention to revise and amend the Articles of Confederation was no new thing in the year 1787. It had been in the minds of the leading American statesmen, and long before any economic evils appeared in the various States. It arose from their patriotic desire for a united Nation, able to take its place with the other Nations of the world. As Edmund Randolph of Virginia strikingly said: "The American spirit ought to be mixed with American pride, to see the Union magnificently triumphant." What they chiefly feared were dissensions of the States and dissolution of the Union, leaving the States open to attack by foreign power. What they desired was to frame some form of Government which, while safeguarding the liberties of the citizens and the rights of the States, should have power to maintain adequately its own authority and independence. These were the objects which occupied all their correspondence. Conventions of the delegates from various States had gathered several times prior to 1787. In 1777, a Convention from New York and the New England States met at Springfield; in 1778, at New Haven, New Jersey and Pennsylvania were represented in addition to New York and New England. In 1780, New York and New England met at Hartford and suggested a General Convention to revise the Articles. The earliest call for a General Convention came from the Legislature of New York in 1782, under the leadership of Alexander Hamilton and General Philip Schuyler. In 1783, the Continental Congress appointed a Committee to consider these New York resolutions for a Convention, but no further action was ever taken. In 1783 also, Washington wrote to Dr. William Gordon suggesting a Convention of the People, as follows:

"To suppose that the general concerns of this country can be directed by thirteen heads, or one head without competent powers, is a solecism, the bad effects of which every man who has had the practical knowledge to judge from, that I have, is fully convinced of; tho' none perhaps has felt them in so forcible and distressing a degree. The People at large, and at a distance from the theatre of action, who only know that the machine was kept in motion, and that they are at last arrived at the first object of their wishes, are satisfied with the event, without investigating the causes of the slow progress to it, or of the expenses which have accrued, and which they have been unwilling to pay—great part of which has arisen from that want of energy in the Federal Constitution, which I am complaining of, and which I wish to see given to it by a Convention of the People, instead of hearing it remarked that, as we have worked through an arduous contest with the powers Congress already have (but which, by the by, have been gradually diminishing) why should they be invested with more? . . . For Heaven's sake, who are Congress? Are they not the creatures of the People, amenable to them for their conduct, and dependent from day to day on their breath? Where then can be the danger of giving them such powers as are adequate to the great ends of Government and to all the general purposes of the Confederation (I repeat the word general, because I am no advocate for their having to do with the particular policy of any State, further than it concerns the Union at large)."

In 1784, Richard Henry Lee, then President of the Congress, wrote to Madison: "It is by many here suggested as a very necessary step for Congress to take, the calling on the States to form a Convention for the sole purpose of revising the Confederation so far as to enable Congress to execute with more energy, effect, and vigor the powers assigned to it," and Madison replied to him: "I have not yet found leisure to scan the project of a Continental Convention with so close an eye as to have made up any observations worthy of being mentioned to you. In general, I hold it for a maxim that the Union of the States is essential to their safety against foreign danger and internal contention, and that the perpetuity and efficacy of the present system cannot be confided in." In 1785, the Massachusetts Legislature passed Resolutions, in response to a message from Governor James Bowdoin, recommending to Congress the calling of a General Convention.

Meanwhile, the sentiments and motives which inspired the desire for a change in the form of Government may be seen in the letters of Washington, Hamilton, Jay, Madison, Jefferson and many others, both in the South and the North. Washington, more than any other man, was responsible for calling the attention of the people to the defects of the Confederation. His letters were filled with appeals for a remedy. As early as

July, 1780, he wrote: "Our measures are not under the influence and direction of one Council, but thirteen, each of which is actuated by local views and politics. . . . We are attempting the impossible." In December, 1780, he wrote that "there are two things (as I have often declared) which, in my opinion, are indispensably necessary to the well-being and good government of our public affairs; these are greater powers to Congress and more responsibility and permanency in the Executive bodies." In 1782, he wrote that if the powers of Congress were not enlarged, "anarchy and confusion must ensue." In 1783, he wrote that: "The experience, which is purchased at the price of difficulties and distress, will alone convince us that the honor, power, and true interest of this country must be measured by a Continental scale, and that every departure therefrom weakens the Union, and may ultimately break the band which holds us together. To avert these evils, to form a Constitution that will give consistency, stability, and dignity to the Union and sufficient powers to the great Council of the Nation for general purposes, is a duty which is incumbent upon every man who wishes well to his Country, and will meet with my aid as far as it can be rendered in the private walks of life." On June 8, 1783, he sent to the Governors of the States a message in which he said:

"There are four things, which, I humbly conceive, are essential to the well-being. I may even venture to say, to the existence of the United States, as an independent power. First. An indissoluble union of the States under one Federal head; secondly. A sacred regard to public justice; thirdly. The adoption of a proper peace establishment; and, fourthly. The prevalence of that pacific and friendly disposition among the people of the United States, which will induce them to forget their local prejudices and policies; to make those mutual concessions, which are requisite to the general prosperity; and in some instances, to sacrifice their individual advantages to the interest of the community. These are the pillars on which the glorious fabric of our independency and National character must be supported."

And these views, he continued to express in the ensuing years, through a voluminous correspondence with friends in the various States. The letters of other leading Americans showed a realization that a truly National Government which should promote the Union of the States was imperative. John Jay of New York wrote to Gouverneur Morris of Pennsylvania, September 24, 1783:

"I am perfectly convinced that no time is to be lost in raising and maintaining a National spirit in America. Power to govern the Confederacy, as to all general purposes, should be granted and exercised. The governments of the different States should be wound up, and become vigorous. America is beheld with jealousy, and jealousy is seldom idle. Settle your boundaries without delay. It is better that some improper limits should be fixed, than any left in dispute. In a word, everything conducive to union and constitutional energy of government should be cultivated, cherished and protected, and all counsels and measures of a contrary complexion should at least be suspected of impolitic views and objects."

Governor John Hancock, in his Message to the Massachusetts Legislature in September, 1783, said: "How to strengthen and improve the Union so as to render it completely adequate, demands the immediate attention of these States. Our very existence as a free nation is suspended upon it." Thomas Jefferson wrote to Madison, in 1784: "I find the conviction growing strongly that nothing can preserve our Confederacy unless the bond of union, their common Council, be strengthened." And to Monroe, Jefferson wrote in 1785: "The interests of the States ought to be made joint in every possible instance, in order to cultivate the idea of our being one Nation." Stephen Higginson, a former Member of Congress from Massachusetts, wrote to John Adams, December 30, 1785, that: "Experience and observation most clearly evince that in their habits, manners, and commercial interests, the Southern and Northern States are not only very dissimilar, but in many instances directly opposed. Happy for America would it be if there was a greater coincidence of sentiment and interest among them. Then we might expect those National arrangements soon to take place which appear so essential to our safety and happiness."

Such were the sentiments which prevailed among the public men of the country, prior to the year 1786, as to the necessity of some alteration in the form of their Government which should promote a more perfect National Union. . . .

THE ARTICLES OF CONFEDERATION
Andrew C. McLaughlin

EDITOR'S NOTE   Andrew Cunningham McLaughlin,
one of the pre-eminent constitutional historians of
his time, was president of the American Historical
Association in 1914, the year after Beard published
his *Economic Interpretation of the Constitution.*
In his book, *The Confederation and the Constitution* (1905), McLaughlin prided himself for not
having neglected economic factors (which he
treated with the utmost conservative bias), but in
his presidential address he denied that constitutional history was merely a phase of economic history; he warned of the oversimplification resulting
from a monolithic emphasis on the materialistic.
Recognizing an almost infinite variety of human
motives and interests, he stressed the importance
of ideals. Nevertheless McLaughlin rejected the
"tone of exaltation" that imbued the works of older
writers on the Constitutional Convention. He also
criticized their denigration of the Articles of Confederation. John Fiske's *The Critical Period of
American History* (1888), for example, had depicted the years 1783–87 as a steady degeneration
into anarchy from which the country was saved by
the right-thinking patriotic framers and their "wonderful" Constitution; it was, said Fiske, an "Iliad,
or Parthenon, or Fifth Symphony, of statesmanship." Censuring Fiske's extremely popular and in-

From Andrew C. McLaughlin, *A Constitutional History of the United
States*, pp. 118–27, 137–46. Copyright 1935 by D. Appleton-Century
Company, Inc. Reprinted without footnotes by permission of Appleton-
Century-Crofts.

fluential book as "altogether without scientific standing," McLaughlin was the first scholar to write with relative objectivity about the Articles and the period of the Confederation. Though a nationalist like Fiske, he emphasized the constructive achievements of the Articles without neglecting their infirmities, and he doubted whether there was such a danger of national dissolution during the so-called "critical period."

McLaughlin's work showed an orderly and logical evolution of the Constitution from the Articles. They were framed, he recalled, during a war against a central government that had claimed the power to tax the colonies and regulate their commerce. Americans, associating liberty with local autonomy or states' rights, understandably withheld the contested powers from the central government of the Union and reserved them to the states. McLaughlin construed the Articles not as the product of ineptitude but as the world's first written constitution establishing a federal system. Considering the novelty of the task, he praised the acumen with which powers were divided between the union and the states. He also praised the government of the Confederation for its wisdom in establishing the principle of nation-building by which a colonial problem was avoided on the American continent: new territories on maturing were to become equal states of the Union. These themes are present in the following selection from McLaughlin's *Constitutional History of the United States* (1935)—the only textbook to win a Pulitzer Prize—and in his other books. Among them are *The Courts, the Constitution, and Parties* and *Foundations of American Constitutionalism*. McLaughlin was a professor of history at the University of Michigan and then at the University of Chicago.

o   o   o   o

WHEN Lee introduced into Congress the resolution for independence (June 7, 1776), it was accompanied by a resolution that steps be taken for the formation of a confederation of the states. The need of organization had long been in the minds of certain leaders, and Franklin the year before had brought in a plan based in some degree on the Albany Plan of 1754. With his plan nothing of importance was done, though it evidently had influence on later proceedings; but after independence was declared, Congress began debating at length articles brought in by a committee and commonly called the Dickinson draft. Pressure upon Congress, as well as some inherent difficulties in the problem, delayed the completion of the task, and consequently not until November, 1777, were the Articles finally adopted by Congress and submitted to the states.

With the announcement of independence, the problem of imperial organization crossed the ocean; it was no longer the problem of organizing the British empire or of ascertaining its constitutional structure, but of organizing America. Nevertheless, in many respects the problem was the old one; reduced to the lowest terms, it was at least the problem of arranging some practicable scheme in which the states would work together for common ends. For there was need of coherence in the war; and as time was soon to show, coherence in peace was quite as necessary and possibly more difficult to maintain. What were the elements in the task, if we take for granted that complete unification, complete absorption of the states into a unitary system, was impossible? The most troublesome problems were again the familiar ones; and central among them was the pivotal question of supply, of finding means of assurance that the states would furnish properly the men and the money for the general needs of the union. If they were to retain a large share of self-government, and of course that was inevitable, what authority should be allowed to the body representing them all? Everybody cried, as he had done twenty years before, that union was absolutely necessary; but when it came to plans of union, there was still distraction.

It is possible that, if a system of union could have been decided upon immediately after independence was announced, the Articles of union would have contained no announcement of state sovereignty. In neither the Dickinson draft (July 12, 1776) nor the draft presented to Congress by the committee of the whole (August 20) was the sovereignty of the states specified; the articles submitted on the latter day declared: "Each State reserves to itself the sole and exclusive regulation and government of its internal police, in all matters that shall not interfere with the articles of this Confederation." The opening paragraphs, it is true, might be construed to signify that nothing was contemplated but a working union of sovereign states. Such glimpses as we can get of the work of construction in the succeeding months, especially in 1777, appear to indicate that, when the Articles were made distinctly to conform to the idea of a coöperative system of sovereignties, the change was the product of a developing sense of separate independence or of growing suspicion. The finished Articles, as submitted to the state legislatures for adoption, announced in plain language the retention of sovereignty by the states.

There were three points on which differences of opinion especially centered: (1) whether the states should have equal voting power in the Congress of the Confederation or should vote in proportion to their population or wealth or some such indication of importance and strength. (2) what should be the basis for determining how much each state should pay into the common coffers; (3) whether the states claiming vast stretches of western lands should continue to hold them in their possession; and this included the subordinate question

—whether or not Congress should be given authority to limit the dimensions of the states.

The debates on the first two questions are of interest to us because they brought out a number of the crucial problems that vexed the men who labored to form a union a decade later; the larger states wished proportional representation; the smaller states wished equal representation. Were the states to be unequally taxed but to have equal voting power in Congress? The debate appears to have been earnest and searching. The outcome of the discussion was the provision that each state should have one vote in Congress, thus securing the complete equality of the states in voting power; but charges of war and all other expenses were to be supplied by the states in proportion to the value of land within each state granted to or surveyed for any person, and the improvements on such land. In other words, equality of the states was accepted as the basis of voting power in Congress, inequality was accepted as the basis for contributions to the treasury. This arrangement was sure to be distasteful to many, and in the long run it proved unsatisfactory. Franklin said in the course of the debates, as John Adams noted them: "Let the smaller Colonies give equal money and men, and then have an equal vote. But if they have an equal vote without bearing equal burthens, a confederation upon such iniquitous principles will never last long."

The western land question presented special difficulty. A suitable solution of the problem was of immense importance. The Congress was engaged in a peculiarly difficult task; under any circumstances, the establishment of a union of states, each cherishing its own interests, must present serious obstacles. And if a union could be formed, what were the prospects that it would endure? In the days when the Confederation was under debate, the critical question was whether a union could be formed at all; and the difficulty of finding an affirmative answer seemed to turn in considerable measure on the dread of the landless states that the landed states would become wealthy and powerful and would overawe and mayhap impoverish their lesser neighbors. But if land were surrendered, it must be governed by somebody; so here again the states, seeking to form a union, were confronted by an essential part of the problem of imperial organization—the problem of imperial expansion. Some of the states claimed that their sea-to-sea charters gave them territory in the west; and New York made assertions of ownership of a considerable region. Other states were within definite limits; Rhode Island, New Jersey, Delaware, and Maryland were comparatively small in area. It is not strange that they should look with jealousy upon their neighbors claiming vast territory, the source of both wealth and power.

It seems remarkable now that the ownership of the transmontane region should have been so hotly contested during those perilous days when the real question was whether the British army would not beat down resistance and the rebellion against the mother country totally fail. But discussed it was; for this western question was a perplexing one, involving much more than merely fixing the western limits of the states. With the question of boundaries went the control of land purchases and the fixing of a land policy as well as direction and control of settlements that might be made beyond the mountains. From the beginning of colonial history, the frontier policy had been for each colony a matter of difficulty, and it was not so easy as it might now seem to cast aside traditions and at once transfer the whole—policy, hopes, plans, government, and lands—into the hands of a central authority as yet untried and indeed unformed. It was characteristic of American optimism, probably, to begin the counting of chickens before they had emerged from the shells.

The problem of the west was an old one, and, like so many others, was associated with the experiences of the old empire. The Albany Plan of Union had proposed a solution. The plan which Franklin presented to Congress in 1775 declared that purchases from the Indians should be made for the general advantage and benefit of the united colonies. The Dickinson draft of a confederation, presented in July, 1776, included even more definite proposals, but they were not included in the draft of the Articles submitted by the committee of the whole the next month. Among the states without large landed possessions, Maryland was the most critical of a system of union which would leave some of the states in possession of western territory. When the Congress was discussing the Articles in the autumn of 1777—for little had been done during many months preceding—a proposal was offered for which Maryland alone voted (New Jersey's vote was divided):

"That the United States, in Congress assembled, shall have the sole and exclusive right and power to ascertain and fix the western boundary of such states as claim to the Mississippi or South Sea, and lay out the land beyond the boundary, so ascertained, into separate and independent states, from time to time, as the numbers and circumstances of the people thereof may require."

The principle of the resolution is significant: the western settlements were not to be held in permanent subordination, but were to become in the course of time independent states, presumably members of the union with equal rights. The proposal, however, was unacceptable, at least as far as it contemplated giving at once to Congress the power to fix boundaries for the large landholding states. Instead of adopting the resolution, Congress added to that paragraph of the Articles which provided for the adjudication of controversies between states the following brief but peremptory statement: "provided, also, that no State shall be deprived of territory for the benefit of the United States."

The Articles were adopted by the Congress, November 15, 1777, and two days later they went forth to the states. Some of the states accepted them fairly promptly, and their delegates signed the Articles under authorization of their respective states. Various amendments were proposed, but the most important dealt with the necessity of settling the western question and especially securing for the use of the United States the crown lands from which revenue could be obtained for paying the debts incurred for the common cause. Maryland renewed her request for power in Congress to ascertain and restrict the boundaries of the large landholding states, and this was supported by Rhode Island, New Jersey, Pennsylvania, and Delaware—none of them having claims to territory in the west. By midsummer of 1778 most of the states had given their assent to the Articles. New Jersey took the step later in the year and was followed by Delaware in May, 1779. Maryland was still obdurate.

The months went by. A union of all the states was highly desirable, not to say imperative; delay was dangerous. Some concession or compromise was necessary. New York, whose claims seemed rather more nebulous than those of the states which asserted rights under sea-to-sea charters, passed a legislative act (February 19, 1780) empowering her delegates "to limit and restrict" her western boundaries. Congress now (September 6, 1780) declared this act was calculated to "accelerate the federal alliance"; the states with western land claims were asked to remove the only obstacle to a final ratification of the Articles. October 10, 1780, Congress passed a momentous resolution: all unappropriated lands ceded to the United States should be disposed of for the common benefit of the United States, "and be settled and formed into distinct republican states, which shall become members of the federal union, and have the same rights of sovereignty, freedom and independence, as the other states." Early in the following year Virginia consented to cede her territory northwest of the Ohio River. She laid down certain conditions and these raised some difficulties which do not need consideration here. Maryland could now feel fairly certain that her chief purpose was attained, and her delegates were authorized to sign the Articles. When this was done (March 1, 1781), the Confederation was complete.

Of great consequence was the final organization of the union, defective though it proved to be; and important also was the spirit of conciliation and national sentiment on which the union rested. Of some consequence, too, was the fact that the thirteen commonwealths, bound in "perpetual" union, jointly possessed a large, unsettled region; such possession probably helped in the development of a sense of common interest and common responsibilities. But of supreme importance was the discovery of the principle of expansion, of nation-building. The principle announced by Congress in 1780 was carried into effect by the famous Ordinance of 1787. Passed in the last months of the dying Confederation, the Ordinance is to-day a lasting memorial, a proof that the Americans had learned a great lesson from their own history. In the building of an empire—though for the time the empire was a confederation of sovereignties—the new settlements should not be permanently treated as dependents unfit to associate on terms of equality with the older members of the union.

It is unnecessary to recount the steps by which the various cessions of western lands were made by the states. In the course of time, those steps were taken. It is significant, however, that the Articles did not contain a provision authorizing the Congress of the Confederation to hold and manage the common territory thus granted or to lay down laws and ordinances for the government of the western settlements. Such powers may, perhaps, be inferred from the general acquiescence in the fact of possession and the circumstances under which the Articles were adopted.

A further view of the Articles is necessary. In Congress and in the states, there appears to have been less discussion concerning the powers delegated to Congress than one might have supposed. Taught by experience in the old empire, by the necessity of carrying on the war, and by earlier plans or discussions of union, the delegates in Congress were enabled to work out the distribution of powers between the central authority and the states with some approach to precision. The powers granted to Congress bear a general resemblance to those exercised by the Crown and Parliament in the old colonial system in which the colonies had grown to maturity; and if one compares the Articles with the Constitution adopted at Philadelphia in 1787, he will find a considerable similarity in the scheme of distribution. Time was to show the defects of the system; but the actual merits of the system agreed upon are noteworthy. No power to lay taxes was bestowed on Congress, and no power to regulate commerce, the two things about which there had been so much dispute in the preceding decade. These omissions were largely instrumental in bringing into existence the Constitutional Convention of 1787.

Without the consent of Congress, the states were expressly forbidden to send an embassy to a foreign state, receive an embassy, enter into any agreement with a foreign power, form any treaty of combination among themselves, maintain ships of war or troops in time of peace—though a militia must be provided and sufficiently armed—or engage in war unless actually invaded or in immediate danger of Indian attack. All charges of war and other expenses incurred for the common defense and general welfare were to be defrayed out of a common treasury supplied by the several states. To Congress was given, among other powers, the general powers of determining on war and peace, carrying on foreign affairs, though with some restrictions, regulating the alloy and value of coin, fixing the standard of weights and measures, regulating the trade and managing all the affairs with the Indians "not members of any of the States," establishing and regulating post offices from one state to another, appointing important army officers and all naval officers, borrowing money, building and equipping a navy, and making requisitions upon the states for troops. For doing the most important things, the vote of nine states in Congress was required, practically a three-fourths vote of the thirteen, a restriction certain to make effective action difficult. No alteration of the Articles could be made unless it be agreed to in Congress and confirmed by the legislatures of all the states. A "committee of the states" could, in the recess of Congress, exercise powers intrusted to it by Congress with the consent of nine states, provided that no power for which the voice of nine states was necessary should be delegated to the committee. One of the delegates could be appointed "to preside"—the predecessor, in fact, of the president of the United States, who does not preside at all.

While the Articles granted to Congress considerable authority, its powers were qualified, in some respects carefully, for the protection of the states' rights. Although Congress was given power to enter into treaties, the states were not totally forbidden to lay imposts, but they were forbidden to levy such duties as might interfere with "stipulations in treaties entered into by the United States . . . in pursuance of any treaties already proposed by Congress to the courts of France and Spain." Congress could make no treaty of commerce whereby the states should be restrained from imposing such imposts on foreigners as their own people were subjected to; and apparently the states could freely prohibit the exportation or importation of any kind of goods. The failure to grant Congress complete power to regulate commerce rendered it difficult or impossible to make a commercial treaty with a foreign nation and to have assurance that the states would comply with its provisions. The years that followed disclosed the fact that the want of authority to make treaties which would bind the states was one of the cardinal defects of the system. . . .

The vicissitudes of the years from the adoption of the Articles to the formation of the federal Constitution deserve more attention than can be given in these pages. Almost everything points in only one direction—toward the need of a competent central government and the necessity of finding a system of union which could maintain itself. Elaborate presentation of details is therefore for our purposes not required. The whole story is one of gradually increasing ineptitude; of a central government which could less and less function as it was supposed to function; of a general system which was creaking in every joint and beginning to hobble at every step. The men who came to Philadelphia in the spring of 1787 had learned the lessons taught by the failings of the Confederation.

One source of the difficulty was the Revolution itself. For the Revolution involved war; it started as a revolt against authority. It had deeply affected the old social order, and although, as we have pointed out, the philosophy on which the movement was founded had within it elements of stability and sobriety, the war left, as war always does, the combatants in a state of mental disquietude; social and economic foundations had been shaken; the full hopes of the conflict could not in the twinkling of an eye be gathered into reality. If a war is fought for liberty, why is it necessary to forge chains of perpetual union and obedience to government? Tom Paine's philosophy, which was permeated by the real spirit of real revolution, had gone beyond the limits of the older doctrines on which the social and political order was supposed to rest; for that ardent propagandist was not fond of picturing the state of nature as a place from which men had emerged for their own greater comfort and security; if his most widely-trumpeted sayings are to be taken at their face value, all things which had grown up since the age of primeval bliss and serenity could have no real sanction for their existence, not even the sanction and support of time—"Government like dress, is the badge of lost innocence; the palaces of kings are built on the ruins of the bowers of paradise." Just how far this new state of nature and all the emanations of this tragic philosophy influenced the average man of those days, no one can say; but their presence is plain enough.

Furthermore, there was the age-old feeling that government is inevitably the enemy of man and not his servant. We cannot neglect the effect of the long struggle in history to curb government lest it act the tyrant. Government in America was not as yet securely in the hands of the people-at-large (if there be any such security anywhere at any time), but a long step forward had been taken. "It takes time," however, as John Jay remarked, "to make sovereigns of subjects"—a wise saying. It took time for the people to realize that the government was their own.

Interstate jealousy did not fail to add to the complexities of the situation. The contest for local rights under the old imperial system had strengthened the sense of state reality; men were conscious of their states; the states were in a sense their own creation. It was difficult, after the strain of war had gone, to feel acutely the reality of America and the dependence of its members one upon another; and as the days went by disorganization rather than integration seemed to be gathering headway, until the more serious patriots and watchers of the night feared for the safety of their country. States with commodious harbors had an advantage over their neighbors, and they did not shrink from using it. Madison, speaking of this condition, declared that at one time "New Jersey, placed between Phil^a. & N. York, was likened to a Cask tapped at both ends: and N. Carolina between Virg^a. & S. Carolina to a patient bleeding at both Arms." The experience of those years brought clearly home to thinking men the need of some general regulation of commerce.

The industrial and commercial conditions after the war were in considerable confusion. Readjustments were necessary, especially for the resuscitation of the New England shipping industry. Some improvement came fairly quickly, and there is evidence that by 1786 the clouds of depression were beginning to lift. But it was hard to make much headway, especially as Britain was not ready to treat her former colonies as if they deserved particular favors or consideration; they had made their own beds, now let them lie there—a condition of retirement not suited to the restless spirit of the New England skippers whose ships were soon plowing the seas, even on to the Orient as well as to the ports of continental Europe. Commercial treaties were desirable, and some steps were taken in that direction; but it was hard to do anything effectively as long as the individual states could not be relied on to fulfill their obligations. Foreign nations naturally queried whether America was one or many, or, perhaps, one to-day and thirteen to-morrow.

The treaty of peace was not carried out. Britain still held the western posts from Lake Champlain to Mackinaw and thus retained control of the northern fur trade and influence over the Indians. Spain holding the mouth of the Mississippi was unwilling to allow free navigation through her territory. Trouble was brewing because of American treatment of the loyalists and because the stipulation in the treaty, that there should be no lawful impediment to the collection of debts due British creditors, received no particular attention. John Jay declared in 1786 that the treaty had been constantly violated by one state or another from the time of its signing and ratification. The Barbary powers, eager to take advantage of a helpless country, to seize American seamen, and to hold them for ransom, entered upon the game with lusty vigor. A nation which was not yet a nation in terms of law and political authority could do nothing to resist scorn and humiliation.

The pivotal problem, the immediate and unrelenting problem, was how to get revenue for the pressing needs of the Confederation. Financial affairs were in a pitiful shape and conditions daily grew worse. At the end of active hostilities the situation was bad enough. "Imagine," wrote Robert Morris who had charge of the newly-created office of superintendent of finance, "the situation of a man who is to direct the finances of a country almost without revenue (for such you will perceive this to be) surrounded by creditors whose distresses, while they increase their clamors, render it more difficult to appease them; an army ready to disband or mutiny; a government whose sole authority consists in the power of framing recommendations." Conditions did not improve; gloom deepened into darkness. The continental paper money ere long became a joke; and the returns from requisitions upon the states soon were lamentably inadequate. A committee of Congress reported in 1786 that the amount received in fourteen months was not sufficient for the "bare maintenance of the federal government on the most economical establishment, and in time of profound peace." The sums due for interest on the domestic and foreign debts were piling up to staggering heights and even the principal of the debts—for, strange as it may seem, Congress had succeeded in borrowing—was increasing ominously. Morris had by this time resigned; he did not wish to be a "minister of injustice." Congress was at its wit's end. ". . . the crisis has arrived," a committee announced,

"when the people of these United States, by whose will, and for whose benefit the federal government was instituted, must decide whether they will support their rank as a nation, by maintaining the public faith at home and abroad; or whether, for want of a timely exertion in establishing a general revenue, and thereby giving strength to the confederacy, they will hazard not only the existence of the union, but of those great and invaluable privileges for which they have so arduously and so honourably contended."

At the very beginning, indeed before the Articles had been signed by the delegates from Maryland, Congress submitted to the states an amendment (February 3, 1781) vesting in Congress a power to levy a duty of five per cent on imported goods, with a few exceptions, and a like duty on "prizes and prize goods." The monies arising from the duties were to be used for discharging the principal and interest of the public debts. The amendment was not adopted, one state, Rhode

Island, failing to ratify. Two years later a similar attempt to obtain revenue was made. In an amendment proposed at this time, certain commodities were designated with various rates of duties; on all other goods a five per cent duty was provided for; the proceeds were to be applied to the discharge of the debts, but the duties were not to be continued for more than twenty-five years. The states were also recommended to take steps for appropriating annually for a like term of years the sum of $1,500,000, the amount to be apportioned among the states. This amendment met the same fate as its predecessor.

In 1784, an amendment was submitted to the states which, if it had been ratified, would have given Congress certain powers over the regulation or restraint of foreign commerce. "Unless the United States in Congress assembled," it was declared, "shall be vested with powers competent to the protection of commerce, they can never command reciprocal advantages in trade; and without these our foreign commerce must decline & eventually be annihilated. . . ." The amendment was ratified by only two states.

Within the individual states, paper money added to the confusion and made recovery of economic stability difficult. Some of the states refused to be drawn down into the whirlpool; but seven of the thirteen had entered upon the scheme. The wise and proper way to get out of debt was to resort to the printing-press; for what forsooth did free government exist? "Choose such men," said one voice crying from the wilderness of poverty and debt, "as will make a bank of paper money, big enough to pay all our debts, which will sink itself (that will be so much clear gain to the state)." Without question, the debtor was in a bad way; but associated with this sort of appeal for relief were all the uneasy spirits whose attitudes of mind, when minds they used, were inimical to steady economic well-being and to stable and competent government. Whether one approves or disapproves the content and the agitation of the whole controversy, the fact remains that conditions were fraught with peril, a peril enhanced by the poverty of debtors and by the mental and spiritual disquietude which, as we all know, are the fruits of war and the companions of the ensuing peace. . . .

But what was the very center of the difficulty? What was the chief problem of the time? The trouble and confusion were manifestly caused by the failure of the states to abide by their obligations. The problem was to find a method, if union was to subsist at all, for overcoming the difficulty, to find therefore some arrangement, some scheme or plan of organization wherein there would be reasonable assurance that the states would fulfill their obligations and play their part under established articles of union and not make mockery of union by willful disregard or negligent delay. That was the *chief problem* of the day. The need of granting certain powers to Congress was plain; in other words, the distribution of powers between the center and the parts was imperfectly provided for in the Confederation. The distribution of powers, however, did not constitute the radical difficulty. If additional "powers" were granted Congress, could there be any assurance that the old trouble would not immediately arise? To the men of 1786—such men as were anxious for national stability —the real remedy appeared to be some application of force, the coercion of recalcitrant states, something more than the grant of naked authority to the central organ of union. The problem of imperial order had been reduced in some respects to fairly simple terms; if the task of distinguishing between powers was no longer especially troublesome, the question remaining was perplexing: could the states be held together in a firm and effective union and what arrangement could be made for securing or assuring obedience to their obligations as members of the union? Plainly enough the men of the time—the men of course who really thought—were troubled and perplexed; but few of them could even then see much further than the need of compulsion—the use of force against disobedient states.

THE IDEA OF A NATIONAL GOVERNMENT
DURING THE AMERICAN REVOLUTION

Merrill Jensen

EDITOR'S NOTE   One of the seminal historians of our
time was Merrill Jensen of the University of Wisconsin, a neo-Beardian whose bold and innovative
books on the years of the Revolution and Confederation have been extremely influential. His un-
failingly fresh insights provoke dispute and gen-
erate excitement. Many historians disagree with
him, but none can ignore him. He is a man to be
contended with. Jensen was the first to demonstrate
that the fundamental constitutional issues of 1787–
88 were fought out during the Revolution and even
had their sources in the pre-Revolutionary period.
Fixing the Articles of Confederation in the context
of the "internal revolution" within the states, he
described the Revolution as a democratic movement and the Articles as its constitutional expression, embodying in governmental form the philosophy of the Declaration of Independence. There
was a conflict, in Jensen's view, between radicals
and conservatives; on the one side there were those
who saw independence as the opportunity to reform the political and economic power structure at
home, and on the other, those who sought to preserve it unchanged. They differed on the kind of
central government there should be for the confederation of states. Most of the conservatives
wanted a strong central government as a means of

From the *Political Science Quarterly*, September 1943, Vol. 58, No. 3,
pp. 356–79. Reprinted by permission of the *Political Science Quarterly*.

preserving the status quo, while the radicals wanted a weak one, preferring strong state governments dominated by their legislatures. The Articles of Confederation represented a victory for the radical position, but the conservative or nationalist position succeeded in 1787. To Jensen, "the Constitution of 1787 was the culmination of an anti-democratic crusade"—a generalization that merits disbelief. That crusade, or, at least the movement for a strong national government, as the following essay definitely shows, began during the Revolution, not after it and not as a result of the "critical period" and the weaknesses of the Confederation. Some of the conservative nationalists were even willing to engage in a *coup d'état* to achieve their objective of a powerful central government. There was a significant connection, according to Jensen, between centralization, land speculation, currency speculation, and the creditor classes. Thus, the Jensen thesis roughly corresponds to the Beard thesis, pushing it back, chronologically speaking, into the years of the Revolution. One can understand the Constitutional Convention, Jensen contended, only by understanding the Galloway Plan, the Dickinson Draft, and other early nationalist efforts. He amplified his views in three books, *The Articles of Confederation* (1940), *The New Nation: a History of the United States during the Confederation, 1781–1789* (1950), and *The Founding of a Nation: a History of the American Revolution* (1968). Readers should observe the note of caution sounded by Jensen in the first of these three: generalizations are statements of tendencies to which there are qualifications and exceptions. Justice Holmes made the same point more pungently: the first mark of a civilized man, he said, is to make generalizations, bearing always in mind that "no generalization is worth a damn."

o   o   o   o

IN July 1783 John Jay wrote to Charles Thomson, secretary of Congress, and urged him to write a history of the Revolution so that posterity might have a true account of it. "I think," he said, "it might be comprized in a small Compass—it need not be burdened with *minute* accounts of Battles, Seiges, Retreats, Evacuations &c—leave those matters to the Voluminous Historians. The *political* Story of the Revolution will be most liable to Misrepresentation, and future relations of it will probably be replete both with intentional and accidental Errors."[1] While Jay's plea went unheeded, an account of the idea of a national government during the Revolution is a commentary on the rightness of his predictions, for the "political story of the Revolution" has been the subject of "misrepresentations" and subsequent accounts of it have been "replete" with "errors."

It is of little moment now whether the errors he foresaw have been intentional or accidental. What is of moment is that ever since the adoption of the Constitution of 1787, Americans, in their effort to explain the nature of the government created, have divided into schools of "states rights" and "nationalism." In the course of bitter, and often violent, controversies which have been both seed and fruit of social and economic tensions in American society, many assumptions have been made concerning the nature of the political struggle in the eighteenth century not warranted by the sources themselves. Historians and political scientists, equally with politicians and legal apologists, have interpreted the past in terms of present hopes and desires. As a result, many questionable generalizations concerning the nature of the American Revolution and its constitutional history have come to be accepted as fact. Thus it is axiomatic that the demand for a strong central govern-

[1] John Jay to Charles Thomson, Passy, July 19, 1783, in Charles Thomson Papers, Library of Congress.

ment after the Revolution arose from the experiences of the Revolution and the "chaos" of the "Critical Period" which resulted from the weakness of the Articles of Confederation. Much of the "chaos" is described as economic in character, even by those looking askance at anything remotely resembling an "economic interpretation" of the Constitution of 1787. Coupled with such assumptions is the almost total ignorance in subsequent times of the clear distinction made by eighteenth-century political leaders between the terms "federal" and "national" as applied to central governments. Today we use the terms interchangeably, but the Founding Fathers of 1776, and the quite different set of Founding Fathers of 1787, suffered from no such confusion. If we are to believe what they said, they believed that a federal government was one created by equal and independent states who delegated to it sharply limited authority and who remained superior to it in every way. They believed that a national government was a central organization with coercive authority over both the states and their citizens. They expressed these beliefs as clearly in 1776 as they did in 1787, and they acted accordingly.[2] Hence it is difficult to maintain that the Articles of Confederation were the result of ignorance and inexperience or that the Constitution was the result of wisdom and experience. Actually both governments were the results of choice by men, very few of whom changed their minds between 1776 and 1787. Differing conceptions of the purpose of government, not igno-

[2]This question of the meaning of terms as used in the eighteenth century has never been studied adequately and does not belong in this paper. The materials are to be found in Thomas Jefferson, Notes on Debates, July 30, 31, August 1, 1776, in *Writings of Thomas Jefferson*, edited by A. E. Bergh (Washington, 1907), I, 33–35; John Adams, Notes on Debates, in *Works of John Adams*, edited by C. F. Adams (Boston, 1850–1856), II, 370–371; Max Farrand, ed., *The Records of the Federal Convention of 1787* (New Haven, 1911–1937), I, 39, 40–42, 19, n. 7. See also Madison's argument in *The Federalist*, no. 39, and Merrill Jensen, *The Articles of Confederation* (Madison, 1940), chap. vii, "The Problem of Sovereignty".

rance, lay at the bottom of the political conflicts and changes of the American Revolution.

The assumption that the demand for a centralized or "national" government with coercive power arose from the experiences of the Revolution, the weaknesses of the Articles of Confederation, and the chaos of the Confederation period is as untenable as the assumption of political ignorance on the part of revolutionary leaders. Actually the idea of a centralized government had its roots deep in the history of the colonies. Plan after plan for a centralized government in the colonies had been proposed from the beginning of the eighteenth century. Most of these plans were concerned with the problems of frontier defense and trade but they also involved the establishment of a central authority with direct control over military affairs and a measure of civil power as well, concentrated in the hands of a powerful executive and a legislative body composed of delegates from the several colonial legislatures. This body had been called a "national assembly" as early as 1698.[3] As the years passed and the tensions in colonial society increased, there began to appear in these plans of union for frontier defense the idea of union for self-defense on the part of the colonial aristocracies. Evidence of this is to be found in a number of queries submitted by Dr. Samuel Johnson, President of King's College, in the year 1760. He frankly disliked the "republican character" of many of the colonial governments and wanted them made uniform with the government of the mother country. The republican form, he said, "is indeed pernicious to them, as the people are nearly rampant in their high notions of liberty, and thence perpetually running into intrigue and faction and the rulers so dependant

[3]These plans have been brought together in Hampton L. Carson, ed., *History of the Celebration of the One Hundredth Anniversary of the Promulgation of the Constitution of the United States* (Philadelphia, 1889), II, 439–486. D'Avenant's plan in which the term "national assembly" is used is on pages 454–455.

on them that they in many cases, are afraid to do what is best and right for fear of disobliging them."[4]

The events of the years 1763 to 1774 served to fortify this type of thinking, for in their dispute with the mother country the colonial ruling classes fatally but inescapably sought the support of the farmers and the "mechanicks." When tax and trade laws could not be evaded by dutiful petitions, popular riots were encouraged by the aristocracy of the towns to give point to their constitutional theories about the right of self-government. But soon leaders came forth to voice popular grievances against local injustices and to demand more self-government within the colonies themselves. These new leaders like Sam Adams and Patrick Henry wrapped themselves in the all-embracing mantle of patriotism, attacked the merchant and planter aristocracies for half-hearted measures in defense of American liberties, and sought to displace them in office and positions of power. The merchant aristocracy of the North was thus faced with an ever more powerful political movement within the towns, while the planter aristocracy of the southern colonies was challenged by an ever-growing back country which expressed itself in such outbursts as the Regulator Movement when constitutional and legal means of relief were denied it.

The growing awareness of the possibility of internal revolution as a concomitant of the struggle against British restrictions caused many members of the aristocracy to become less ardent in their opposition to Great Britain, while it caused others to turn to the idea of a voluntary surrender of a portion of their local authority in a closer union with the mother country. In the spring of 1774, Thomas Wharton of Philadelphia expressed this attitude. He said there should be a union on

[4]*Ibid.*, II, 483. Dr. Johnson suggested the appointment of a viceroy to be located in New York. He should meet with delegates from the various colonial legislatures from time to time to consult on war and trade and veto or approve "laws passed in each government."

constitutional principles with a central legislature in the colonies and with an executive appointed by the King and with more power than the colonial governors. This "supreme legislature" should have the power "to make Laws relative to the General Police of America," for, said Wharton, such power "would have a tendency of checking a Turbulent Spirit in any one of the Colonies & give England as well as the Colonies a greater Security than they would otherwise have."[5] This same attitude was expressed with characteristic frankness by Gouverneur Morris, a witness of the controversy in New York in 1774. In the years just past, he wrote, the aristocracy had gulled the mob, but the mob now had leaders of its own and could not be fooled forever. If the disputes with Great Britain were to continue, the aristocracy would lose all power and be ruled by a riotous mob. Therefore Morris declared himself for peace at almost any price, for he said that the English constitution was the guarantee of the position of the wealthy people in the colonies.[6]

It was with such an attitude that many representatives of the conservative elements in American society came to the first Continental Congress in the fall of 1774. Here they were met with two ideas they abhorred. The revolutionary group[7]

[5]Thomas Wharton to Thomas Walpole, Philadelphia, May 2, 1774, in Thomas Wharton Letter-Book, 1773–1784. pp. 34–35, in the Pennsylvania Historical Society. Many a colonial was well aware of the practical advantages of the British connection, as well as of the irritants arising from it. Many, for instance, were not averse to having British troops stationed in the colonies, where they could be and were used to suppress local outbreaks against established authority. See, for instance, John Penn to William Murray, Philadelphia, January 29, 1764, in the Emmett Collection, no. 3116, New York Public Library.

[6]Gouverneur Morris to ... Penn, New York, May 30, 1774, in Peter Force, ed., *American Archives* (Washington, 1837–1853), 4th ser., I, 342.

[7]It is difficult, though necessary, to provide some label for the opposing parties during the Revolution, because readers at once attach to such labels a content derived from their own experience rather than the content which should be derived from the facts of the period for which they are used. Those called conservatives in this study were members

proposed that the law of nature be made the basis of colonial rights, whereas the conservatives naturally preferred the certainties offered by the British constitution and the colonial charters. Equally abhorrent, especially to representatives of the mercantile interest, was the proposal to stop all trade with Great Britain. Such measures would result only in independence and chaos.

Because of their desire to stay within the empire and its certainties, and, as Galloway said, "to probe the ultimate designs of the republicans" to see if they were willing to stop short of independence, the conservatives united in drafting a plan for a centralized government in the colonies. In his speech prefacing the plan Galloway presented the general argument for centralization consistently used by those conservatives who, unlike Galloway, finally chose the revolutionary side when forced to make a choice by the Declaration of Independence. The colonies, said Galloway, were "so many inferior societies, disunited and unconnected in polity." They deny the authority of Parliament, and yet in their relations with one another they are in a perfect state of nature and destitute of any supreme direction or decision whatever, even to the settlement of differences among themselves. Only the authority of Parliament had prevented civil war between colony and colony in the past. Therefore there must be either an Ameri-

---

of that group who wished to retain the British connection, but, failing that, and choosing to become revolutionists, wished to retain the political and economic structure of the colonial period unchanged in the new states. The revolutionary group, or party (the "radicals"), wanted independence from the beginning of the struggle. Their motives were extremely various. Some wanted power; some wanted political and social change in varying degrees; some had special grievances of various kinds. But on the whole one thing is clear: they disagreed with the "conservatives" on the issue of the nature of the central government to be adopted for the American states. Most of the conservatives saw in a powerful central government the means of maintaining the status quo, and they saw this from the start.

can parliament or a surrender of authority to the King or to Parliament.[8]

Galloway thus expressed the conviction of all those who assumed the necessity of coercive centralized authority. Behind the assumption lay many motives, ranging all the way from the disinterested patriotism of men as different as Washington and Thomas Paine to the economic and political opportunism of Alexander Hamilton and Gouverneur Morris. This complexity of motivation perhaps goes far toward explaining the relative ineffectiveness of the conservative group during the Revolution, for all too often those who urged more power for Congress in the interest of the "good of the whole" could be and were charged with using such arguments as a cloak for private gain at the expense of "the whole."

The revolutionary group defeated the Galloway plan, but it did not object to some form of central organization, especially as a means of shoving the colonies in the direction of independence. As early as 1766, Sam Adams expressed his delight with the Stamp Act because it made possible a union of the colonies.[9] Likewise the revolutionary group welcomed the first Continental Congress. In 1775 and in 1776 they supported plans of confederation which were in turn defeated by the conservatives. The paradox was only a seeming one, for in 1775 and 1776 the idea of confederation was a part of the radical program of achieving independence by indirection. Men like John Dickinson, James Wilson, Robert Morris and Robert Livingston knew this, and hence their opposition.[10]

But when it became apparent that independence could no longer be avoided, the conservatives, led by John Dickinson, switched their tactics once more. They argued eloquently the

[8]Joseph Galloway, *Historical and Political Reflections on the Rise and Progress of the American Rebellion* (London, 1780), pp. 70–77.

[9]Sam Adams to Christopher Gadsden, Boston, December 11, 1766, in Samuel Adams Papers, New York Public Library.

[10]Jensen, *Articles of Confederation*, pp. 84, 87–88.

need of sovereign authority over the new states-to-be; they pictured the horrors of civil war; they deplored the fact that people felt at liberty to do as they pleased at any time; they insisted on the necessity of centralized authority to regulate trade and western lands, and to suppress civil war.[11] When the motion for independence and confederation was made early in June 1776, the conservatives, led by John Dickinson, dominated the committee appointed to draft articles of confederation. This committee offered to Congress the draft of a constitution with enormous potentialities, for in it no restrictions were placed on the authority of Congress and no guarantees of rights were made to the states. In addition, Congress was given power to establish state boundaries and to control western lands, the chief source of potential wealth in the eighteenth century.

All these features were eventually deleted from the Articles. Southern conservatives like John Rutledge, who had not felt the force of internal revolution, were afraid that the South would be at the mercy of the "democratic" states of New England; landholding states wanted no interference with their claims; and above all the "federalists" wanted no power superior to the power of the individual state governments. The Articles of Confederation when completed left ultimate power in the hands of the creating states. The central government was given specific and sharply circumscribed powers. And most important of all, the creating states retained for themselves that vast area of unspecified, unenumerated powers, the twilight zone wherein constitutional governments function most largely.[12]

The political groups who brought on the Revolution thus won a sweeping victory, but those conservatives who chose the revolutionary side, so far as independence was concerned, did not surrender their ideals of government. Their experience with revolutionary enthusiasms and more democratic forms

[11]*Ibid.*, pp. 112–116.
[12]*Ibid.*, chapters v-viii.

of state government confirmed them in the fears they had expressed before the Declaration of Independence. Hence their desire for a national government was intensified rather than diminished, and they showed no more intention of accepting the Articles of Confederation as a permanent constitution than they did of accepting the more democratic constitutions adopted in some of the states.[13]

For a time the Revolution swept many of the conservatives from positions of effectiveness, although enough remained in legislative seats to voice from time to time the demand for centralized authority. They could not change the Articles of Confederation, now before the states for ratification, but they could and did seek to establish precedents upon the basis of which they could argue the sovereignty of Congress. Gouverneur Morris had proposed such strategy as early as 1775. He had then urged Congress to consider the case of James Rivington, the Tory printer in New York City. Morris declared that by such action Congress would acquire judicial power just as the Association had given it legislative power. The canny Morris was keenly appreciative of the importance of precedent. "The power of Government as of man," he said, "is to be collected from small instances; great affairs are more the object of reflection and policy. Here both join."[14]

[13]Edward Rutledge wrote to John Jay, November 24, 1776, advising a strong executive for New York, because, he said, "a pure democracy may possibly do, when patriotism is the ruling passion; but when the state abounds with rascals, as is the case with many at this day, you must suppress a little of that popular spirit." In *The Correspondence and Public Papers of John Jay*, edited by H. P. Johnston (New York and London, 1890–1893), I, 94. The bitter opposition of conservatives like Dickinson, Wilson and Morris to the Pennsylvania Constitution of 1776 was such that for months at a time it prevented any effective action on behalf of the war by the Pennsylvania legislature. Richard Henry Lee was convinced that the people who opposed the Declaration of Independence were also opposed to the completion of the Articles of Confederation, because it would complete the independence of the American states. To Sam Adams, July 12, 1777, in Samuel Adams Papers.

[14]Gouverneur Morris to Richard Henry Lee, May 1775, in Force, *American Archives*, 4th ser., II, 726.

Time and again the small minority of conservatives who remained in Congress tried to "collect" the power of government "from small instances." One such instance was the report of a price-fixing convention in New England in 1777 which was laid before Congress. James Wilson and others argued that the approval of Congress was necessary. His opponents were convinced that the purpose of this approval was to secure for Congress the power of disapproval of other state acts at a later time, and so defeated the proposal.[15] Many of the revolutionary group were as well aware as the conservatives of the subtle power of precedents once established.

Closely related to the forces behind such strategy were the land companies, whose members sought to profit from lands lying west of the Alleghenies. The issue was clear: if states with charter claims like Virginia retained control, her own speculators would have first chance; if Congress got control, the speculators from the landless states organized in companies like the Indiana, Illinois, and Wabash might have better hopes of success. These companies had appealed to a central government—the British—before the Revolution to separate the West from Virginia and to give it to them. Once the Revolution broke out, it was natural for them to appeal to Congress, which in all hopefulness they pictured as the inheritor of British sovereignty. The appeal was tangible as well as theoretical, for they distributed shares of their stock to members of Congress.[16]

The Dickinson draft of the Confederation gave the desired power to Congress, but it was taken completely away by the landed states before the Confederation was completed. Thus

[15]Thomas Burke, Abstract of Debates in Congress, February 12, 1777, in Edmund C. Burnett, ed., *Letters of Members of the Continental Congress* (Washington, 1921–1936), II, 249; Benjamin Rush, Diary, February 4, 1777, in *ibid.*, II, 234–235; William Ellery to the Governor of Rhode Island, February 15, 1777, in *ibid.*, II, 255.

[16]See Merrill Jensen, "The Cession of the Old Northwest," in the *Mississippi Valley Historical Review* (June 1936), XXIII, 27–48.

defeated in practical politics, the land companies sought support for their claims both from Virginia and from Congress, the direction of the appeals being determined from time to time by the apparent chances of success. When Virginia's actions finally made it plain that there was little to be gained from her, representatives of the land companies evolved tenuous theories in support of the sovereignty of Congress in general and over western lands in particular. An Indiana Company memorial in 1779, for instance, declared that the West had been set up as a separate government under the sovereignty of the King, and that now the jurisdiction over that land was in the hands of "the whole United States in Congress assembled, in whom the Sovereignty is now vested."[17] Other memorials were even more explicit. One of them declared that "all the Rights and all the obligations of the Crown of Great Britain respecting the lands and governments devolve upon the *United States* and are to be claimed, exercised and discharged by the United States in Congress Assembled."[18]

This subtle doctrine of the devolution of sovereignty was the creation of the nationalists, for such men as James Wilson and Robert Morris were leading members of the land companies. But no such doctrine, however subtle, could mislead the representatives of the landed states. And when Virginia denied all jurisdiction of Congress in such matters, William Trent replied for both the Indiana and Vandalia companies with utter frankness that the "Question of the jurisdiction of Congress" was the very essence of their claims, and that it was "of infinite consequence to the American Union as well as to your memorialists."[19]

Repeated defeats such as these by no means abated the

[17]Papers of the Continental Congress, no. 77, folios 234–236, in the Library of Congress. This was presented by George Morgan.

[18]Walpole Company Memorial presented by William Trent, September 11, 1779, in Papers of the Continental Congress, no. 41, X, folios 79–86.

[19]October 13, 1780, Papers of the Continental Congress, no. 77, folios 230–233.

determination of those who saw in the creation of a powerful centralized government the answer to their needs and desires. It was not, however, until 1781 that they appeared in Congress in numbers sufficient to indicate conservative victories in many of the states in 1780.[20]

The stresses of the year 1780 gave strong grounds for their activity both in the state governments and in Congress. Public finance seemed an insurmountable problem. British success in the South was frightening. Men were casting desperately about for political remedies for economic and military problems that no political scheme could solve. In private letters, newspaper essays, and in state politics the nationalists urged their program with more force than ever, for now they had behind them a new and powerful interest created by the Revolution—the public creditors who held evidences of debt issued by state and central governments. Great riches lay in the masses of depreciated paper used to finance the war if Congress could acquire the power of taxation and forcible collection. The nationalists did not look upon this debt as a handicap, but agreed with Hamilton who declared in 1781: "A national debt, if it is not excessive, will be to us a national blessing. It will be a powerful cement of our Union."[21] There was no novelty, even then, in this concept of a creditor group as a powerful nationalizing force, for, as early as May 1775,

[20]Robert Morris was elected to the Pennsylvania legislature; a conservative constitution was written in Massachusetts; Thomas Jefferson was replaced by Thomas Nelson, a conservative, as governor of Virginia. These are but a few samples of the changes which were taking place in 1780 and 1781, and which were being reflected in the changing personnel of Congress.

[21]Hamilton to Robert Morris, April 30, 1781, in *The Works of Alexander Hamilton*, edited by John C. Hamilton (New York, 1851), I, 257. The debt was rapidly concentrating in the North. Hamilton wrote Governor Clinton on May 14, 1783, that at least four-fifths of the domestic debt was due to the citizens of the states from Pennsylvania and north. *The Works of Alexander Hamilton*, edited by Henry Cabot Lodge (New York and London, 1904), IX, 342.

the New York Provincial Congress had concerned itself with currency problems and accepted a report drafted by Gouverneur Morris. This report declared that Congress should control all currency. One of the reasons given for this proposal was "that whenever a Paper currency has been emitted, and obtained general credit, it will be a new bond of union to the Associated Colonies. . . ."[22] In 1776, Joseph Hawley of Massachusetts urged the creation of a confederation, because "without a general Superintending Legislative what will become of us with regard to our Paper Medium?"[23] And, as the war neared its end, Robert Morris, from his eminence as superintendent of finance, wrote to John Jay, "Finance, my friend, the whole of what remains of the American Revolution grounds there."[24]

It is evident that men saw a connection between centralization and currency during the Revolution. It is also evident that some of them looked upon the public debt and debt funding as involving more than economics or justice. Hamilton and Gouverneur Morris early realized that the creditor group might be consolidated behind a movement for the imposition of a national government upon the states. The demand for more congressional power over finance grew ever stronger with depreciation and with the concentration of the public debt in fewer and fewer hands. There was talk of dictatorship —of giving Washington power to extract from state governments by force that which could not be acquired by persuasion. There was a demand that strong men be given charge

[22] Force, *American Archives*, 4th ser., II, 1264. Report of the Committee on the Expediency of Continental Currency.

[23] Joseph Hawley to Sam Adams, Watertown, June 2, 1776, in Samuel Adams Papers. See also [Samuel Savage] to Sam Adams, August 22, 1776, in Samuel Adams Papers.

[24] Jared Sparks, *The Life of Gouverneur Morris* (Boston, 1832) I, 234. Robert Morris wrote to Hamilton July 2, 1782, that "what remains of the war, being only a war of finance, solid arrangements of finance must necessarily terminate favorably. . . ." Hamilton, *Works* (Hamilton ed.), I, 285.

of government departments. There was talk of forcing people to accept distinctions in rank.[25] Then, in the fall of 1780, Alexander Hamilton embodied most of such proposals in a concrete program of action presented to James Duane, a persistent nationalist.

The root of evil, Hamilton said, was that Congress lacked the power to act upon the states collectively. To get around this fact, he conjured up the idea that Congress should use "undefined powers." Such powers could be limited only by the object of the establishment of Congress, which was the freedom and independence of America. The Confederation could be ignored, since it had not been ratified, and, furthermore, it was defective because of the idea of "uncontrolled sovereignty in each State over its internal police. . . ." Congress must perform innumerable acts for the general good which would interfere with this power of the states.

There were two ways to get power. The first was to assume that Congress had once had and used discretionary power limited only by the end for which Congress had been organized. Hamilton was too realistic to suppose that such an assumption would be accepted by "the generality of Congress," and his second proposal showed that the nationalists had learned much from radical tactics. Hamilton proposed that a convention be called, that it be given power to draw up and adopt a new government without reference to Congress, the states, or the people. This government would be a

[25]See Jared Sparks's summary of Gouverneur Morris' essays of "An American" which appeared in the *Pennsylvania Packet* in February and March 1780. Sparks, *Morris*, I, 218–233.

The scheme to give Washington dictatorial powers in the year 1780 is hidden in a fog of cryptic remarks, but it was apparently a real effort. See Philip Schuyler to Hamilton, Philadelphia, April 8, 1780, in Hamilton, *Works* (Hamilton ed.), I, 135–136; General Nathaniel Greene to Joseph Reed, Norristown, May 20, 1780, in Joseph Reed Papers, New York Historical Society; James Lovell to Elbridge Gerry, November 20, 1780, in Burnett, *Letters*, V, 452; Matthews to Washington, September 15, 1780, in *ibid.*, V. 373.

"solid, coercive union" with "complete sovereignty" over the civil, military and economic life of the thirteen states. Its economic power was to be assured by permanent revenues in the form of land taxes, poll taxes, duties on trade, and the ownership of all unoccupied western lands.

In the meantime Congress must take two immediate steps to secure power. The committees in charge of foreign affairs, war, marine, trade and finance must be replaced by single executives who should be "men of first abilities, property, and character in the continent. . . ." The second step was for Congress to consolidate behind it the power of the army, which, like the creditors, Hamilton described as an "essential cement to the union. . . ." The army should be reformed. Hamilton said it was "a mob rather than an army, without clothing, without pay, without provisions, without morale, and without discipline." Congress could attach the army to it by providing clothing and by giving the officers half pay for life. "Congress would then have a solid basis of authority and consequence; for, to me, it is an axiom, that in our constitution, an army is essential to the American Union."[26] Hamilton's belief in the use of force provided by the creditors and the army to achieve political ends foreshadows the attempted *coup d'état* of 1783, not to mention the willingness of some nationalists to use force in 1787, had that been necessary to achieve their ends.[27]

No general convention was called, but in November 1780, groups of delegates from New York and the New England states met at Hartford, ostensibly to deal with the problem of

[26]Hamilton to Duane, September 3, 1780, in *Works* (Hamilton ed.), I, 150–168.

[27]See the letter of Benjamin Rush to Richard Price, June 2, 1787, in the Massachusetts Historical Society *Proceedings*, 2nd ser., XVII, 367–368. Rush said that time, necessity and reason would wear down the opposition to the constitution when it appeared but that if those failed, "force will not be wanting to carry it into execution; for not only all the wealth, but all the military men of our country (associated with the society of Cincinnati) are in favor of a wise and efficient government."

raising troops in the North. Far more than this was involved, for General Schuyler had said before the convention met that there would be a proposal to ask for the appointment of a dictator, with "Vice-Dictators" in each of the thirteen states.[28] The convention did not go that far, but it did urge that Washington be given dictatorial power to collect supplies from the states and that Congress be given the power of taxation, in order to pay the interest on the public debt. It declared that the lack of coercive power in the "General Government of the Continent" was the greatest defect. To remedy it, the idea of implied powers was propounded. The powers of Congress had never been defined, said the convention, but there was a "necessarily implied compact" between the states at the beginning of the war. From this it "may certainly be inferred that Congress was vested with every power essential to the common defense. . . ." However, the convention was willing to waive argument on this point. The important thing was to exercise power now, and, though the idea might seem harsh, a weak and inefficient government could never answer the ends of society. These the convention defined as defense against foreign invasion.[29]

Such ideas were startling to men like James Warren, who wrote to Sam Adams:

if one of them [the resolutions] does not astonish you I have forgot my political catechism. Surely history will not be credited when it shall record that a convention of Delegates from the four N England States & from the next to them met at Hartford in the year 1780 and in the heighth of our contest for public Liberty & security solemnly Resolved to recommend to their several States to Vest the Military with Civil Powers of an extraordinary

[28]Schuyler to Hamilton, September 10 and 16, 1780, in Hamilton, *Works* (Hamilton ed.), I, 183, 184–185.

[29]"Proceedings of the Hartford Convention, November 8–14, 1780," in the *Magazine of American History* (October 1882), VIII, pt. 2, 688–698.

kind & where their own Interest is concerned, no less than a compulsive power over deficient States to oblige them by the point of a Bayonet to furnish money & supplies for their own pay & support.[30]

Congress refused to consider such schemes in 1780, but by 1781 significant changes took place in the complexion of that group. Nationalists were beginning to appear there in significant numbers. John Dickinson was elected from Delaware, although he did not attend. James Duane, James Wilson, Robert R. Livingston, James Varnum, James Madison and Alexander Hamilton all appeared and became the dominant figures in congressional affairs from 1781 to 1783. The presence of these men and many lesser ones who followed their lead helps to explain, as much as the distresses of the months before Yorktown, the measures taken by Congress in 1781. It also helps to explain the temporary subsidence of proposals for revolutionary action by the nationalist group. Once back in Congress they sought to achieve their ends by amendments to the Confederation, by administrative changes, and by a variety of ingenious interpretations of the Confederation.

The ideas expressed in newspaper essays, at the Hartford Convention and in private letters were now adopted in some detail. An amendment giving Congress a limited revenue for an unlimited time was sent to the states for ratification. Committees of Congress were replaced by men to whom both circumstance and design gave dictatorial power. Robert Morris became superintendent of finance with Gouverneur Morris as his assistant. Robert R. Livingston became secretary of foreign affairs. Benjamin Lincoln became secretary of war. Robert Morris, as banker, as merchant, and as a public official controlling the finances of Congress, represented more power than the American states had yet seen in the hands of a single man. He appointed collectors of federal requisitions in each of the states. He started a private bank with money Congress

[30]Plymouth, December 4, 1780, in Samuel Adams Papers.

borrowed in France. He made the office of superintendent of finance the center around which rallied all the multifold interest desiring authoritarian government.[31]

In the long run, even such far-reaching steps were inadequate, for the Articles of Confederation hedged Congress within narrow bounds. From the nationalist point of view, the essential power lacked was the power of coercion over the states and their citizens. It was *power*, not powers, that they wanted. Given the power of coercion, all other powers could be taken for granted, for few of the nationalists were hampered by regard for either democratic spirit or forms. These nationalists actually looked upon the ratification of the Confederation as of doubtful value for fear that it would encourage the idea that Congress had thereby gained enough power.[32]

As soon as ratification of the Confederation was complete, a committee was appointed to prepare plans for making it effective. James Duane, James Madison and James Varnum, three outstanding nationalists, were the committee, and their report coincides more nearly with their ideas than it did with the realities of the moment, for, short of revolutionary action, all the states would have to approve. The committee used the idea of implied powers differently than Hamilton and the Hartford Convention had used it the year before. They now declared that the Confederation itself gave Congress "a gen-

[31]Jennings B. Saunders, *Evolution of the Executive Departments of the Continental Congress, 1774–1789* (Chapel Hill, 1935), contains a brief account of this movement. All the treatments of Morris are highly partial one way or another and none of them gives an adequate account of his rôle as superintendent of finance.

[32]Hamilton to ———?, February 7, 1781, in *Works* (Lodge ed.), IX, 230–231. Such sentiments were also to be found in the newspapers. See "An Independent American" to "The People of America" in the *Pennsylvania Gazette*, March 14, 1781. This writer argued that the importance of the ratification of the Articles of Confederation not be exaggerated, because such covenants or confederations on paper were of no consequence unless supported by virtue and honor.

eral and implied power" to carry the Articles of Confederation into effect in the states, but that because no "determinate and particular provision" to that effect was in the Confederation, they were ready to propose a new amendment. This amendment gave Congress the specific power to use the army and navy to force the states to abide by the decisions of Congress. This and many other amendments to free Congress from dependence on the states were proposed, but the demands were so extreme that Congress delayed consideration of them repeatedly, until circumstances once more played a conclusive rôle.[33]

The battle of Yorktown in the fall of 1781 and the peace negotiations under way gave no joy to the nationalists. Their arguments for centralization and the supposed efficiency and economy that would result depended heavily on the continuance of the war, and they knew it. Shortly after Yorktown Gouverneur Morris wrote General Greene that the acquisition of power by Congress was a difficult matter, but that "To reinforce the reasonings, to impress the arguments, and to sweeten the persuasions of the public servants, we have that great friend to sovereign authority, a foreign war." But he said, if the war stopped, he had little hope that the "government would acquire force."[34] Robert Morris agreed with this view. He declared that he would welcome peace so that he might be rid of his job but that, if he were to speak as a patriot, he would wish that the war would continue until the central government acquired more power.[35]

The approaching end of the war thus forced the nationalists to realize that one of their best arguments for increased centralized authority would soon disappear, and this realization

[33]*Journals of Congress*, XIX, 239; XX, 469–471, 773; Papers of the Continental Congress, no. 24, folios 49–51.

[34]Philadelphia, December 24, 1781, in Sparks, *Morris*, I, 239–240.

[35]To Matthew Ridley, October 6, 1782, in *The Confidential Correspondence of Robert Morris* (Stan V. Henkels Catalogue, No. 1183), 41.

was accompanied by a growing desperation as one after another of their measures failed of success. Evidence of this desperation was the fact that once more they took refuge in constitutional theories and talk of conventions. In July 1782, the New York legislature adopted a recommendation drafted by Hamilton for a convention to give Congress both power and money.[36] The public creditors in New York held a meeting in September and talked of a creditors' convention for the state, and even of one for all the states.[37] Hamilton told Governor Clinton of New York that since Congress had the power to determine the amount of money to be paid into the public treasury, it therefore had the constitutional power of taxation.[38]

The urbane Robert Morris became almost plaintive in arguing with the governor of Rhode Island, who insisted that it was unconstitutional to ask for an impost amendment. Morris replied that "if a thing be neither wrong nor forbidden it must be admissible"; that the requisition was not forbidden and certainly not wrong for "it can not be wrong to do that which one is obliged to do, be the act what it may." And even if one admitted that the request might be contrary to the Confederation, the Confederation itself was created by general consent and by general consent might be altered. "The requisition therefore, if complied with, will by that very compliance become constitutional."[39]

Such arguments and theories reveal more of the desires of their users than they do of the nature of the Constitution. Far more to the point was a scheme of revolutionary action which a variety of events brought to a head. In January 1783, Vir-

[36]Hamilton to Robert Morris, Poughkeepsie, July 22, 1782, in *Works* (Lodge ed.), IX, 265.

[37]Hamilton to Robert Morris, September 28, 1782, in *ibid.*, IX, 293.

[38]February 24, 1783, in *ibid.*, IX, 315.

[39]October 24, 1782, in Francis Wharton, ed., *The Revolutionary Diplomatic Correspondence of the United States* (Washington, 1889), V, 830–832.

ginia withdrew her ratification of the impost amendment of 1781 and thus joined Rhode Island in opposition. A member of Congress wrote in the same month that "Congress are, and have been exceedingly embarrassed by the urgent, and reiterated Demands made upon them by the publick Creditors, holding Certificates and liquidated accounts. . . ."[40]

Virginia's repeal was a bitter blow to their hopes. Robert Morris offered his resignation as superintendent of finance, partly if not wholly as a means of forcing Congress to take some action on behalf of the creditors.[41] During this same time, the discontent[42] which had been smoldering among the officers of Washington's army at Newburgh came to a head with the appointment of three men who were sent to Congress to demand a settlement of accounts. When this committee, headed by General McDougall, appeared in Philadelphia, two kinds of meetings took place: official meetings with a committee of Congress, and unofficial meetings with certain of the nationalist politicians, including Gouverneur Morris and Alexander Hamilton. These men saw in the clamors of the creditors and the discontent of the officers an opportunity to unite the two groups in a *coup d'état* to establish the kind of government they had been unable to establish through either constitutional processes or interpretations.[43]

As a result of the unofficial negotiations, the army commit-

[40]Samuel Wharton to the Delaware Council, January 6, 1783, in Burnett, *Letters*, VII, 2–4.

[41]Arthur Lee to Sam Adams, March 15, 1783, in Burnett, *Letters*, VII, 68; *Pennsylvania Gazette*, March 5, 1783; North Carolina Delegates to the Governor of North Carolina, March 24, 1783, in Burnett, *Letters*, VII, 99; Hamilton to Washington, April 1783, in *Works* (Lodge ed.), IX, 334–335.

[42]Rufus Putnam to Sam Adams, Boston, October 18, 1782, in Samuel Adams Papers. Putnam said that the temper of the army was such that it should not be trusted with arms.

[43]There are but two accounts of this scheme worthy of attention. The oldest is that of George Bancroft, *History of the Formation of the Constitution of the United States* (New York, 1882), chap. v, "A Plan

tee was convinced that it should throw in its lot with Congress, rather than to turn to the states for a settlement of accounts.[44] A delegate was sent back to the army officers at Newburgh, apparently with instructions to keep Washington in the dark.[45] General McDougall was perfectly frank in reporting the situation to General Henry Knox. He listed all the difficulties in the way of securing a settlement and then asked: "Under these apprehensions, as well as others of general concern to the Confederacy, what if it should be proposed to unite the influence of Congress with that of the Army and the publick Creditors to obtain permanent funds for the United States which will promise most for the ultimate security of the Army?"[46] Meanwhile Gouverneur Morris was predicting, prematurely but revealingly, that "much of convulsion will ensue" and that it "must terminate in giving to government that power, without which government is but a name." No grant of funds would be made by the states, he said, unless the army united with the other public creditors to obtain it.[47] To General Knox he wrote that the only thing the army could do was to unite with the creditors of every kind, both foreign and domestic, and urge the granting of permanent funds. "The

---

to Force a Stronger Government". Within the limits of his materials Bancroft does a much better job than subsequent historians who have covered the same ground. The other account is that of John Corbin, in his *Two Frontiers of Freedom* (New York and London, 1940), part 2, chap. iii, "Fascism—1783". In this study, as in his biography of Washington, Corbin deals with facts that historians have usually ignored and he comes to some extraordinary conclusions.

[44]Gouverneur Morris to General Nathaniel Greene, February 15, 1783, in Sparks, *Morris*, I, 250–251.

[45]John Armstrong, Jr., to General Horatio Gates, Philadelphia, April 29, 1783, in Burnett, *Letters*, VII, 155, n. 3. This letter, written after the failure of the scheme, predicts that civil war will follow.

[46]January 19, 1783, in Burnett, *Letters*, VII, 14, n. 2. See also McDougall's letter of February 19, in *ibid.*, VII, 50, n., and McDougall and Ogden to Knox, February 8, in *ibid.*, VII, 35, n.

[47]Morris to John Jay, January 1, 1783, in Sparks, *Morris*, I, 249.

army may now influence the Legislatures and if you will permit a Metaphor from your own Profession after you have carried the Post the public Creditors will garrison it for you."[48] Meanwhile Arthur Lee wrote to Sam Adams that "the terror of a mutinying army is played off with considerable efficacy."[49]

The key figure in any such scheme was Washington, and Hamilton undertook to sound him out. In his letter, Hamilton was more than a little circuitous, for Washington's reactions were not to be predicted in spite of his reiterated demands for a stronger central government. Hamilton discussed the inadequacies of Congress, the necessity of the army supporting itself if the war continued, and of supporting itself to secure justice if peace were declared. How to keep a suffering army in bounds was the question, and this only Washington could do. He should take direction of the army's efforts to obtain redress, and he should endeavor to retain the confidence of the army without losing that of the people. Hamilton insinuated that Washington was suspected of not being sufficiently interested in the welfare of the army. He concluded by saying that the "great *desideratum* . . . is the establishment of general funds which alone can do justice to the creditors of the United States. . . . In this the influence of the army, properly directed, may operate."[50]

Washington refused to accept the responsibility. He refused to believe that the discontent of the army was as serious as the nationalists tried to convince him it was. He said flatly that he did not believe the army would exceed "the bounds of reason and moderation, notwithstanding the prevailing sentiment in the Army is, that the prospect of compensation for past Services will terminate with the War."[51] And finally

[48]February 7, 1783, in Burnett, *Letters*, VII, 34, n.

[49]January 29, 1783, in *ibid.*, VII, 28.

[50]February 7, 1783, in *Works* (Lodge ed.), IX, 310.

[51]To Hamilton, March 4, 1783, in *The Writings of George Washington from the Original Manuscript Sources, 1745–1799*, edited by John C. Fitzpatrick (Washington, 1931–41), XXVI, 135–188.

he charged that the whole affair was a plot of politicians in Philadelphia.[52]

Washington was either unaware how far the plans had gone among his officers, or else he chose to ignore them until anonymous petitions were circulated among the officers urging them to refuse to fight if the war should continue and to refuse to lay down their arms if peace should be declared, until they had secured some settlement of their accounts. Washington then took charge and in a dramatic speech to the officers he defeated the scheme, for without him and the officers who were sure to follow him nothing could be done.[53]

In spite of this crucial defeat, the nationalists remained active until the official cessation of hostilities. Once more the basic weakness of their plans was apparent, for, as usual, they failed to take into account the political realities they faced, so ridden were they by their own desires. Only a group of officers had been involved whereas any such measure needed an army to make it successful. And it was perfectly obvious that the common soldiers had but one desire and that was a desire to go home which they demonstrated by insubordination, riots and desertion. Washington, faced with a disintegrating army, suppressed the riots, flogged the soldiers, and asked Congress for advice. Congress evaded the issue and shifted the responsibility back to him by allowing him to grant furloughs or discharges as he pleased. His officers demanded that he keep the soldiers in camp until their accounts had been settled, but Washington refused to do so, and on June 13, 1783, most of

[52]To Joseph Jones, March 12, 1783, in *Writings*, XXVI, 213–215; to Hamilton, March 12, in *ibid.*, pp. 216–217. Once the plot had failed, Hamilton denied that he had ever contemplated the use of force, although he admitted that he considered it would be well to unite the army and the creditors. To Washington, March 17, in *Works* (Lodge ed.), IX, 323–326.

[53]The Newburgh proceedings are in the *Journals of Congress* for April 29, 1783. Washington's account of this affair is to be found in his letters to the President of Congress, March 18, in *Writings*, XXVI, 229–232, and to Joseph Jones in *ibid.*, pp. 232–233.

the common soldiers and many of the officers started for home without formality or farewell.[54]

The possibility of an armed revolution vanished with the common soldiers who probably knew nothing of what had been intended for them. With them vanished the hopes of the nationalists, and one by one they too returned to private life. Alexander Hamilton and Gouverneur Morris are two examples. Robert Morris, in spite of repeated threats to resign, stayed on as superintendent of finance until the spring of 1784. His place was taken by a committee of three, one of whom was Arthur Lee who had openly charged Morris with corruption. The nationalists did not surrender their hopes or their plans with their positions in Congress: they merely moved back to the states to continue the work for a national government.

The idea of a national government was thus an integral part of the American Revolution. The ideas of the nationalists had been fully shaped by the end of the war. Their oft-defeated schemes and plans indicate the methods by which they were ultimately to achieve success, and are a commentary on their political philosophy, for those plans involved the use of force if necessary, the support of the public creditors, and the exploitation of Washington's prestige to bring about a political revolution. Their ends were the creation of a centralized government with coercive authority and the consolidation behind that government of the creditor groups whose prospects of increased wealth would furnish solid support.

The significance of these facts for the interpretation of the American Revolution is that these ideas, plans and ends were the product, not of a period of post-revolutionary chaos, necessity and governmental weakness, but of the history of the American Colonies, and, more particularly, of the Revolution itself.

[54]Louis C. Hatch, *The Administration of the American Revolutionary Army* (New York, 1904), chaps. viii-ix, has the best general account of these events. The relevant documents are in Burnett's *Letters* and in Washington's *Writings*, XXVI.

THE BEARD THESIS ATTACKED:
A POLITICAL APPROACH

Robert E. Brown

EDITOR'S NOTE Amidst the uproar of outraged
patriotism that greeted the appearance of Beard's
An Economic Interpretation of the Constitution,
there was one critical review that foreshadowed a
substantial segment of present day scholarly opinion. Writing in the *History Teachers Magazine*
(February 1914), Edward S. Corwin, the distinguished constitutional scholar of Princeton, lodged
a reasoned dissent. Focusing upon the principal
point in the Beard thesis, the influence of personalty interests, particularly public securities, Corwin
claimed that Beard's conclusions "scarcely survive"
scrutiny. Analyzing Beard's statistics, Corwin observed that at least one-third of the total security
holdings of the framers were evidences of state, not
United States, indebtedness, the payment of which
the Constitution did not even suggest. Of the remaining two-thirds, most was held by five men, in-
conspicuous figures at the Constitutional Convention except for Elbridge Gerry who possessed the
lion's share—and he *opposed* the Constitution. The
holdings of the leading members of the Convention
amounted to nothing or almost that. More impor-
tantly, "Beard's whole argument," Corwin pointed
out, "rests upon a totally unallowable assumption,"

namely that the framers did not speculate in public securities between 1787 and 1790 and after; therefore, the Treasury Department records which Beard used to identify security holders proved the existence of their holdings in 1787, although the records were from 1790 and after. This, said Corwin bluntly, "is the most unmitigated rot"—and it was. Corwin did not deny that a leading purpose of the Convention was to secure property interests against state attacks, but he noted that everyone knew that. Even George Bancroft and the older writers whom Beard depreciated had recognized that fact, and that the opponents of the Constitution rarely objected to the provisions of Article One, Section 10, by which this objective had been fulfilled. Rejecting the notion that the movement for the Constitution was a species of *coup d'état*, Corwin pointed out that the Congress of the Confederation—the legitimate government that was being superseded —had voluntarily forwarded the Constitution to the states for ratification; moreover, it was achieved by popularly elected state conventions. Corwin also challenged the contention that property qualifications disfranchised most adult males. He noted too that the Constitutional Convention had been chosen by the same legislatures that had been voting paper money and stay laws, and that the state conventions were chosen by the same electors who had chosen those legislatures.

Despite Corwin's criticisms, the book survived and grew in stature. Twenty years after its appearance—during the New Deal, when an emphasis on class conflict in historical interpretation was fashionable—Beard was elected president of the American Historical Association. The honor reflected a belated and widespread professional acceptance of the Beard thesis. A token of its influence is the fact that it was one of the two most prominently mentioned books by a symposium of liberal intellectuals who in 1938 described "Books That Changed Our Minds." By that time, moreover, the vast majority of college texts in American history adopted the Beard thesis. Important scholars like Corwin, Warren, and McLaughlin rejected it, and Beard himself, shortly after, became an apostate to the Beard thesis, but it continued to prevail. In the early 1950's a few isolated scholars began to chip away at it. Robert Thomas showed that, contrary to Beard, the Virginians who favored the Constitution held substantially the same kinds and amounts of property as those who opposed it; Douglass Adair showed that Beard had misconstrued Madison's famous *Federalist* #10; and Cecilia Kenyon showed that the Anti-Federalists were less democratic and more in favor of checks-and-balances than the supporters of the Constitution.

Then, in 1956, Robert E. Brown of Michigan State, published his distempered, wholesale critique, *Charles Beard and the Constitution.* Its object was to prove that the emperor wore no clothes. Though the Beard thesis emerged with considerably more than a fig-leaf to cover its believability, Brown had effectively discredited it. He subjected the great book to a close textual analysis and proved that much of it, though scarcely all as Brown contended, was, as Corwin had said, "unmitigated rot." Beard's facts were not necessarily accurate, nor did they bear out his conclusions. Scholars who had accepted the Beard thesis were, at the least, forced to admit that they had been uncritical. Beard may not have been wrong, but Brown demonstrated that he had not proved his case. Uneasy Beardians argued that the basic "insight" of the economic interpretation was essentially correct, notwithstanding Brown. But "insight" is a word that scholars, like critics and intellectuals, use when they do not have the evidence to support a perception that transcends or substitutes for empirical data, leaving them with the dumb belief that there must be more than the known evidence shows.

Brown not only aimed at demolishing the Beard thesis; he sought to replace it with a thesis of his own, that the Constitution was essentially a democratic document framed by democratic methods for a democratic society. In two books, *Middle Class Democracy and the Revolution in Massachusetts, 1691–1780* (1955) and *Virginia 1705–1786: Democracy or Aristocracy?* (1964, written with his wife), Brown argued that the colonies on the eve of the Revolution were functioning democracies, at least that they were far more democratic than scholars like Beard and Jensen had believed. Although Brown proved that property qualifications on the right to vote did not have a widespread disfranchising effect, his focus on the right to vote exposed him to the criticism that democracy means much more than that. Brown considerably overstated his case. It would have been enough to demonstrate that the Constitution was not an undemocratic document, was more democratic than the Articles of Confederation, and did not impede the development of democracy. To claim that the Constitution itself was a democratic document strained the evidence. To claim that it was written for a democratic society was to indulge in an absurd and fanciful anachronism. But to claim that it was democratically framed and ratified was supportable. In 1963 Brown published his Bacon Lectures, epitomizing his books. The following extract is from the section covering the making of the Constitution.

o o o o

THE WRITING AND RATIFICATION OF THE CONSTITUTION

HAVING examined briefly the structure of colonial society and the nature of the American Revolution, we have now arrived at our final problem, the writing and ratification of the Constitution. And since this document was the joint product of colonial society and the Revolution, a suspicion that we have altered our views about the Constitution would be well-grounded. Today many historians do not look upon this era of our history as they did ten years ago, although again it should be pointed out that not all historians have accepted the latest interpretation.

The interpretation of the Constitution that was accepted until recently had its origins in the reform era and Progressive Movement during the early years of the twentieth century. One of the first writers, and one who never received full recognition for his ideas, was J. Allen Smith, who published *The Spirit of American Government* in 1907. Far better known was another writer, Charles A. Beard, whose book, *An Economic Interpretation of the Constitution of the United States* (New York, 1913), virtually achieved the status of the gospel among most historians and political scientists after its publication in 1913.

As with colonial society and the Revolution, the emphasis in the old interpretation of the Constitution was on class conflict. According to this view, the adoption of the Constitution represented something of a Thermidor—a conservative upper-class counter-revolution designed to reverse the democratic gains achieved by the Revolution.

In more detail, the argument went something like this. The lower classes, having won the Revolution, proceeded to democratize American society in their state constitutions and in the constitution of the general government. Under these democratic governments, the lower classes passed debtor laws, paper money acts, and various other legislation for the benefit of the lower classes. Those elements of the upper classes that had not become Loyalists, and especially the owners of personal property in the form of money, public securities, manufactures, and trade and shipping, became dissatisfied with governments that did not protect their property. Unable to amend the Articles of Confederation to suit their economic purposes, they engineered what amounted to a *coup d'état* in eliminating the Articles and adopting the Constitution.

According to the old interpretation, then, the Constitution was something of a conspiracy by these upper-class, personal property interests to put over a conservative, property-oriented government on the lower classes. Men representing money, public securities, manufactures, and trade and shipping were originators of the move. They were personally interested in and derived economic advantages from the outcome of their labors. No popular vote was taken to call the Constitutional Convention and the propertyless masses, because of property qualifications, were excluded from participation. The Constitution was essentially an economic document based on fundamental beliefs in the rights of private property. Either because of disfranchisement or indifference, only about a fourth of the adult men voted on ratification of the Constitution and probably not more than a sixth of the adult men voted favorably. Men who supported ratification in the state conventions had the same economic interests as the men who wrote the Constitution, and in ratification, the division for and against the Constitution was between substantial personalty interests on one hand and small farmers and debtors on the other.

In short, the argument was that the Constitution was put over undemocratically in an undemocratic society, and the *coup d'état* or conspiracy was carried out by substantial holders of personal property as opposed to small farmers and debtors.

Undoubtedly because recent scholarship has caused a change

in our interpretation of colonial society and the Revolution, historians are now focusing more attention on the Constitution, and with similar results. The class-struggle view of the Constitution does not appear to hold up any better than does a similar interpretation of colonial society and the Revolution. Let us look at these points one by one to see what the evidence reveals.

The first thing that we encounter is a tremendously complicated contradiction in the old interpretation. If the Revolution was a successful social movement by the lower classes, why did the new state constitutions retain their old property qualifications for voting and often impose even higher qualifications for holding office? And if this kept the suffrage as restricted as it was before the Revolution—and logically this must have been true—how was it possible for the lower classes to control the state legislatures and to pass debtor laws and paper money acts? On the other hand, if the state legislatures *were* controlled by the lower classes, how can we say that the mass of the people could not participate in the adoption of the Constitution? Or again, if state legislatures could pass debtor and paper money laws, why would they elect delegates representing creditor interests to draw up a constitution that would restrict future debtor and paper money laws?

The historian cannot have his cake and eat it too. Either the American Revolution was a social movement which brought great gains for the common man who in turn controlled the state legislatures, the election of delegates to the Constitutional Convention, and the ratification of the Constitution, or the Revolution was not a great social movement and the common man did not gain these things. If the Revolution achieved democracy, then we must explain the Constitution as the product of a democratic rather than an undemocratic society. If we explain the Constitution as the product of an undemocratic society, we must, perforce, discard the interpretation of the Revolution as a great democratic movement.

In the old interpretation, the Articles of Confederation have been considered democratic, but just how democratic were they? If democracy has some relation to majority rule, the Articles were not very democratic. Each state had one vote, regardless of population, and we have long considered our Senate with two votes for each state as one of the more un-democratic features of the Constitution. Under the Articles, Rhode Island carried as much weight as Virginia or Massachusetts. For another thing, important legislation under the Articles required a vote of nine of the thirteen states, not just a simple majority. And finally, amendment to the Articles required unanimous approval, even more conservative than the three-fourths required under the Constitution.

If one argues, as has been done, that the Articles were really democratic because they permitted the states to practice democracy without let or hindrance, then one gets back to the fundamental contradictions again. If the states were practicing democracy under the Articles, we cannot explain the Constitution in terms of the disfranchised masses, and we must also say that the delegates to the Constitutional Convention represented popular will since they were elected by popularly-elected legislatures. Again we cannot use democracy to explain the Revolution and an absence of democracy to explain the Constitution as the old interpretation does.

The fact that there was no popular referendum for the calling of the Constitutional Convention and no popular election of delegates to the Convention has been used by adherents of the old interpretation to bolster the thesis that the Constitution was undemocratic, but this argument is easily answered. Traditionally, colonial and state legislatures had elected delegates to intercolonial or interstate meetings and there had never been a popular referendum on whether such a meeting should be held. The Stamp Act Congress which adopted the extremist Stamp Act Resolves, the First Continental Congress which adopted the extremist Suffolk Resolves, and the Second

Continental Congress which adopted the Declaration of Independence and wrote the Articles of Confederation were all called without popular referendums and without popular election of delegates. If the Constitution was undemocratic because the people did not vote either on holding the convention or on the election of delegates, then by the same token the Declaration of Independence and the Articles of Confederation were also undemocratic. In addition, the Articles were even more undemocratic, for they were submitted to ratification by state legislatures which were not elected for this purpose, and at least the Constitution was ratified by special conventions elected for this purpose only.

As far as popular sentiment at the time was concerned, the sources indicate that the people were about as agitated over the fact that they did not elect the Constitutional Convention delegates as are the people of this country today over their failure to elect delegates to the United Nations. I would venture to guess that the number of people who lose sleep over their failure to vote for our United Nations delegates would not be very impressive. In fact, I would suppose that not many people even *know* how our United Nations delegates are selected.

Given the nature of the Articles of Confederation, one might suggest that popular elections of delegates to a convention to amend the Articles would have been unthinkable if not unconstitutional. In the first place, the Confederation was one of states, not peoples, and since the Confederation government did not act directly on the people, it would have been strange had the people demanded direct action instead of leaving confederation problems to their state legislatures. And in the second place, the Articles provided for amendment by states, not the people. No alteration was to be made in the Articles unless such alteration was "agreed to in a congress of the united states, and be afterwards confirmed by the legislatures of every state." Instead of looking upon the election of delegates to the Constitutional Convention by state legislatures as something of a conspiracy against the people, we might easily say that a popular election would have been in the nature of a political revolution.

As for the election of the delegates themselves, we need only repeat a previous question that if state legislatures could pass "radical" debtor laws and paper money bills, why did they elect personalty interests to represent them in the Constitutional Convention?

When we turn from the contradictions in the old interpretation to the evidence itself, what do we find?

In the debates of the Constitutional Convention are to be found the best accounts of American society in 1787 as the delegates saw that society. And unfortunately for the old interpretation, most of the evidence, while supporting a thesis that economic factors are important in constitution making, disproves the particular kind of economic interpretation that we have accepted in the past.

First of all, the debates indicate that there was a great deal of democracy, both economic and political, in the United States in 1787. Charles Pinckney of South Carolina stated it this way:

> The people of the U. States are perhaps the most singular of any we are acquainted with. Among them are fewer distinctions of fortune & less of rank, than among the inhabitants of any other nation. Every freeman has a right to the same protection & security; and a very moderate share of property entitles them to the possession of all the honors and privileges the public can bestow; hence arises a greater equality, than is to be found among the people of any other country, and an equality which is more likely to continue, because in a new Country, possessing enormous tracts of uncultivated lands, where every temptation is offered to emigration & where industry must be rewarded with competency, there will be few poor and

enjoy an equal power of arriving at the supreme offices & few dependent—Every member of the Society almost, will consequently of dircting the strength & sentiments of the whole Community. None will be excluded by birth, & few by fortune, from voting for proper persons to fill the offices of Government—the whole community will enjoy in the fullest sense that kind of political liberty which consists in the power the members of the State reserve to themselves, of arriving at public offices, or at least, of having votes in the nomination of those who fill them.

Pinckney went on to point out that because of their middle-class society, Americans could never copy the British constitution even though that constitution was the best. There were few rich men here for a house of lords, and the genius of the people and their general mediocrity of fortune would mitigate against distinctions of rank. Cheap land and the elimination of entail and primogeniture would long preserve the equality of condition which so eminently distinguished the American people. Equality, he said, was the leading feature of the United States, and among the great body of the people there were few of wealth or poverty.

James Madison also supported Pinckney's view of American society. Madison said that the United States had "not reached that stage of Society in which the conflicting feelings of the Class with, and the class without property, have the operation natural to them in Countries fully peopled." Madison was worried about the future when a dangerous propertyless proletariat might develop in this country, a development that would endanger all property.

On the subject of political democracy in 1787 the debates in the Convention leave no doubts in the reader's mind. Elbridge Gerry of Massachusetts said that the people of England would probably lose their liberty from the smallness of the vote, while in America the danger came from the opposite extreme. Roger Sherman of Connecticut declared that an equal distribution of liberty among all ranks meant that the poor were equal to the rich in voting.

In showing the extent of political democracy, some of the delegates expressed a desire that voting be limited to freeholders, a strange desire coming from men who were supposedly writing a constitution to protect personalty. John Dickinson of Delaware argued that restriction of voters to freeholders would be popular because the great mass of citizens were freeholders and would be pleased by the restriction. Gouverneur Morris supported this idea on the ground that nine-tenths of the people were freeholders and would be pleased by a freehold qualification. These men, and many others, showed no fear whatever in entrusting political power to the small farmers, and of course their statements also indicate that most men were voters.

In addition, there were other delegates who revealed no fear of a "city proletariat" or working class, and in the process demonstrated that these people were also qualified voters at the time. George Mason of Virginia reminded the Convention that eight or nine states had already extended the suffrage to others besides freeholders, and what would these people say if they were disfranchised? Nathaniel Gorham of Massachusetts said that there had never been any inconvenience from allowing non-freeholders to vote, though it had long been tried. Elections in New York, Philadelphia, and Boston, where merchants and mechanics voted, were at least as good as elections participated in by freeholders only. The people had long been accustomed to this right in various parts of America, Gorham concluded, and would never allow it to be abridged. There is no evidence in the Convention debates to support the statement that there was a mass of disfranchised men in 1787.

Some of the Convention delegates undoubtedly deplored

the fact that American society was democratic, but they never doubted that democracy was there to be reckoned with. Gerry said, "The evils we experience flow from an excess of democracy," and George Mason, while admitting that there had been too much democracy, declared that he did not want to go to the opposite extreme. "The democratick spirit runs high," said Paterson of New Jersey, "the democratic licentiousness of the state legislatures proved the necessity of a firm senate," echoed Randolph of Virginia, and Alexander Hamilton could see evils operating in the states that would soon cure the people of their fondness of democracy, for the country needed to be rescued from democracy.

Not only did the delegates recognize the presence of democracy at the time but they were also fully aware of the fact that any constitution which they constructed must meet the approval of the people. In fact, there was scarcely a feature of the Constitution which was not favored or opposed with the argument that it would please or displease the people. James Madison, who called the freeholders the "safest depositories of Republican liberty," said that his reaction to restricting the vote to freeholders would depend on how much opposition came from those states where others besides freeholders had the vote. Benjamin Franklin also pointed out that the common people had the vote and would resent any effort to deprive them of it. Edmund Randolph of Virginia objected to a single executive on the ground that "the sentiments of the people ought to be consulted—they will never bear the semblance of monarchy." But James Wilson of Pennsylvania argued just the opposite because he saw no antipathy among the people to a single executive. Roger Sherman believed that an executive council would be necessary to make the new government acceptable to the people.

George Mason was particularly outspoken in his belief that the convention must consider the views of the people if they expected the Constitution to be accepted:

"Do gentlemen mean to pave the way to hereditary monarchy?" he asked. "Do they flatter themselves that the people will ever consent to such an innovation? If they do, I venture to tell them they are mistaken. The people will never consent. And do gentlemen consider the danger of delay, and the still greater danger of a rejection not for a moment but forever, of the plan which shall be proposed to them. Notwithstanding the oppressions & injustice experienced among us from democracy; the genius of the people is in favor of it, and the genius of the people must be consulted."

There might be differences of opinion over what the people thought about government, but there was no disagreement that the voice of the people would be decisive. Pierce Butler of South Carolina objected to the strong court system in the Constitution on the ground that the people would oppose it. Said he: "The people will not bear such innovations. . . . Supposing such an establishment to be useful, we must not venture on it. We must follow the example of Solon who gave the Athenians not the best Govt. he could devise, but the best they wd. receive." George Read of Delaware then countered with the argument that the people at large were wrongly suspected of being averse to a general government. If Paterson of New Jersey could argue that the delegates must follow the people for the people would not follow the delegates—that the plan of government must consult the genius, temper, habits, and prejudices of the people—Madison could say that the Convention should devise the best government possible without reference to the people, for no one knew their opinions. Then Madison was answered by Gerry, who declared that the Convention had to consider what the people thought, as all legislators had done, regardless of their desires.

One thing that we can be fairly sure of, then, is that the Constitution was not written for, nor adopted by, an undemocratic society.

There are numerous other important concepts to be found in the Convention debates which are still our best source for understanding the Constitution.

In the Convention, delegates often expressed frank views as to the purpose of government, and when we add up the total of these views, we find that government was designed to do many things, not just protect personal property. Some of the delegates emphasized the protection of property as the fundamental function of government, while others placed the emphasis on human rights. Usually the combination of human and property rights went together, a fact that should not be too surprising in a middle-class society that had long accepted life, liberty, and property as the natural rights of man.

The views of James Madison are particularly relevant on the question of the purpose of government, for Madison has often been used as the cornerstone of the economic interpretation of the Constitution. Madison insisted that:

> [I]t was politic as well as just that the interests & rights of every class should be duly represented & understood in the public councils. It was a provision everywhere established that the country should be divided into districts & representatives taken from each, in order that the Legislative Assembly might equally understand & sympathize, with the rights of the people in every part of the Community. It was not less proper that every class of citizens should have an opportunity of making their rights be felt & understood in the public Councils.

Then Madison described the three classes in the country as "the landed, the commercial, & the manufacturing," that is, vertically structured property groups rather than groups horizontally divided between rich and poor. What he wanted, he said, was some voting qualifications besides land so the commercial and manufacturing groups would be protected.

If the conflict between human rights and property rights ever reach proportions where one or the other had to be sacrificed, Madison said, it would have to be property rights rather than human rights. If the right to vote, fundamental in a republican government, were confined to property, persons would be oppressed, he declared, and if it were confined to persons, property would be oppressed. Both had to be protected, but limitation of the vote to freeholders would violate the vital principle of free government that those bound by the laws should help make them. Then Madison concluded that if ever the choice came between universal suffrage and limitation of voting to people with property, the decision would have to be for universal suffrage at the expense of property. But in this country, Madison added, the actual distribution of property, especially land, and the universal hope of acquiring property created much sympathy in the country for property.

We have tended in the past to think of the Founding Fathers as men coldly motivated by their own economic interests, but the *Debates* do not substantiate this view. These men were much bigger than our former interpretation would admit. Here we find Madison, a Virginia planter, believing that commercial and manufacturing interests had equal claims to protection and participation in government, and if the showdown ever came, property rights would have to be sacrificed to universal suffrage. One might even hazard an opinion that the world's really great men—and women—have been those who were willing to stand by their principles whenever there was a conflict between principle and interest.

It was also Madison who saw the really fundamental conflict in American society at the time, and this conflict was not one of class. After talking about divisions between sections or commercial and non-commercial states, Madison got down to the real basic issue in this country—the division between slave and free states, between North and South. He contended that the states were divided in interests depending on whether or not they had slaves. The North against the South formed the great division in the United States, and the great danger to the general government was this opposition of great northern and southern interests, as the sectional voting in Congress had demonstrated. Later in the debates Madison declared that he had always conceived the great difference of interests in the United States to be between the two sections. And finally he went so far as to say that it was pretty well understood in the Convention that the real difference of interests lay not between large and small states but between northern and southern, with the institution of slavery and its consequences forming the line of demarcation.

The Civil War proved only too well how right Madison was, but this kind of evidence does little to support the type of economic interpretation that we have had for the past half-century.

We have long believed that checks and balances were devices by which conservatives protected their property from the onslaughts of democratic majorities, but the facts are that all sorts of people advocated checks and balances for different reasons. There were many different interests in the country—horizontal and vertical divisions, commercial against agricultural states, large states against small and free against slave. And of course these different interests desired checks and balances to protect themselves. Even Jefferson, generally considered a liberal, believed that the Virginia Constitution was defective because it failed to provide checks against legislative tyranny by pitting different interests against each other. One of the chief complaints of the colonists had been that they had no effective checks on Great Britain. As Gunning Bedford of Delaware said, "I do not, gentlemen, trust you." Bedford believed that any group with unlimited power would probably abuse it, and he wanted the small states protected from the large ones.

Far from believing that the Constitution was an effective check and balance system to curb democracy, some men in the Convention did not think that the proposed plan of govern-

ment really provided effective checks and balances. Alexander
Hamilton looked on the Randolph Plan as one in which a
democratic house checked a democratic senate and both of
these were checked by a democratic executive. Since all three
ultimately came from the same source—the people—even
though they came by different routes, they would not provide
effective checks. James Wilson also pointed out that the landed
interest controlled the state legislatures which elected senators and therefore the Senate would not provide checks against
the landed interest.

Under the old interpretation, we were also led to believe
that the delegates to the Constitutional Convention were
holders of the kind of personal property that the Constitution
supposedly protected, but on examination this generalization
does not hold together. A delegate by delegate analysis of
property-holding indicates that to the extent to which property can be determined, the delegates were overwhelmingly
owners of real rather than personal property. In order to show
that some of the delegates were owners of personalty, it has
been necessary to take what they held after, not before, the
Constitution was adopted, and this property, especially public
securities, could easily have been purchased after the Constitution was ratified.

When we examine ratification of the Constitution, we again
find that the evidence does not support the old interpretation.
That interpretation would have us believe not only that the
Constitution was ratified as a sort of conspiratorial *coup
d'état* by the upper classes in a society where the lower classes
were excluded from politics, but also that the process of ratification elicited some of the hottest political contests that the
country has ever seen. The question, then, is whether the evidence supports this interpretation.

Before we look at the evidence, however, we must first
examine briefly the connotations of the term *coup d'état*.
Webster defines it as "a sudden forceful stroke in politics; es-

pecially the sudden forceful overthrow of a government." We know that regardless of instructions, most of the delegates came to Philadelphia with the idea of discarding the Articles of Confederation. George Mason said that "the most prevalent idea" among the delegates even before the Convention met was "a total alteration of the present federal system, and substituting a great national council of parliament." But did this constitute a *coup d'état*?

There are many arguments against the use of *coup d'état* to describe what happened. Whether or not the Convention was legal under the Articles is open to question. Throughout the Articles the phrase "the united states in congress assembled" is used whenever reference is made to congress under the Articles. But in Article XIII where provision is made for amendments to the Articles, there is the statement that no alteration was to be made "unless such alteration be agreed to in a congress of the united states, and afterwards confirmed by the legislatures of every state." Did this mean any congress or did it mean only the Confederation Congress? Or did it merely imply that a meeting other than the Confederation Congress could propose alterations but that such alterations would not be legal unless first approved by the Confederation Congress? One could argue that the Convention was "a congress of the united states" and was therefore legal, even though it was not "the united states in congress assembled." Or the argument could be made that the Convention was not an illegal body as long as its proposals were passed on by the Confederation Congress.

There is no doubt, however, that what the Constitutional Convention finally proposed was illegal under the Articles. The Constitution was not an amendment to the Articles, and it was not to be ratified by the legislatures of every state. In this sense, we could say that the Convention was staging a political *coup*.

But there are other considerations. There were statements in the Convention of a general feeling among the people that the Confederation was inadequate and would have to be changed, and others that the people expected something substantial from the Convention. Throughout the debates, the thought was uppermost in the minds of the delegates that their proposals would have to meet the approval of the people. Furthermore, the delegates wanted to by-pass the state legislatures where, according to the old interpretation, the interests of the upper classes were especially protected by property qualifications for voting and office-holding. Instead, they planned to submit ratification to conventions elected for this specific purpose. And to all this we must add the facts that the Convention sat for several months, that the people knew it was in session, that the people had considerable time to deliberate on ratification, and that they could have defeated it.

When the evidence is all in, the adoption of the Constitution does not appear as a *coup d'état* staged by the holders of personal property. Since ratification was accomplished by conventions elected by the people for this specific purpose, and not by state legislatures as was the Articles of Confederation, and since the evidence seems to indicate that most men were voters, it would be more logical, perhaps, to say that the Constitution represented a *coup d'état* in the interests of the people.

I doubt that the term *coup d'état* applies in either case. A more logical explanation would be that the people had recently been through a revolution based on natural rights and the compact theory, and they believed that they could change governments whenever these governments failed to protect life, liberty, and property. They had recently gotten rid of such a government and had, in fact, set up others. Hence there was nothing unreasonable in discarding what they had established for something new. And Shays' Rebellion was stark evidence that the owners of personal property were not the only property owners who suffered under the Confederation. The movement for the Constitution originated with men who were or at various times had been elected as leaders by the people, the delegates to the Convention were practically all men who had served in public office, and the men who ratified the Constitution were popularly elected and for the most part had previously held elective offices. Under these circumstances, it would not seem too strange, or revolutionary, that the people would ratify the Constitution.

When we turn to the evidence on ratification, the whole fabric of the old interpretation disintegrates. Theoretically, ratification should have been quickest and easiest in those states where personal property carried the most weight and most difficult in the agricultural states. But of the first four states to ratify, three (Delaware, New Jersey, and Georgia) were almost entirely agricultural and all three ratified unanimously. The fourth, Pennsylvania, voted two to one in favor of the Constitution. Among the first nine states to ratify, the vote was close in two only, Massachusetts and New York, both of which should have been weighted in favor of personalty, and even in those states the winning percentage was more than 55 to less than 45. The total vote of the first nine ratifying states was 725 for and 361 against, or 66.75 per cent in favor of ratification. The vote of the eleven states that had ratified when Washington took office in 1789 was 844 for and 467 against, or 64.37 per cent for the Constitution. This was a greater margin than the 1936 victory of Franklin D. Roosevelt who won by less than 63 per cent or of Dwight D. Eisenhower in 1956 who won by less than 58 per cent. An overwhelming victory of the proportions achieved by the Constitution would soothe the heart of any politician, unless perhaps he came from Maine or Georgia.

Far from being a hot contest, as the old interpretation led us to believe, ratification of the Constitution could better be considered as virtually no contest. In Boston, for example, where the statement has been made that "the fight was rather warm," only 760 voters out of some 2,700 or more who were qualified even bothered to vote, and these 760 voted overwhelmingly in favor of the Constitution. Philadelphia provides an even more striking example of both indifference on the part of the voters in general and heavy preference for the Constitution among those who did vote. In the City of Brotherly Love, only some 1,450 brothers voted out of about 5,500 who were qualified, and the leading candidate for the Constitution received 1,215 votes while the leading opponent received only 235. A winning margin of more than five to one is anything but a hot political contest, and the margin by which the Constitution won in Philadelphia would tempt anyone to go into politics.

Two contemporary views tell us much about the feelings of the people at the time, and given the vote on the Constitution, probably represented the feelings of many others besides the writers themselves. One was John Quincy Adams, who recorded the following in his diary:

> February 7, 1788. This day, at about noon, the news arrived in this town [Newburyport] that the Federal Constitution was yesterday adopted and ratified by a majority of nineteen members in our State Convention. In this town the satisfaction is almost universal; for my own part, I have not been pleased with this system, [meaning the new Constitution] and my acquaintance have long since branded me with the name of an antifederalist. But I am now converted, though not convinced. My feelings upon the occasion have not been passionate nor violent; and, as upon the decision of this question I find myself on the weaker side, I think it is my duty to submit without murmuring against what is not to be helped. In our government, opposition to the acts of a majority of the people is rebellion to all intents and purposes; and I should view a man who would now endeavour to excite commotions against this plan, as no better than an insurgent who took arms last winter against the Courts of Justice.

The next day Adams recorded the reception which was given to the delegates on their return from the ratifying convention. They were met by "a number of very respectable citizens, and a number who were not very respectable," an indication that class elements were missing, and escorted into town to the ringing of bells and expressions of joy on the part of "the mob." It seemed to Adams that every man expected to acquire an independent fortune because of the adoption of the Constitution. For his part, Adams, as might be expected, "pass'd [sic] the evening at home in reading and writing."

In Adams' entire account there is no hint that the Constitution was illegal or the result of a *coup d'état*, or involved class conflict. To him, it met the necessary test of popular approval.

The other contemporary observer was Richard Henry Lee of Virginia who opposed the Constitution and who wrote as follows:

One party is composed of little insurgents, men in debt, who want no law, and who want a share of the property of others; these are called levelers, Shaysites, etc. The other party is composed of a few, but more dangerous men, with their servile dependents; these avariciously grasp at all power and property; you may discover in all the actions of these men an evident dislike to free and equal government, and they go systematically to work to change, essentially, the forms of government of this country; these are called aristocrats, moneyites, etc. Between these two parties is the weight of the community; the men of middling property, not in debt on the one hand, and men, on the other, content with republican governments, and not aiming at immense fortunes, offices, and powers.

In 1786 the little insurgents, the levelers, came forth, invaded the rights of others, and attempted to establish governments according to their wills. Their movements evidently gave encouragement to the other party, which in 1787 has taken the political field and with its fashionable dependents, and the tongue and the pen, is endeavoring to establish, in great haste, a politic kind of government. These two parties are really insignificant, as compared with the solid, free, and independent part of the community.

"It was this group for whose support both sides bid." Lee also said that the best men in Virginia would scrutinize the Constitution in the state's ratifying convention, and if they accepted it after a close scrutiny, he would be satisfied with it. In short, the attitude of both Adams and Lee was anything but intransigent.

If we were to edit out parts of this Lee statement, we would have a perfect account of the economic interpretation of the Constitution—the aristocrats against the debtors. But when we include the entire quotation, the important group is not the small upper class on one side or the small lower class on the other, but the great middle class that I have emphasized in these lectures. This great middle class was the group which decided the fate of the Constitution.

The *Federalist Papers* have been used by advocates of the old interpretation to substantiate a class-conflict view of the Constitution, but when we examine *The Federalist*, we find meat for various interpretations. *The Federalist*, a series of newspaper articles written by Hamilton, Madison, and Jay in favor of the Constitution, indicates that the promoters of the Constitution were appealing to a wide variety of interests, not merely those of an upper class. If we take only *Federalist* No. 10 by Madison, and edit out the parts that do not prove economic determinism, as has been done in the past, a good case can be made for the economic interpretation. But he who uses *The Federalist* to prove what the Constitution was all about is not entitled to edit out the parts of No. 10 that do not prove economic determinism. Furthermore, we must either use all eighty-five *Federalist* numbers, not just No. 10, or we must prove that No. 10 was more important than the others. If

Madison emphasized horizontal economic class conflict in No. 10, he also divided society into vertical economic groups and emphasized conflict there too. We have already noted his belief that class division had not yet developed in this country and his statement that the real division here was between slave and free states. In any event, Hamilton, Madison, and Jay appealed to all kinds of people in *The Federalist*.

Under the old interpretation we were led to believe that the Constitution represented a conservative check and balance system that would curtail democracy. But what did contemporaries think? Far from opposing the Constitution on this ground, the antifederalists objected to the new system because it did not contain sufficient checks. One of the big tasks of the authors of *The Federalist* was to convince the people that the Constitution did provide adequate checks and balances.

In conclusion, then, it seems clear that whatever future research does to clarify the issues surrounding the Constitution and its ratification, we cannot assume, as we have in the past, that the Constitution was adopted undemocratically in a undemocratic society and that it was put over on the people as a sort of *coup d'état* or conspiracy by holders of personal property. For good or bad, America in 1787 was a country in which· most men were middle-class property owners, especially the owners of real estate, and because they were property owners, they were also qualified voters. Having fought the Revolution to preserve a society based on the natural rights of life, liberty, and property, it is not at all surprising that they would adopt a Constitution which provided for the protection of property. In fact, had the people suspected that the Constitution would not protect property, I doubt that it would have had the slightest chance of adoption. And certain it is that if the common people had opposed, there would have been no Constitution.

THE BEARD THESIS ATTACKED, II:
A POLITICAL-ECONOMIC APPROACH

Forrest McDonald

EDITOR'S NOTE   Robert E. Brown, working with a
gifted, critical intelligence, a copy of Beard, and a
copy of the *Records of the Federal Convention*,
tried to prove Beard wrong. Forrest McDonald of
the University of Alabama, eschewing so negative
an approach, went back to the primary sources to
test the validity of the Beard thesis. Beard had admitted in his 1913 preface that his work was "frankly
fragmentary," its purpose to encourage other scholars to study in greater depth the economic forces
that condition political movements. McDonald's
*We the People: The Economic Origins of the Con-
stitution* (1958), which ranks among the master-
pieces of American historical scholarship, was a
work of prodigious research intended to supersede
Beard by filling in the details, not only on the economic interests of the delegates to the Constitutional
Convention but of most of the members of the state
ratifying conventions, a topic that Beard had neglected. Like Brown, McDonald concluded that
Beard was wrong; but, McDonald did not, like
Brown, reject the primacy of economic forces and
in that respect is a neo-Beardian. He rejected
Beard's particular economic interpretation as rigid
and simplistic, suggesting in its place a complex,
pluralistic economic interpretation that would ac-

From Forrest McDonald, *We the People: The Economic Origins of the
Constitution*, pp. 93–110, 349–57. Copyright 1958 by The American
Research Center, Inc., Madison, Wisconsin. Reprinted without footnotes
by permission of the author.

count for the variety of local, state, regional, and factional differences among diverse interest groups, some of which were split internally by intramural conflicts, others by an allegiance to a multiplicity of interests which were by no means only economic in character.

McDonald contended that with few exceptions the delegates to the Constitutional Convention represented a cross-section of the geographical areas and shades of political opinion in the United States in 1787. He disagreed with Beard, too, in his findings that realty rather than personalty was the dominant type of wealth in the Convention; that its members, like those in the state ratifying conventions, did not vote as consolidated economic groups; that holders of public securities were almost as numerous among opponents of the Constitution as among its framers and advocates; and that generally there were no significant property differences between the two sides.

Despite his several very suggestive hypotheses concerning the nature and utility of a pluralistic economic interpretation of the making of the Constitution, McDonald's *E Pluribus Unum: The Formation of the American Republic, 1776–1790* failed to follow through. His lively account of political factors was more eccentric and perverse than original. He construed the Virginia Plan, for example, as a mere alteration of the form, though not the substance, of the Confederation, while he depicted the Paterson Plan as the one that would have made the national government truly sovereign. Most surprising, however, was his interpretation of economic factors in the Beardian mode. "Commerce, debts, and lands: stir them one way," said Mc-Donald, "and the Union would be cemented, stir them another and it would be dissolved." "Debtors and creditors, public and private," he added, "had been and would continue to be the most dynamic elements in American politics." The Constitution would have shifted the tax burden from land to commerce, with the result, said McDonald, that whether one favored or opposed the Constitution "depended upon who owed whom, how much and under what conditions." He even followed Beard when discussing the appeal of the Constitution to special interest groups: shippers and shipowning merchants, holders of public securities, and land speculators. Moreover, McDonald adopted the Beardian line when regarding the federal debt as the crucial force accounting for the movement for constitutional revision along the lines of expanded national powers. Thus the most sophisticated critic of Beard not only verged on an economic determinism in his own interpretation, but he actually coincided with the Beard thesis on several vital points. In still another book on the making of the Constitution, *Novus Ordo Seclorum* (1985) [New Order of the Ages], McDonald has given us a superior history of the intellectual origins of the Constitution. In the selections that follow from *We the People,* chapters four and eight, McDonald appears in his earlier role, that of the revisionist critic of the Beard thesis.

o   o   o   o

ECONOMIC INTERESTS AND VOTES IN THE CONVENTION

ANY analysis of the relationship between personal economic interests and political behavior in the Convention must necessarily be tentative. For one reason, as the data in the preceding chapter reveal, the interests represented by given delegates do not always permit of placing them in mutually exclusive categories—a delegate might not only have been a farmer but he might also have had a large investment in public securities; or he might have been a merchant who was likewise a debtor in desperate straits. For another and perhaps more important reason, the delegates in the Convention did not vote as individuals but by states, with the result that, except for the most prolific speakers, their conduct as individuals is somewhat obscured.

Despite these obstacles, however, certain observations may be made with respect to the connection between economic interests and political outlook. If, to be consistent with Beard's system, all the merchants and their attorneys, together with the larger holders of public securities, are considered as one group, and all the farmers, debtors, country lawyers, and holders of state offices who held no securities, mercantile property, or other significant personalty are considered as another, the delegates can be divided into two quite different camps with respect to their economic interests. The first group could be styled the "Personalty Group," the second the "Realty Group." The lines of division would then fall as follows:

State	Personalty Group	Realty Group
N.H.	Langdon and Gilman	None
Mass.	King, Gerry, Strong, and Gorham	None
Conn.	Sherman and Ellsworth	Johnson
N.Y.	Lansing and Hamilton	Yates
N.J.	Dayton	Paterson, Livingston, Brearley, Houston
Pa.	Clymer, Fitzsimons, Franklin, Ingersoll, Mifflin, Wilson, Robert Morris, and Gouverneur Morris	None
Del.	Bedford	Bassett, Dickinson, Read, and Broom
Md.	Luther Martin and Mercer	Jenifer, Carroll, and McHenry

STATE	PERSONALTY GROUP	REALTY GROUP
Va.	Randolph, McClurg, Mason, Blair, and Wythe	Washington and Madison
N.C.	Williamson	Alexander Martin, Blount, Davie, and Spaight
S.C.	C. C. Pinckney	Charles Pinckney, Rutledge, and Butler
Ga.	Pierce and Baldwin	Few and Houstoun

Perhaps a few of the delegates could be classified otherwise, but it would not greatly change the basic alignment. Johnson could perhaps be shifted to the personalty group, but his state of Connecticut is already so classified. Dickinson likewise could be shifted, on the grounds of his earlier associations, but that would not change the Delaware majority. Wythe could be shifted on the ground that his public security holding was too small to have influenced his stand on issues, but since Wythe was absent most of the time the question is a purely academic one. McHenry could conceivably be transferred from the realty to the personalty group. This shift alone would change the complexion of a delegation. It would have little effect on the present analysis, however, since McHenry, too, was frequently absent—more than half the time the Convention was in session.

The table indicates that the personalty interests were in a clear majority in the Convention: thirty-one members as against twenty-four in the realty group. More important for immediate purposes, it will be seen that all the states except Maryland were decisively dominated by one group or the other (Georgia, split 2–2 in the table, must be regarded as a personalty state because Houstoun attended only for the first week or two). Seven were personalty states: Massachusetts, New Hampshire, Connecticut, New York, Virginia, Pennsylvania, and Georgia; four were realty states: New Jersey, Delaware, North Carolina, and South Carolina.

If the economic interests represented by the delegates were the dominating element, or even one of several dominating elements, in the making of the Constitution, one would expect to find an alignment inside the Convention along the above lines. Not on all issues, of course, for there were necessarily issues on which no economic interests were at stake or on which such interests conflicted; nor should one expect to find these exact alignments on any particular issue, for parliamentary strategy also had its effect. In general, however, as votes on all issues piled up in the day-to-day business of the Convention, the basic, underlying pattern of voting behavior should show the personalty states standing on one side, the realty states standing on the other, and Maryland vacillating between these two groups.

The table on the next page puts this proposition to the test. The figures cited are from the Convention votes as recorded in Madison's notes and the official journal of the Convention. A glance at the table indicates that there were distinct voting patterns in the Convention, but that they hardly coincided with the personalty and realty interests groups as listed above. The most conspicuous alignment is that of the extreme northern states with the extreme southern states: New Hampshire, Massachusetts, North Carolina, South Carolina, and Georgia. This alignment is shown in the tabulation below, in which the percentages represent, as in the table on page 96, the proportion of the issues voted upon by two states that elicited the same vote.

	New Hampshire Per Cent	Massachusetts Per Cent	North Carolina Per Cent	South Carolina Per Cent	Georgia Per Cent
New Hampshire ..	......	73.1	61.4	65.7	62.8
Massachusetts	73.1	......	64.4	63.3	59.5
North Carolina	61.4	64.4	......	65.2	65.0
South Carolina	65.7	63.3	65.2	.....	71.8
Georgia	62.8	59.5	65.0	71.8	......

Considered as a unit, the bloc voted with Connecticut 55 per cent of the time; with New York 47 per cent; New Jersey 51 per cent; Pennsylvania 54 per cent; Delaware 49 per cent; Maryland 45 per cent; and Virginia 59 per cent of the time.

VOTES OF STATES IN THE PHILADELPHIA CONVENTION*

	New Hampshire	Massachusetts	Connecticut	New York	New Jersey	Pennsylvania	Delaware	Maryland	Virginia	North Carolina	South Carolina	Georgia
New Hampshire		177–242 73.1%	159–262 60.6%	none	130–222 58.5%	154–258 59.6%	133–251 52.9%	121–260 46.5%	150–262 57.2%	150–244 61.4%	171–260 65.7%	161–256 62.8%
Massachusetts	177–242 73.1%		219–401 54.6%	46–106 43.3%	178–352 50.5%	245–396 61.8%	214–388 55.1%	182–390 46.6%	244–401 60.8%	252–391 64.4%	254–399 63.3%	233–391 59.5%
Connecticut	159–262 60.6%	219–401 54.6%		47–106 44.3%	224–361 62.0%	214–415 51.5%	218–408 53.4%	220–410 53.6%	221–421 52.4%	222–401 55.3%	220–419 52.5%	220–409 53.7%
New York	none	46–106 43.3%	47–106 44.3%		55–93 59.1%	44–104 42.3%	56–105 53.3%	44–97 45.3%	50–106 47.1%	51–104 49.0%	48–106 45.2%	53–103 51.4%
New Jersey	130–222 58.5%	178–352 50.5%	224–361 62.0%	55–93 59.1%		193–356 54.2%	226–350 64.5%	194–353 54.9%	171–361 47.3%	173–352 49.1%	163–359 45.4%	196–357 54.9%
Pennsylvania	154–258 59.6%	245–396 61.8%	214–415 51.5%	44–104 42.3%	193–356 54.2%		220–403 57.0%	204–404 50.4%	275–415 66.2%	212–396 53.5%	201–413 48.6%	206–404 50.9%
Delaware	133–251 52.9%	214–388 55.1%	218–408 53.4%	56–105 53.3%	226–350 64.5%	220–403 57.0%		215–386 55.7%	212–408 51.9%	190–388 48.9%	189–406 46.5%	182–398 45.7%
Maryland	121–260 46.5%	182–390 46.6%	220–410 53.6%	44–97 45.3%	194–353 54.9%	204–404 50.4%	215–386 55.7%		227–410 55.3%	180–392 45.9%	167–408 40.9%	192–399 48.1%
Virginia	150–262 57.2%	244–401 60.8%	221–421 52.4%	50–106 47.1%	171–361 47.3%	275–415 66.2%	212–408 51.0%	227–410 55.3%		262–401 65.3%	235–419 56.0%	245–409 50.9%
North Carolina	150–244 61.4%	252–391 64.4%	222–401 55.3%	51–104 49.0%	173–352 49.1%	212–396 53.5%	190–388 48.9%	180–392 45.9%	262–401 65.3%		261–400 65.2%	256–392 65.0%
South Carolina	171–260 65.7%	254–399 63.3%	220–419 52.5%	48–106 45.2%	163–359 45.4%	201–413 48.6%	189–406 46.5%	167–408 40.9%	235–419 56.0%	261–400 65.2%		294–409 71.8%
Georgia	161–256 62.8%	233–391 59.5%	220–409 53.7%	53–103 51.4%	196–357 54.9%	206–404 50.9%	182–398 45.7%	192–399 48.1%	245–409 50.9%	256–392 65.0%	294–409 71.8%	

*The table reads like the conventional mileage chart. The sets of two figures on the first line following the name of the state at the left represent a comparison of its voting record with that of the states given at the head of the several columns. The first figure indicates the number of times the two states voted on the same side of issues, and the second the total number of times they voted on the same issues. The percentage given on the second line is the ratio of the first to the second figure above—that is, the percentage of the total number of issues voted upon by the two states that elicited the same vote from both of them.

A second alignment was Delaware and New Jersey, and a third was Pennsylvania and Virginia. Delaware and New Jersey tended to vote with the northern states on most issues, but on less than half the issues did they vote with their fellow realty states, the Carolinas. Pennsylvania and Virginia split on only a third of the issues they both voted upon; when they did, Pennsylvania voted with the personalty states to the north and Virginia with her realty neighbors to the south. New York, a personalty state, voted more than half the time only with Delaware and New Jersey, realty states, and Virginia, a personalty state. Maryland and Connecticut acted as two lone wolves, Maryland opposing the basic five-state bloc and voting only with her neighbors, and Connecticut barely tending to break even with everyone, though voting consistently with personalty-dominated New Hampshire and realty-dominated New Jersey.

In short, the voting patterns of the state delegations in the Convention by no means followed the lines of a basic economic cleavage into realty and personalty interests.

A second way to test alignments inside the Convention affords a considerably closer view. Though delegates voted by states, it is possible to ascertain how individuals voted on a number of key issues. One source of data is Professor Max Farrand's monumental *Records of the Federal Convention*, in which he gives an attendance list, a record of the dates on which given delegates were known to be absent from the Convention. Recorded speeches, motions, and other expressions of attitude reveal how given individuals voted on given issues. Further, Madison and some of the other delegates who took notes in the Convention occasionally recorded the votes of individual delegates. By a process of elimination the attitudes of a remarkably high percentage of the delegates on specific issues can be ascertained.

On June 8, for example, the Convention voted on a motion that the national legislature in the contemplated new government be given an absolute veto power over any and all state laws which it judged improper; this was a test of the extent of extreme nationalism in the Convention. Gerry spoke out strongly against this proposal, but since Massachusetts voted as a state in favor of it, delegates Gorham, King, and Strong, all in attendance, must have voted for it. Ellsworth of Connecticut had made a strong speech a few days earlier in favor of a similar proposal, but since his state voted against it, Sherman and Johnson must both have voted no. It is probable that Hamilton of New York voted for the motion, since it was in his original plan and, according to Yates, he had voted for it a week earlier. Since New York's vote was negative, Yates and Lansing must both have voted against the motion; Lansing's opposition is attested by his condemnation of the idea in his later report to New York's Governor Clinton. Of the New Jersey delegation, Dayton and Houston were absent; the state voted no, which means that at least two of the three attending delegates voted no, and that it is a two-to-one probability that any of the three voted against it. Further, since the New Jersey delegation was indecisively split on only one of the 361 votes it cast in the entire Convention, it is quite likely that all three opposed the motion. Delaware's vote was divided: Madison records that Broom was absent, that Dickinson and Read voted for the proposal, and that Bedford and Bassett voted against it. Four members of the Maryland delegation, McHenry, Martin, Carroll, and Mercer, were absent; the remaining delegate, Jenifer, cast the state's vote against the proposal. Virginia's vote is recorded by Madison: Mason and Randolph were against the motion; McClurg, Blair, and Madison were in favor of it; and Washington abstained from voting. Of the North Carolina delegates, Blount was absent, Williamson spoke against the proposal, and at least two of the remaining three, Spaight, Davie, and Martin, must also have opposed the measure since the state's vote was cast against it. Charles Pinckney of South Carolina favored the proposal, being the author of the motion; since his state voted against it, it follows that Rutledge, Charles C. Pinckney, and Butler all opposed it. Baldwin of Georgia was absent, and all three of Georgia's remaining delegates undoubtedly voted against the motion. This may be inferred from the fact that on the three occasions when the motion came up (with Georgia voting against it each time), the four Georgia delegates were in and out of the house in such combinations as to make it a certainty that all of them voted no on the question at least once. Neither of New Hampshire's delegates was in attendance.

In this manner the vote of every delegate can be, at least inferentially, accounted for on this issue, except, unfortunately, the votes of Pennsylvania's eight delegates. Only two of these, Wilson and Gouverneur Morris, spoke out on any great number of the issues. It is probable that some of the delegates were occasionally absent from the house, but their residence in Philadelphia makes it impossible to determine whether any of them had gone home for a week or so, as delegates from other states sometimes did. Thus whereas the votes of delegates from other states on a number of issues can be ascertained by these methods, those of the Pennsylvanians cannot.

For the purpose of testing the proposition that the personalty interests in the Convention were a consciously cohesive faction, however, it is not necessary to know how individual Pennsylvanians cast their votes. The Pennsylvania delegation was exclusively one of personalty interests, so that however much dissension there may have been inside the delegation—indications are that there was very little—the vote of the state was invariably on the side of those interests. If, therefore, the proposition is sound, delegates representing personalty interests would have tended, with few exceptions, to have sided with Pennsylvania on a great majority of the critical and fundamental questions voted upon. By the same token, delegates representing realty and agrarian interests would have voted against Pennsylvania.

On sixteen such key questions there is internal evidence of the probable votes of individual delegates. These votes are depicted in the table on pages 124–25. In general, all sixteen questions bear directly upon Gouverneur Morris' classic statement of the "great question" (September 17), "shall there be a national Government or not?"[1]

On the basis of the summaries at the right of the table, indicating the number and percentage of votes in agreement with Pennsylvania's, the delegates may be divided into three more or less distinct categories. The first consists of twenty-six delegates who voted with Pennsylvania on a majority or all of the issues; exactly half of them were primarily or exclusively representatives of the personalty interests, and the other half representatives of realty and agrarian interests. A second category comprises the fourteen men who manifestly did not side with Pennsylvania; none of them voted with Pennsylvania on more than half the questions. Seven of these were representatives of the personalty interests, seven were representatives of the realty interests. The third group, numbering six, was indecisive; these delegates voted with Pennsylvania on just over half the issues. Four of them were representatives of the realty interests, two of the personalty interests.

The conclusion is inevitable, then, that in so far as can be ascertained from the votes of individual delegates, no alignment of *personalty interests* versus *realty interests* existed in the Convention.

A third test bears more directly on economic matters. At the heart of Professor Beard's interpretation of the Constitution as an economic document is a statement that the critical

[1]Six of the votes pertain to the fundamental issue whether sovereignty should continue to remain in the hands of the states or should be transferred to a new general government, five relate to restrictions on state governments, three are on economic clauses in the Constitution, one concerns the process of ratification, and one is on a proposal to make the Constitution unamendable.

VOTES OF DELEGATES IN AGREEMENT WITH AND VOTES OPPOSED TO THOSE OF THE PENNSYLVANIA DELEGATION ON SIXTEEN KEY ISSUES

X—vote in agreement with Pennsylvania; o—vote opposed to Pennsylvania; P—personalty; r—realty

VOTE OF:	1	2	3	4	5	6	7	8	9	10	11	12	13	14	15	16	TOTAL VOTES CAST	In Agreement with Pennsylvania No.	Percentage
PENNSYLVANIA	N	Y	N	N	N	N	N	N	Y	Y	N	N	N	N	Y	N			
McClurg (P)	X	X	X	X	—	X	—	—	—	—	—	—	—	—	—	—	5	5	100
Hamilton (P)	X	X	X	—	—	X	—	—	—	—	—	—	—	—	—	—	3	3	100
Houston (r)	—	—	X	—	—	—	—	—	—	—	—	—	—	—	—	—	1	1	100
Langdon (P)	—	—	—	X	X	X	X	X	X	X	X	o	X	X	X	X	13	12	92.3
Gilman (P)	—	—	—	X	X	X	X	X	X	X	X	o	X	X	X	X	13	12	92.3
Dayton (P)	—	—	X	—	—	X	X	X	—	X	o	o	X	X	X	X	12	11	91.6
Gorham (P)	X	X	X	X	X	X	o	X	o	—	o	X	X	X	X	X	15	12	80
Washington (r)	X	—	X	X	o	X	X	X	o	o	o	o	X	X	X	X	15	12	80
Madison (r)	X	X	X	X	X	X	X	X	o	X	o	o	X	X	X	X	16	12	75
King (P)	X	X	X	X	X	X	X	X	X	—	o	o	X	X	X	X	15	11	73.3
Livingston (r)	o	o	o	—	X	X	X	X	—	X	X	o	X	X	X	o	14	10	71.4
Brearley (r)	o	o	X	—	X	X	X	X	—	X	o	o	o	X	X	o	14	10	71.4
Few (r)	X	o	X	—	—	X	o	X	X	X	o	X	o	o	X	X	14	10	71.4
Dickinson (r)	o	X	X	—	X	X	X	o	o	X	o	X	X	X	—	—	13	9	69.2
C. Pinckney (r)	X	o	X	X	X	X	o	X	X	X	o	X	o	o	X	X	16	11	68.7
Blair (P)	X	X	X	X	X	X	o	X	o	o	X	X	o	o	X	X	16	11	68.7
Baldwin (P)	—	o	X	X	o	X	o	X	X	X	X	X	o	o	X	X	15	10	66.6

	1	2	3	4	5	6	7	8	9	10	11	12	13	14	15	16	A	B	C
Read (r)	o	X	X	o	X	o	X	X	X	X	o	o	X	X	X	?	15	10	66.6
Blount (r)	—	—	o	—	—	X	o	X	X	X	X	o	X	o	X	X	12	8	66.6
Strong (P)	X	X	o	X	X	o	—	—	—	—	—	—	—	—	—	—	6	4	66.6
Pierce (P)	X	o	X	—	—	—	—	—	—	—	—	—	—	—	—	—	3	2	66.6
Williamson (P)	X	o	o	X	o	X	o	X	X	X	X	o	X	o	X	X	16	10	62.5
Spaight (r)	o	o	o	X	o	X	o	X	X	X	X	o	X	X	X	X	16	10	62.5
Rutledge (r)	o	o	o	X	X	X	o	X	X	X	o	X	o	X	X	X	16	10	62.5
C. C. Pinckney (P)	o	o	o	X	X	X	o	X	X	X	o	X	o	X	X	X	16	10	62.5
Butler (r)	o	o	o	X	X	X	o	X	X	X	o	X	o	X	X	X	16	10	62.5
Broom (r)	o	—	X	o	X	o	X	X	X	X	o	o	X	X	o	?	14	8	57.1
Carroll (r)	—	—	X	o	X	o	o	o	X	o	X	o	o	o	X	X	14	8	57.1
Jenifer (r)	X	o	X	X	X	X	o	o	X	o	X	o	o	o	o	X	16	9	56.2
Randolph (P)	X	o	X	X	X	o	o	X	X	o	X	o	o	o	o	X	16	9	56.2
Bedford (P)	o	o	X	o	X	o	X	X	X	X	o	o	X	X	o	?	15	8	53.3
Bassett (r)	o	o	X	o	X	o	X	X	X	X	o	o	X	X	o	o	15	8	53.3
Ellsworth (P)	o	X	o	o	X	X	o	o	X	o	X	o	X	—	—		14	7	50
Davie (r)	X	o	o	X	o	X	—	—	—	—	—	—	—	—	—	—	6	3	50
Lansing (P)	X	o	—	—	—	—	—	—	—	—	—	—	—	—	—	—	2	1	50
Johnson (r)	o	o	o	o	X	X	o	o	X	o	X	X	o	X	X	o	16	7	43.7
Sherman (P)	o	o	o	o	X	X	o	o	X	o	X	X	o	X	X	o	16	7	43.7
A. Martin (r)	X	o	o	X	o	X	o	—	—	—	—	—	—	—	—	—	7	3	42.8
Paterson (r)	o	o	X	X	—	—	—	—	—	—	—	—	—	—	—	—	5	2	40
Houstoun (r)	X	o	o	X	o	—	—	—	—	—	—	—	—	—	—	—	5	2	40
Mason (P)	X	o	X	X	o	o	o	o	X	o	X	X	o	o	o	X	16	7	37.5
McHenry (r)	—	—	—	—	—	X	o	o	o	o	X	X	o	o	o	X	11	4	36.3
Yates (r)	X	o	o	—	—	—	—	—	—	—	—	—	—	—	—	—	3	1	33.3
Gerry (P)	o	o	o	o	o	o	o	o	X	—	o	X	o	X	o	X	15	4	26.6
L. Martin (P)	—	—	o	o	—	—	o	o	o	o	X	X	o	o	o	—	11	2	18
Mercer (P)	—	—	—	—	o	o	—	—	—	—	—	—	—	—	—	—	2	0	0
Wythe (P)	—	—	—	—	—	—	—	—	—	—	—	—	—	—	—	—	—	—	—

economic features of the instrument were certain positive grants of power and certain negative clauses, restrictions against attacks on property. Specifically, the most important positive features were the grant to Congress of exclusive power to regulate commerce and to fund the war debt. The key negative clauses were those prohibiting the issue of paper money by states and declaring that states could pass no laws impairing the obligation of contract—that is, laws staying executions for debts or making fiat money or goods legal tender for debts.

An analysis of the attitudes revealed while these four significant features of the Constitution were in the process of adoption should, therefore, throw additional light on the question whether the delegates were creating a system to promote and protect special interests "which they felt in definite, concrete, form." Each of the features is considered briefly in the following paragraphs.

At first almost every delegate was agreed that the new government should have the power to regulate and levy duties on commerce. The working out of the details of the subject, however, revealed basic conflicts of interests and differences of opinion almost sufficient to break up the Convention.

Two limitations on congressional control of commerce did find their way, after bitter struggles, into the finished Constitution: the temporary restriction against regulation of the slave trade and the prohibition of duties on exports. Three other important proposals were the subject of intense controversy in the Convention. On August 28 Massachusetts, Connecticut, Pennsylvania, Maryland, Virginia, South Carolina, and Georgia voted against Madison's proposal to make absolute the restriction against state import duties. On the next day Maryland, Virginia, North Carolina, and Georgia voted for a proposal so to tie the hands of Congress that no laws respecting commerce could be passed without a two-thirds majority of both houses. This proposal, which would have prevented the adoption of the first national commercial system and almost every major tariff bill passed before the Civil War, was also favored by South Carolina, though all the South Carolinians except Charles Pinckney voted against it, in keeping with the bargain they had made for northern support on the slave trade. Finally, on September 15, a spectacular last-ditch proposal was made which might have destroyed the entire commercial system being established. This proposal, which would have removed from congressional control all import and export duties levied by states, had the support of Virginia, North Carolina, and Georgia, and half the Pennsylvania delegation.

This conflict over the proposal to grant to Congress exclusive power over commerce was partly one of personal interests, partly one of state and sectional interests, and partly one of opinions based on little more than abstract philosophy. Every state except New Hampshire voted for at least one of the three crippling proposals mentioned above, two states voted for two of them, and two others voted for all three. All but a handful of the delegates present voted for at least one of them; only Gilman, Langdon, Madison, possibly Washington, and perhaps two or three others voted consistently to give Congress exclusive power over commerce.

One would expect that if there was unanimity on any issue in the Convention, it would have been on the payment of the war debts, because of the large number of security holders among the delegates. On the contrary, however, there was much disagreement, and the discussions were, in a way, a preview of the great debates that were to take place in Congress over the adoption of Hamilton's funding plan in 1790. With one minor exception nothing was said in the Convention on the subject of the debts until thirty days before adjournment. At that time, on August 18, the report of the Committee of Detail, summarizing the Convention's expressed sentiments, revealed, among other things, that no provision regarding the debt had been made. Thereupon, Madison and Charles Pinckney moved that a catch-all committee be set up to consider a number of miscellaneous additional powers. Pinckney, who was not a security holder, included in his list a power "to secure the payment of the public debt." Rutledge, who likewise owned no securities, added a motion that power to assume the war debts of the states should also be considered by this committee.

The question of the public debt was discussed intermittently for a week, at the end of which the clauses in the Constitution respecting public obligations were agreed upon. During the week's debate twenty-two men made their attitude on the subject more or less clear. Eight of them expressed strongly the sentiment that all public creditors should be taken care of, and fourteen expressed reservations regarding the payment of all or parts of the public debt.

Gerry, the largest holder of securities in the Convention, was the most outspoken champion of public creditors, urging that Congress be expressly required to pay the national debt, and favoring the assumption of state debts (August 18, 21, 22, 25). King, a large holder of the public debt of New York, spoke strongly in favor of assumption (August 18), and Sherman, a creditor of Connecticut, argued in behalf of specific requirements for the payment of both national and state debts (August 18, 25). Rutledge and Charles Pinckney, neither of whom held any securities, were advocates of the assumption of state debts (August 18). Gouverneur Morris, who held no securities, was almost as emphatic as Gerry in his insistence that the new Congress be specifically required to pay the public debt.

On the other hand, Ellsworth, who held continental but no state securities, was against the assumption of state debts, but he urged that it be specifically required that continental debts be paid (August 18, 25), which was exactly coincident with his personal interests. John Langdon, the third largest public creditor in the Convention, voted against assumption of state debts and argued against any special provisions for any public creditors, saying that he "wished to do no more than to leave the creditors in the statu quo" (August 18, 25). Gilman, another security owner, joined Langdon in voting against assumption (August 18) and any special provisions for continental creditors (August 25). The Delaware delegation present, including Bedford, Broom, and Read, all holders of securities, and Bassett, who held none, voted against assumption (August 18). The New Jersey delegation present, including Dayton, a substantial security holder, Brearley, a nominal security holder, and Livingston, who held no public paper, joined Delaware in voting against assumption (August 18). Randolph, one of the larger creditors in the Convention, Mason, only nominally a public creditor, and Johnson, not a holder of securities, expressed sentiments similar to Langdon's that no special provisions should be made for public creditors, and they were all against expressly requiring Congress to pay the public debt (August 25). Butler, not a creditor, joined the latter delegates, and he stated further that he was against making "payment as well to the Bloodsuckers who had speculated on the distresses of others, as to those who had fought & bled for their country" (August 23, 25).

Thus four men—Gerry, King, Sherman, and Ellsworth—were obviously working ardently for the interests represented by their own investments. Except for these four, neither public creditors nor non-creditors evinced anything like consistent attention to the personalty interests they represented.

With respect to the negative clauses—the restrictions against attacks on property by state legislatures—it was observed earlier that a fourth of the delegates had voted for just such "attacks." It is therefore not surprising to find that when the clauses forbidding paper money and establishing the sanctity of contracts came up for a vote on August 28, many of the delegates opposed the prohibition of such legislation.

The vote against paper money was overwhelming: only Virginia opposed the restriction and Maryland was divided. Of the five Virginians present, at least three must have voted against the restriction. Mason and Randolph had expressed extreme disapproval of paper on August 16, but Madison had indicated his unwillingness to have it cut off altogether. If the Virginia vote was split, then, it must have been Washington, Madison, and Blair who opposed the restriction and Mason and Randolph who favored it, though it is conceivable that the latter two may also have voted in the negative. Apparently the distribution of Maryland's split vote was McHenry and Martin against the restriction, Carroll and Jenifer for it. In addition to these five (or seven) opponents of the restriction, two other delegates expressed similar sentiments: Gorham, in the debate, and Mercer, who was not present but who had declared himself "a friend of paper money" on August 16. Thus from seven to nine delegates opposed this protection of property.

There was considerably more opposition to the contract clause. Rufus King's motion that there be "a prohibition on the States to interfere in private contracts" immediately evoked a barrage of criticism. After some discussion the Convention approved a substitute motion, made by Rutledge, from which King's proposal was deliberately omitted and which provided instead only that *ex post facto* laws and bills of attainder be prohibited. The votes of individuals are indicated in the table above, as issue number 10. Though the votes of a dozen or so men are only highly probable, not certain, it appears from recorded statements and a process of elimination that no fewer than twenty-seven of the thirty-eight delegates present voted for Rutledge's motion to scrap the sanctity-of-contracts clause. They were Dayton, Livingston, Brearley, Madison, Williamson, Blount, Spaight, Butler, Charles and Charles C. Pinckney, Rutledge, Baldwin, Few, Dickinson, Read, Bassett, Bedford, Broom, Clymer, Robert and Gouverneur Morris, Franklin, Fitzsimons, Mifflin, Ingersoll, Langdon, and Gilman.

If one adds to this list the six delegates who opposed the restriction on paper money but who favored the contract clause, it is apparent that at least thirty-three of the forty-one delegates whose attitudes are ascertainable voted against one or both of the critical constitutional safeguards against attacks on property. Eighteen of the thirty-three belonged to the "Personalty Group," fifteen had realty-agrarian interests. Of the eight who voted for both restrictions. five were men having personalty interests, three had realty-agrarian interests.

There remains a fourth and final criterion of Professor Beard's proposition that the members of the Philadelphia Convention were significantly influenced in their deliberations by the personal property interests they represented. This criterion is the relation between the economic interests of the delegates and their attitudes toward the finished Constitution.

To attempt to ascertain with what measure of satisfaction each member viewed the Constitution is, unfortunately, to work with too nebulous a subject. That some of the delegates —for example, King, Wilson, and Madison—were enthusiastic about the finished product is obvious both from their utterances in the Convention and from their later conduct. That others were lukewarm toward it or even signed it against their better judgment is also obvious. Blount signed only after the style of the signatures was changed from one indicating individual approval to one merely attesting that the state delegations present unanimously approved the Constitution. McHenry was "opposed to many parts of the system" but was prepared to support it because it was amendable. "I distrust my own judgment," he said. Franklin said there were many parts he did not approve and would never approve. Dayton considered the Constitution defective and derided those who thought it would be a panacea for the nation's ills. Some delegates thought the Convention had gone too far; others, Hamilton among them, that it had not gone far enough. But the attitudes of too few individuals are known, and the shades of opinion are too ephemeral, to be subjected to systematic scrutiny.

Some progress in this direction can be made, however, by considering the interests of those definitely opposed to the new system. Suppose the Convention had been a ratifying convention; in that event, at least seven members would have voted against the adoption of the Constitution: Gerry, Lansing, Yates, Mercer, Luther Martin, Randolph, and Mason.

These seven men constituted almost an all-star team of personalty interests. All except Martin were members of high rank in their local aristocracies; all except Yates had very large incomes. Two of them were lawyers with large mercantile clienteles, three had large mercantile interests. Three had extensive landholdings in the west. Mason was the largest private creditor in the Convention, Gerry the largest public creditor. Five of the group were among the larger public security holders in the Convention: they held approximately a third of all the securities owned by the delegates, in terms of both market and face value, and they made more than $31,000 by the appreciation of those securities after the establishment of the new government. The market value of their securities in 1787 was sufficient to have bought the security holdings of forty-three members of the Convention—all but five—and Mason's money at interest would have bought the remainder with $5,000 to spare.

On this basis one could venture to argue, speciously, and almost make a convincing case of it, that the internal conflict in the Philadelphia Convention lay between the men of considerable personalty interests, who opposed the Constitution, and men having realty-agrarian interests, a band of debtors, and a few men having modest personalty interests, who favored the Constitution.[2]

[2]Of the thirty-nine signers of the Constitution, twenty were men whose primary interests were in the form of personalty, nineteen had primarily realty-agrarian interests. If the six men in the personalty group who were

Professor Beard made no attempt at a systematic analysis of the role of economic interests inside the Philadelphia Convention. Instead, he predicted what such an analysis would show if it were made: "A thorough treatment of material forces reflected in the several clauses of the instrument of government created by the grave assembly at Philadelphia would require a rewriting of the history of the proceedings in the light of the great interests represented there."

The foregoing analysis would seem to indicate that anyone wishing to rewrite the history of those proceedings largely or exclusively in terms of the economic interests represented there would find the facts to be insurmountable obstacles.

A REVALUATION OF THE BEARD THESIS
OF THE MAKING OF THE CONSTITUTION

PROFESSOR BEARD interpreted the making of the Constitution as a simple, clear-cut series of events. When all the groups that became Federalists are brought together and analyzed, he asserted, and all the anti-Federalists are brought together and analyzed, the events can be seen as mere manifestations

---

debtors in a desperate plight and/or speculators in lands who suffered from the funding of the debts under the Constitution are shifted to the realty-agrarian group, the group takes on a quite different complexion. Then only fourteen of the thirty-nine signers would have belonged to the class for whose benefit, according to Professor Beard's thesis, the Constitution was written. The remaining twenty-five belonged to the group comprising farmers, men with realty interests, debtors, and immediate losers. Thus, to carry further the analogy of the Philadelphia Convention to a ratifying convention, only 36 per cent of the thirty-nine men favoring the Constitution are classifiable as members of the personalty interests group, whereas 86 per cent of those who would have voted against the Constitution are so classifiable. The seven opponents held two and a half times as much in securities (face value) per capita as the thirty-nine proto-Federalists, and their holdings of other forms of personalty were also more than twice as much per capita as those of the proto-Federalists.

of a fundamentally simple economic conflict. His analysis led him to formulate three basic propositions, one regarding the Philadelphia Convention and two regarding the contest over ratification. In the light of the data in the foregoing chapters, we may now focus our attention upon these three key propositions of Beard's economic interpretation of the Constitution.

The Philadelphia Convention

From his analysis of the Philadelphia Convention, Beard concluded that the Constitution was essentially "an economic document drawn with superb skill" by a "consolidated economic group . . . whose property interests were immediately at stake"; that these interests "knew no state boundaries but were truly national in their scope."

From a thorough reconsideration of the Philadelphia Convention, however, the following facts emerge. Fully a fourth of the delegates in the convention had voted in their state legislatures for paper-money and/or debtor-relief laws. These were the very kinds of laws which, according to Beard's thesis, the delegates had convened to prevent. Another fourth of the delegates had important economic interests that were adversely affected, directly and immediately, by the Constitution they helped write. The most common and by far the most important property holdings of the delegates were not, as Beard has asserted, mercantile, manufacturing, and public security investments, but agricultural property. Finally, it is abundantly evident that the delegates, once inside the Convention, behaved as anything but a consolidated economic group.

In the light of these and other facts presented in the foregoing chapters, it is impossible to justify Beard's interpretation of the Constitution as "an economic document" drawn by a "consolidated economic group whose property interests were immediately at stake."

The Contest over Ratification, First Proposition

Beard asserted that the ultimate test of the validity of an economic interpretation of the Constitution would rest upon a comparative analysis of the economic interests of all the persons voting for and all the persons voting against ratification. He made an analysis of the economic interests of some of the leaders in the movement for ratification and concluded that "in the ratification, it became manifest that the line of cleavage for and against the Constitution was between substantial personalty interests on the one hand and the small farming and debtor interests on the other."

For the purpose of analyzing this proposition it is necessary to employ Beard's own definitions of interest groups. In the paragraphs that follow, as in the foregoing chapters, the term "men of personalty interests" is used to mean those groups which Beard himself had in mind when he used the term, namely money, public securities, manufacturing and shipping, and western lands held for speculation.

From a thorough reconsideration of the contests over ratification the following facts emerge.

1. In three states (Delaware, New Jersey, and Georgia) the decisions of the ratifying conventions were unanimous, and it is therefore impossible to compare the interests of contending parties. The following analyses of the conventions in these three states may be made, however.

In Delaware almost 77 per cent of the delegates were farmers, more than two-thirds of them small farmers with incomes ranging from 75 cents to $5.00 a week. Slightly more than 23 per cent of the delegates were professional men—doctors, judges, and lawyers. None of the delegates was a merchant, manufacturer, banker, or speculator in western lands.

In New Jersey 64.1 per cent of the delegates were farmers, 23.1 per cent were professional men (physicians, lawyers, and college presidents), and only 12.8 per cent were men having personalty interests (one merchant, three iron manufacturers, and one capitalist with diversified investments).

In Georgia 50 per cent of the delegates were farmers (38.5 per cent slave-owning planters and 11.5 per cent small farmers), 11.5 per cent were frontiersmen whose economic interests were primarily agrarian, 19.2 per cent were professional men (lawyers, physicians, and professional officeholders), and only 11.5 per cent had personalty interests (all merchants). The interests of 7.7 per cent of the delegates were not ascertained.

Beard assumed that ratification in these states was pushed through by personalty interest groups before agrarian and paper-money groups could organize their forces. The opposite is true. In each of these three states agrarian interests dominated the conventions. In each state there were approximately equal numbers of delegates who had voted earlier for and against paper money.

2. In two states in which the decision was contested (Virginia and North Carolina) the great majority of the delegates on both sides of the question were farmers. In both states the delegates who voted for and the delegates who voted against ratification had substantially the same amounts of the same kinds of property, most commonly land and slaves. A large number of the delegates in the Virginia convention had voted on the question of repudiation of debts due British merchants, and the majority of the delegates who had favored such repudiation voted for ratification of the Constitution. Large numbers of delegates in both North Carolina conventions were speculating in western lands. In the first convention a great majority of these land speculators opposed the Constitution; in the second a substantial majority of them favored ratification.

Beard assumed that ratification in these states represented

the victory of wealthy planters, especially those who were rich in personalty other than slaves, over the small slaveless farmers and debtors. The opposite is true. In both states the wealthy planters—those with personalty interests as well as those without personalty interests—were divided approximately equally on the issue of ratification. In North Carolina small farmers and debtors were likewise equally divided, and in Virginia the great mass of the small farmers and a large majority of the debtors favored ratification.

3. In four states (Connecticut, Maryland, South Carolina, and New Hampshire) agrarian interests were dominant, but large minorities of delegates had personalty interests.

In Connecticut 57.8 per cent of the delegates who favored ratification and 67.5 per cent of those who opposed ratification were farmers. Ratification was approved by 76.2 per cent of all the delegates, by 81.8 per cent of the delegates having personalty interests, and by 73.3 per cent of the farmers in the convention. Here, then, four delegates out of five having substantial personalty interests favored the Constitution. On the other hand, three of every four farmers also favored the Constitution.

In Maryland 85.8 per cent of the delegates who voted for ratification were farmers, almost all of them wealthy slave-owning planters; 27.3 per cent of the opponents of ratification were farmers, all of them substantial slave-owning planters. The opponents of ratification included from three to six times as large a proportion of merchants, lawyers, and investors in shipping, confiscated estates, and manufacturing as did the delegates who favored ratification. It is to be observed, however, that because the vote in the Maryland ratifying convention was almost unanimous (63 to 11), statistics on the attitudes of the various interest groups would show that every major interest group except manufacturers favored the Constitution. A majority of the areas and of the delegates that had advocated paper money also favored the Constitution.

In South Carolina 59 per cent of the delegates who voted for ratification were large slave-owning planters and 10.7 per cent were lesser planters and farmers. Of the delegates who voted against ratification, 41.7 per cent were large slave-owning planters and 34.2 per cent were lesser planters and farmers. Merchants, factors, and mariners favored ratification, 70 per cent to 30 per cent, a margin almost identical to the vote of the entire convention—67 per cent for, 33 per cent against—and manufacturers, artisans, and mechanics were unanimous in support of the Constitution. On the other hand, 35.7 per cent of the delegates who favored ratification were debtors who were in a desperate plight or had borrowed paper money from the state. Only 15.1 per cent of those who voted against ratification were debtors or had borrowed paper money from the state. No fewer than 82 per cent of the debtors and borrowers of paper money in the convention voted for ratification.

As respects New Hampshire, comparisons are difficult because of the lack of adequate information concerning 28.2 per cent of the delegates. Of the delegates whose interests are known, 36.9 per cent of those favoring the Constitution and 25 per cent of those opposing it were farmers; of the known farmers in the convention 68.7 per cent favored ratification. If it is assumed, however, that all the delegates whose interests are not ascertainable were farmers (as in all likelihood most of them were), then 49.1 per cent of the delegates favoring ratification were farmers, 54.3 per cent of those opposing ratification were farmers, and 52.8 per cent of the farmers in the convention voted for ratification. Delegates whose interests were primarily in personalty (merchants, tradesmen, manufacturers, and shipbuilders) voted in favor of ratification, 60.9 per cent to 39.1 per cent. Delegates from the towns which had voted for and against paper money divided almost equally on the question of ratification: 42 per cent of the towns that had voted for paper money and 54 per cent of those that had voted against paper sent delegates who voted for the Constitution.

Beard assumed that in these states ratification was the outcome of class struggles between commercial and other personalty groups (Federalists) on the one hand and farmers and advocates of paper money (anti-Federalists) on the other. This generalization is groundless. In each of these states a majority of the men having personalty interests favored ratification, but in each of them a similar majority of the farmers also favored ratification. In one of these states there was no great demand for paper money, in another a large majority of the friends of paper money favored ratification, and in the other two the advocates of paper money were divided almost equally on the question of ratification.

4. In four states (Massachusetts, Pennsylvania, New York, and Rhode Island) men having personalty interests were in a majority in the ratifying conventions.

In Massachusetts, in the popular vote (excluding that of Maine) men whose interests were primarily non-agrarian favored the Constitution by about three to two, and men whose interests were primarily agrarian opposed the Constitution by about 55 per cent to 45 per cent. In the ratifying convention 80 per cent of the merchants and shippers engaged in waterborne commerce, 77 per cent of the artisans and mechanics, and 64 per cent of the farmers favored ratification. About 83 per cent of the retail storekeepers, 85 per cent of the manufacturers, and 64 per cent of the miscellaneous capitalists opposed ratification. One-fourth of those favoring and one-sixth of those opposing the Constitution were farmers. Of the personalty groups combined, 57.5 per cent opposed and 42.5 per cent favored ratification. The realty groups combined, including artisans and mechanics, favored ratification by 67 per cent to 33 per cent.

In Pennsylvania only 34.8 per cent of the delegates favoring ratification were farmers, and only 26.1 per cent of the opponents were farmers. Almost three-fourths—72.7 per cent—of the farmers in the convention favored ratification. The great majority of the delegates on both sides, however, 84.7 per cent of those favoring and 91.3 per cent of those opposing the Constitution, had substantial investments in one or more of Professor Beard's four forms of personalty.

New York delegates are difficult to classify as farmers because almost all farmers in the convention were also landlords with tenants. Delegates to the state's convention may be classified as elected Federalists, converts from anti-Federalism, delegates who abstained from voting, and anti-Federalists. Of the delegates about whom there is sufficient data on which to generalize, fewer than 20 per cent of each group consisted of farmers who had no tenants and who owned none of Beard's four forms of personalty.

Rhode Island delegates do not lend themselves to occupational classification because almost everyone in the state normally combined in his own economic activities several kinds of functions. Only 11.8 per cent of the delegates favoring ratification and only one of the delegates opposing ratification were found to have no interests except farming. The early opponents of paper money formed the original core of those favoring ratification, yet in the final vote 62 per cent of the delegates voting for ratification and 63 per cent of those opposing ratification were men who had borrowed paper money from the state.

Beard's thesis—that the line of cleavage as regards the Constitution was between substantial personalty interests on the one hand and small farming and debtor interests on the other —is entirely incompatible with the facts.

The Contest over Ratification, Second Proposition

Beard was less certain of the foregoing point, however, than he was of this next one:

Inasmuch as so many leaders in the movement for ratification were large security holders, and inasmuch as securities constituted such a large proportion of personalty, this economic interest must have formed a very considerable dynamic element, if not the preponderating element, in bringing about the adoption of the new system. . . . Some holders of public securities are found among the opponents of the Constitution, but they are not numerous.

This proposition may be analyzed in the same manner that Beard's more general personalty-agrarian conclusion was analyzed. To repeat, Beard asserted that public securities were the dynamic element within the dynamic element in the ratification. This assertion is incompatible with the facts. The facts are these:

1. In three states (Delaware, New Jersey, and Georgia) there were no votes against the Constitution in the ratifying conventions, and hence no comparisons can be made. If public securities were the dynamic element in the ratification, however, it would be reasonable to expect that the great majority of the delegates in these states which supported the Constitution so unreservedly should have been security holders. But the fact is that in Delaware only one delegate in six owned securities, in New Jersey 34 per cent of the delegates, and in Georgia only one delegate.

2. In two states (New Hampshire and North Carolina) the numbers of security holders among the delegates were very small. In New Hampshire only 10.5 per cent of those who voted for and only 2.2 per cent of those who voted against ratification held securities. In the first North Carolina convention only 2.4 per cent of the friends and only 1.1 per cent of the opponents of ratification held securities. In the second convention only 2.0 per cent of those favoring and only 3.9 per cent of those opposing the Constitution were security holders. Superficially these facts tend to substantiate Beard's

thesis, for these virtually security-less states were slow to ratify the Constitution. It has been shown, however, that actually the reluctance of these states to adopt the Constitution and their vulnerability to raids on their securities by outsiders were both merely surface manifestations of the same underlying conditions—the isolation, the lack of information, and the lethargy of the majority of the inhabitants of North Carolina and New Hampshire.

3. In three states (Rhode Island, Maryland, and Virginia) where there were contests and considerable numbers of security holders, the advocates and the opponents of ratification included approximately the same percentages of security holders: in Rhode Island, 50 per cent of the advocates and 47 per cent of the opponents; in Virginia, 40.5 per cent of the advocates and 34.2 per cent of the opponents; and in Maryland, 17.4 per cent and 27.3 per cent respectively. The facts relative to these three states clearly contradict Beard's thesis.

4. In two states (Massachusetts and Connecticut) the advocates of ratification included a considerably larger percentage of holders of securities than did the opponents. In Massachusetts 31 per cent of the ratificationists and only 10.1 per cent of the anti-ratificationists were security owners, and in Connecticut 36.7 per cent and 15 per cent respectively. The situations in these two states, and in these two states alone, tend strongly to support Beard's thesis.

5. In three states (Pennsylvania, South Carolina, and New York) a considerably larger percentage of the delegates opposing ratification than of the Federalist delegates held public securities. In Pennsylvania 73.9 per cent of the opponents and 50 per cent of the supporters of ratification were security owners, in South Carolina 71 and 43 per cent respectively, and in New York 63 and 50 per cent respectively. The facts pertaining to these states not only fail to harmonize with Beard's thesis but indicate that there the precise opposite of his thesis is true.

In the light of the foregoing facts it is abundantly evident that there are no more grounds for considering the holding of public securities the dynamic element in the ratification than for considering this economic interest the dynamic element in the opposition. There were, indeed, some holders of public securities among the opponents of the Constitution and, contrary to Beard's assertion, they were as numerous as the security holders among the supporters of the Constitution.

On all counts, then, Beard's thesis is entirely incompatible with the facts. Beard's essential error was in attempting to formulate a single set of generalizations that would apply to all the states. Any such effort is necessarily futile, for the various interest groups operated under different conditions in the several states, and their attitudes toward the Constitution varied with the internal conditions in their states.

THE BEARD THESIS DEFENDED

Jackson T. Main

EDITOR'S NOTE Jackson Turner Main of the State
University of New York, Stony Brook, is the country's foremost authority on the class system of our
early national history and its relationship to political behavior. His first book, *The Antifederalists:
Critics of the Constitution, 1781–1788* (1961), originally a doctoral dissertation done under the guid-
ance of Merrill Jensen, argued that the political
alignment on the Constitution substantially followed class lines. Unlike Robert E. Brown who
assumed the existence of a virtually classless or all-
one-class society, and unlike Forrest McDonald
who recognized the existence of classes but denied
significant class differences among proponents and
opponents of the Constitution, Main was close to
Beard in his emphasis on class conflict—and he had
the evidence of contemporary testimony on his
side. His interpretation of the ratification controversy allowed for important exceptions to his thesis;
in the towns, for example, all classes overwhelmingly supported the Constitution.

If class politics was not always determinative in
Main's view, an economic interpretation was. Main
broadly construed mercantile interests to include
most townspeople (merchants, shipowners, common seamen and laborers, and craftsmen) and a
special type of rural people (planters and farmers

From Jackson T. Main, "Charles A. Beard and the Constitution: A
Critical Review of Forrest McDonald's *We the People*," *William and
Mary Quarterly*, January 1960, 3rd Ser., XVII, pp. 86–102. Reprinted
without footnotes by permission.

who relied upon the towns as markets for their crops). All were united in their common dependence on trade. "The mercantile interest," Main wrote, "understood in this broad sense, is the key to the political history of the period. Its counterpart is the noncommercial interest of the subsistence farmer. This is a socio-economic division based on a geographical location and sustains a class as well as a sectional interpretation of the struggle over the Constitution." Main explored those socioeconomic divisions in depth in his superb pioneering study, *The Social Structure of Revolutionary America* (1965).

In the following article Main defends Beard's *Economic Interpretation* against McDonald's attack. McDonald's apparent thoroughness and rich detail had had an intimidating effect on his readers who not unreasonably, yet uncritically, assumed that his facts were reliable, just as an earlier generation had assumed that Beard's were. If Main does nothing else in his critique of McDonald, he refreshes the spirit of skepticism that all students of history should have when reading a secondary account without having a personal mastery of the primary sources on which it is, or should be, based. That same spirit of skepticism should apply to Main's critique. As McDonald pointed out in a rejoinder, Main passed over the fourth chapter in which McDonald proved that there was virtually no correlation between economic interests and voting behavior in the Constitutional Convention. McDonald dismissed Main's criticisms of his treatment of the ratification controversy in Connecticut and Massachusetts, on the ground that the Beard thesis was basically sound for those two states, but only for those two. He claimed that nothing Main wrote altered the fact that in both Pennsylvania and South Carolina, more Anti-Federalists held securities than Federalists and in greater amounts, contrary to Beard. Finally, McDonald concluded that even if one conceded all points to Main with respect to the states which he interpreted differently, there were still seven other states for which Main had not attacked the data, "which means," said McDonald, "that Main concedes that Beard was wrong in at least seven of the thirteen states." Here was proof, he concluded, that the Beard thesis, like any other monolithic interpretation of a complex event, cannot be sustained. Readers should note, however, that Main's critique is necessarily fragmentary because it is only the length of an article and could not, therefore, touch on McDonald's treatment of the ratification controversy in all the states.

o   o   o   o

IT IS A little strange that, when dozens of monographs during two score years have profitably used Beard's interpretation of the Constitution, an attempt utterly to refute him has aroused scarcely a whimper of protest. Nobody would insist that Beard's thesis be accepted in its entirety, but his fundamental idea—that the Constitution reflected the economic interests of the large property holders who wrote it—has survived much research, and any book which challenges it ought to be examined with a cautious and skeptical eye. If Forrest McDonald's *We the People: The Economic Origins of the Constitution* (Chicago, 1958), is so scrutinized, it will be found that Beard has survived the attack. Since a complete criticism would require a volume of equal length, this discussion will review only a few of the most important aspects.[1]

[1]This essay is based upon material gathered for a study of post-Revolutionary politics. The objective is not to defend Beard *in toto*, for much that he wrote has been proved erroneous, nor is it to present

Beard's work was an early attempt to test the hypothesis "that economic elements are the chief factors in the development of political institutions." He therefore assembled data concerning the real and personal property owned by those who wrote the Constitution and those who favored its ratification. Since, as he wrote, a complete survey "would entail an enormous labor," Beard relied chiefly on secondary accounts and published documents, except that he did undertake to identify the holders of the Federal debt. In addition, he discussed the political ideas of the members of the Federal Convention insofar as these related to his general purpose. This chapter is not discussed by McDonald. Beard found that most of the members of the Convention were lawyers, that they came from towns or regions near the coast where public securities were concentrated, that they were not farmers, and that they would be economically benefited by ratification because they possessed public securities, land held for speculation, money at interest, slaves, or property in commerce, manufacturing, and shipping. The same observations applied to the Federal members of the various state ratifying conventions. In general, the division on this issue "was between substantial personalty interests on the one hand and the small farming and debtor interests on the other."

McDonald set himself the task of testing Beard's conclusions. In doing so he made far greater use of primary materials and has substantially increased our knowledge, especially concerning the economic interests of the men involved. It is this contribution which immediately impresses the reader and has led to the general praise which the book has hitherto received. Nevertheless the research is far from complete. The facts cited are those which tend to refute Beard, while those which would support his views are often omitted; and the interpretation of the facts is likewise open to dispute.

---

an alternative hypothesis, but to examine critically this particular attack upon Beard's thesis and thereby to clear the way for future interpretations.

The first part of the book attempts to prove that the Federal Convention, far from reflecting exclusively the ideas of certain well-to-do economic groups, was a truly representative body. McDonald seeks first to show that the delegates came from most of the major geographical areas; second, that they reflected all "shades of political opinion"; and third, that they themselves were of diverse economic interests, often in debt, less rich than Beard had suggested, and less influenced by ownership of public securities.

The first contention is "proved" by defining geographical areas in a way which achieves the desired result and by counting as present at the Convention anyone who was chosen as a delegate even when he did not attend. This faulty methodology may be illustrated by the case of Massachusetts. On the basis of physical location one might expect that the major areas would be described as (1) the maritime coast and its immediate hinterland, (2) Maine, and (3) the agricultural, upland interior, with perhaps (4) the Connecticut Valley towns distinguished as a fourth section. Such a division would reflect political and economic realities, for the seacoast towns were in fact usually opposed to those of the interior, while the lower Connecticut Valley usually supported the east and Maine went its own way. If this were done, then of the four delegates who attended, three came from the east and one from the Valley, leaving most of the state, including Maine and all of the interior, unrepresented. However, McDonald divides the coastal towns into four separate areas in such a way that all but one of them were represented; counts Rufus King as doubling for Maine as well as Newburyport, although King no longer lived in either place (being in fact a resident of New York and had left Maine when he was twelve); considers that a group of interior towns connected with Boston were present through Francis Dana, although Dana did not attend the Convention; and concludes that six out of nine areas into which he divides the state were represented at Philadelphia. In this manner the fundamental fact, which Beard recognized, is concealed, namely, that the commercial east coast was represented and the agrarian west was not. In like fashion he says that three out of four New Hampshire regions were represented, although the only two delegates who attended were from Portsmouth and Exeter, both within ten miles of the coast!

In Virginia as in Massachusetts, McDonald divides the Tidewater eastern part of the state into four separate areas, all represented; in addition the "Upper James" is counted present through Edmund Randolph who lived in Richmond, a fall-line town; and the rest of the interior is also considered to be present through Patrick Henry, who did not attend. McDonald can then cheerfully concede that the three sections west of the Blue Ridge were not represented, for he has discovered a majority of six out of nine. It can be argued with equal if not superior evidence that in truth all of Virginia's delegates to the Convention represented only one section: the Tidewater, or perhaps more accurately the eastern river valley area, leaving four sections to be counted as not present.

McDonald's proof that "all shades of political opinion" were present rests upon his division of the country into "factions," which are supposed to include all political groupings. He then finds that most of the major factions were represented. The argument depends, of course, upon whether the idea of "factions" adequately describes post-Revolutionary politics, and whether his particular identification of factions is valid. His conclusions therefore follow only if his definitions be accepted and if in addition it is granted that all those chosen as delegates should be counted even though they rejected the election. Massachusetts may again serve as an illustration. McDonald finds two major factions, led by John Hancock and James Bowdoin, and several minor ones headed by Samuel Adams, Theodore Sedgwick, Benjamin Lincoln, Benjamin Austin, and the Cushing family. Since both of the major factions were represented, he declares his point proved. But Massachusetts politics cannot be explained in terms of the personal leadership of individuals, of whom all but one lived near the coast, and that one (Sedgwick) a supporter of the conservative, commercial Bowdoin group. What about the vast majority of small interior towns? Surely a delegation which contained not a single man to express the views of small farmers —not a Shaysite or Shaysite sympathizer—did not reflect all of the various political opinions, but fundamentally only one. Similarly in Virginia, McDonald declares that "all four major and three independent factions were represented." But R. H. Lee and Henry did not attend, so that even accepting his definition of factions the true figure is two out of four major groups. Moreover, once again there was not a single delegate who spoke for the small farmers. In state after state the only "factions" represented were those of the mercantile, large landholding, well-to-do easterners, and it certainly is not true that the Convention represented all shades of political opinion. Once again Beard's analysis is the more nearly correct one.

The attempt to refute Beard's views concerning the property interests of the delegates is equally open to question, even though McDonald has gathered much additional data. The refutation is attempted by placing the emphasis upon those facts which depreciate the property held and by continually minimizing the delegates' wealth. Now every historian is required to select such facts as he believes significant and to arrange them in such a way as to convey a meaning: to interpret. Yet it is not always easy for the reader to remember that he is being presented an interpretation rather than an exact re-creation of reality. It will be instructive to compare, in a few cases, the accounts given by Beard and McDonald. The latter emphasizes that Robert Morris was heavily in debt and died bankrupt; Beard barely mentions this and concentrates upon describing his great wealth in 1787. Beard stresses James Wilson's large estate, McDonald his debts and ultimate poverty. To McDonald, Hamilton was "perpetually in debt"; to Beard, he is the principal spokesman for the rich, who "lived well, and had a large income." Madison is depicted by Mc-Donald as the owner of "560 ill-kept acres," by Beard as the son of a wealthy planter, relieved thereby from the necessity of earning a living (actually the Madison estate included 5,748 acres and 99 slaves). Richard Bassett appears in *We the People* as a man of moderate means who lived "in comfort"; in Beard he is one of the wealthy men of the state who "entertained lavishly." In a number of other instances the two accounts differ, sometimes radically.[2]

Throughout *We the People*, men of means are made to appear quite the opposite. Hamilton, Robert Morris and Wilson were not the only ones to die in debt; so also did Nathaniel Gorham, who in 1787—the date that matters—was one of the country's wealthiest men. We read that Pierce Butler, who owned 143 slaves, was "in rather desperate circumstances." William Houstoun, "the richest member of the Georgia delegation," could scarcely support himself, the implication being that the rest of the delegates from that state must have been truly impoverished; yet in truth Houstoun was one of the wealthy planter aristocracy with extensive lands. Gouverneur Morris's family estate is called "magnificent" when he fails to inherit it, but in the next paragraph, having passed into Morris's hands, it becomes "debt-laden. Jared Ingersoll, we read, had in 1787 "besides a wealthy father-in-law, a moderately successful practice, a fourth interest in a 30-ton sloop in the coasting trade, *and little else*" (italics mine). Edmund Randolph was in "great need," "beset with economic difficulties," impoverished it seems by thousands of acres and over a hundred slaves. Indeed to McDonald the rich man had less wealth than the poor, for we learn that John Rutledge's 243

[2] See the treatment of Ellsworth, Ingersoll, King, and Wythe. Incidentally the last had, in addition to the property assigned to him by McDonald, 800 acres and 28 slaves in Elizabeth City County.

slaves "were apparently more of a burden than an asset." When a man's basic wealth enabled him to borrow money in a time of great currency shortage, this is interpreted as a sign of poverty. Washington becomes "land- and slave- poor," a debtor, who borrowed £10,000 to cover expenses when he went to New York as President. McDonald lists thirteen members who were "debtors for significant amounts" and whose condition "ranged from acute embarrassment to desperation and outright bankruptcy," including such impecunious figures as Rutledge, Robert Morris, James Wilson, Washington, Madison, Randolph, Butler, Houstoun, and both Pinckneys.

This is absurd. If the reader will take the trouble to examine the facts which McDonald himself provides, the true situation will become apparent. The fact is that over two dozen of the sixty-five elected delegates, and more than half of those who signed the Constitution, were rich, and others were well-to-do. Not more than nine—less than one-seventh of the elected delegates—were of only modest means. Almost all of the delegates, moreover, were merchants, large landholders, or lawyers representing these groups, comprising precisely what Beard said they were: a "consolidated economic group."

McDonald also attempts to disprove the influence of public securities upon the Founders. The real question, it might be urged, is not whether a member of the Convention held securities, but the distribution of these in the country at large and the extent to which delegates reflected the desires of security holders.[3] However, since Beard did not do this, McDonald is justified in restricting his inquiries to the holdings of the delegates. In doing so he emphasizes that few of them held large amounts, and he tries, by gratuitous remarks, to disparage the importance of the profit received. Nicholas Gilman made $500 which is "roughly $10 per month from 1787

[3]The distribution of the debt and its great political significance are examined in detail by E. James Ferguson in a book soon to be published. He has kindly made available the results of his research.

to 1791." Rufus King made "only" about $1,300 in four years. Thomas Fitzsimons retained "only" $2,668.10 worth. Oliver Ellsworth's profit of $3,240 "would hardly seem large enough to write a Constitution to protect," and McDonald's concession that in Ellsworth's case the motive probably did exist merely emphasizes the impression he conveys that in all other cases no such amount would suffice. It was Beard's point, however, that even a small holding might well create sympathy with the needs of public creditors. The question was not, he wrote, "how many hundred thousand dollars accrued to them," but whether they represented "distinct groups whose economic interest they understood and felt in concrete, definite form through their own personal experience with identical property rights." Furthermore the stake of the delegates was by no means as small as McDonald implies. No argument can conceal the fact that nearly half of the delegates made over $500 each from the appreciation of these certificates, and no fewer than thirteen held $5,000 worth apiece (face value) in 1787. It would certainly seem that once again Beard is closer to the mark than McDonald.[4]

In addition to this effort to reinterpret the nature of the Convention, McDonald tries to disprove Beard's contention concerning the alignment for and against ratification—"to test," as he puts it, "the validity of Beard's class struggle interpretation," by demonstrating through a description of the members

[4]There are other interpretations in these chapters which might be challenged. The author is eager to note whenever a delegate voted for paper money or on behalf of debtors, ignoring any contrary behavior. The reader is usually not informed of the circumstances, which perhaps were not always known to McDonald. Langdon's vote for paper money was actually cast in behalf of a measure which was favored by many creditors as an alternative to something worse: a paper money plan so conservative that it was negatived by all of the soft money towns. Moreover Langdon spoke out strongly against state issues of paper money. See Richard B. Morris, "Insurrection in Massachusetts," in *America in Crisis*, ed. Daniel Aaron (New York, 1952), p. 48. The quote from Beard is from *An Economic Interpretation*, p. 73.

of the ratifying conventions that men on both sides had the same economic interests and the same amount of property. In his anxiety to prove his point, McDonald sometimes (1) minimizes the property held by Federalists and exaggerates that owned by Antifederalists; (2) defines, in ways open to question, the professions of men on both sides so as to make it appear that they were of similar status; (3) omits, doubtless inadvertently, some relevant biographical data; (4) prints summary tables which appear to support his views, but neglects to publish tables which might have proved the contrary; and lastly (5) includes those facts which support his opinions but overlooks some which do not. The reader is drawn into an uncritical acceptance of all this because McDonald has done some excellent research and goes into great detail upon subjects which uphold his interpretation.

The first chapter of the three (chapters five, six, and seven) devoted to this subject is the least liable to objection. Most of the states discussed did not contain a large Antifederal party, and so, few challenging comparisons are made. There are, however, some doubtful generalizations,[5] and the discussion of the Connecticut ratifying convention introduces the line of argument which McDonald follows throughout. It is emphasized that the wealthy Federalist merchant Jeremiah Wadsworth had to give up some of his tax-delinquent land, and this is evidently supposed to cast doubt upon his financial difficulties of the period. The question therefore is not who was in financial straits at the time—everybody was—but whether Federalists or Antifederalists had more property. In this case the fact of greatest significance is that Wadsworth was the richest man in the state. In the ratifying convention, we are

[5]McDonald theorizes that the states which were weak supported, and those which were strong opposed, the Constitution. There may be some validity to this, although an attempt to prove it universally true forces the author to insist, against much contrary evidence, that Connecticut and Maryland were weak whereas Rhode Island and New Hampshire were strong.

told, both sides came from "similar economic backgrounds" in spite of the fact that twenty-nine out of thirty-three lawyers and ten out of twelve merchants were Federalists. The admission that among Antifederalists "less than half as many were public security holders" turns out to be McDonald's way of expressing the fact that forty-five Federalists and only six Antifederalists held part of the national debt.

Chapter six will furnish most of the examples of the way in which the true situation is disguised. The treatment of the alignment in Pennsylvania is typical Property held by the Federalists is minimized. Robert Coleman is listed merely as the "proprietor of an ironworks"; one would not guess that this was the Elizabeth Furnace, which covered part of a 4,000-acre property, and that Coleman was one of the wealthy men of the state. Less than justice is done to the holdings of such men as Yeates and Rush, while Neville and Scott certainly cannot be characterized merely as frontier farmers, for both were men of means, economic leaders of their community. Colonel Thomas Bull, whom McDonald calls a farmer, managed an iron furnace so successfully that he was able to erect a fine mansion, a gristmill, a sawmill, and a blacksmith shop, and to retire.[6] On the other hand, among the Antifederalists, Nicholas Lotz, who was a weaver, becomes "the proprietor of a clothing business." Adam Orth is called an iron manufacturer although he did not own a forge until 1793. James Martin is stated to have been engaged in "miscellaneous promotional and speculative deals" elevating him above the farmer rank, but these high-sounding phrases mean, upon examination, only that he owned a couple of small farms and some public securities. Federalists such as Barclay, Neville, and Scott, who outdealt Martin by a wide margin, remain merely "farmers."

[6] J. Smith Futhey and Gilbert Cope, *History of Chester County, Pennsylvania* (Philadelphia, 1881), pp. 489–490. McDonald here contradicts Beard, but it is Beard who is correct The county histories, not used by McDonald, contain much information on these men.

Summarizing his information in a table, McDonald introduces an occupation called "manufacturing capitalist," which turns out to mean someone who had a mill, the idea evidently being that these small property holders should be considered among the economic elite. Six Federalists and seven Antifederalists are placed in this category, which makes it appear that, if anything, the Antifederalists were more likely to be "capitalists." But the fact is that six additional Federalists, identified only as farmers, also had mills (Allison, Bull, Hannum, J. Morris, Wynkoop, and Yardley). In addition, if the Antifederalist Whitehill is elevated out of the farmer ranks because he owned an inn, the same ought to apply to the Federalist Barclay. The total result is that McDonald's summary table is misleading, for whereas it states that 35 per cent of the Federal ratifiers were farmers, the true figure, accepting his definition of what constituted a farmer, is 15 per cent.

McDonald also tries to demonstrate that the Antifederalists held more public securities than their opponents by comparing the certificates held by the delegates. The fact that a few of the important Antifederalists owned certificates really proves little. Popular parties typically derive their leadership from men of large property, and in nearly every state, including Pennsylvania, the Antifederalists were led by men of means. A few of them were indeed large holders, but the evidence is strong that most of the securities were owned by Federalists. Philadelphians owned as much as 90 per cent of the debt, and Philadelphians of all professions and classes were Federal; pro-Constitution candidates to the ratifying convention received an average of 1,200 votes each compared with 160 each for the Antifederalists.[7] Among the largest ($10,000 plus)

[7] McDonald argues that this vote represented the decision of mechanics, artisans, and tradesmen, but clearly the merchants had voted the same way. Contemporary testimony is unanimous on this point. For example, David Redick to William Irvine, Sept. 24, 1787, Irvine Papers, Vol. IX, Historical Society of Pennsylvania, Philadelphia; statement of George Bryan, Bryan Papers, *ibid.*

THE BEARD THESIS DEFENDED

holders whose political affiliations could be determined, three out of five were Federalists.[8]

Finally (and this is the most important point of all), whereas only two or three Antifederal delegates were men of large property, more than a dozen of their opponents were wealthy. In short the delegates on both sides did not hold "about the same amounts of the same kinds of property." Again Beard is more nearly correct than McDonald.

A similar procedure is followed in the case of Massachusetts. Federalists are downgraded and their property minimized. Elijah Dwight was more than a retail shopkeeper; he was a prominent and wealthy judge. Ebenezer Janes, who is called a maker of gravestones, was also a miller and a deacon who had an imposing house. T. J. Skinner, "carpenter," was a prominent Williamstown merchant. John Ashley, identified by McDonald merely as a farmer, was a merchant, a lawyer, and a large landowner (and Harvard, 1754). Noah Porter, also called a farmer, had the first chair in town, later added a chaise, had £100 loaned at interest, was Harvard 1761, and was sheriff of Hampshire County. Tristam Dalton was not just a lawyer but a wealthy merchant who married the daughter of another wealthy merchant. Morison writes that when Dalton went to New York as one of Massachusetts' first senators, he drove "in Newburyport style, in his own four-horse coach, emblazoned with the Dalton arms, and attended by servants in the Dalton livery." Other examples could be given. Among the Federalists whom McDonald could not identify, George Payson of Walpole and Moses Richardson of Medway were both innkeepers, while John Winthrop and Caleb Davis were both prominent merchants of Boston. On the Antifederal side there are also some errors in the assigning of occupations.

An important question of interpretation concerns the category of "gentleman-capitalists," who were "men of means,

[8]E. James Ferguson kindly made available his extensive material on the Federal debt.

large landowners, renters, money-lenders, and investors in various local business ventures." Among the thirteen Federalists identified as such, many undoubtedly belong to this group, among them Francis Dana, Benjamin Greenleaf (who was from Newburyport, incidentally, not Salem), Nathaniel Barrell, Benjamin Lincoln, William Pynchon, William Heath, and Richard Cranch. Whether all or even any of the fifteen Antifederalists are properly assigned to this category is of course a matter of judgment, but it is clear from the records that they did not as a group compare in wealth with their Federal equivalents.

McDonald's summary table and his conclusions, being based in part upon doubtful facts, can be seriously challenged. If the changes in occupation noted above are made, it appears that thirty merchants and tradesmen favored ratification and only eight opposed it. At the other end of the social scale most of the men whose occupations are unknown may safely be presumed to have been farmers, and if they are added to those known to have been such, then 38 per cent of the Federalists and 58 per cent of the Antifederalists were farmers. Therefore, despite McDonald, the Federalists were not more successful in winning the support of these men. McDonald omits any mention of the relative property holdings of the opposing sides, but it is certainly important to observe that almost all of the wealthy men in the convention were Federal. He does concede that the vast majority of public security holders favored ratification. His figures (in assembling which he has done a real service) show, indeed, that only three Antifederalists held $500 worth whereas forty-one Federalists did so. Outside of the convention, virtually all of the securities were concentrated in Boston and a few other seacoast centers; most of the large owners were merchants and, insofar as their politics are known, they were Federalists.

South Carolina is discussed without providing the usual table summarizing the alignment. Had such a table been con-

structed it might have caused McDonald to modify his conclusions. Two key generalizations are offered. First, "The majorities by which merchants, factors, lawyers, planters, and
farmers favored ratification was for each group about the same
as the overall majority in the convention—about two to one."
Let us accept the data given, but among the Federalists
changing John Chesnut and Henry Laurens from planters to
merchants and John Kean from unknown to merchant. The
proportions are as follows: merchants, 3:1 for ratification;
among artisans and merchants, 7:1, lawyers 5:1, doctors 5:1,
and large planters 3:1, but in significant contrast small
planters and farmers 2:1 *against* ratification. The truth therefore is diametrically opposed to his statement. Secondly, he
continues, "They had, proportionately, about the same amounts
of the same kinds of property." Let us construct our own table
of slaveownership, since none is furnished:

	Federalists	Antifederalists
unknown	18	8
none	2	2
1–9	16	21
10–19	25	14
20–49	23	13
50–99	30	12
100 plus	35	3

It will be seen that 43.6 per cent of the Federalists and only
20.5 per cent of the Antifederalists owned fifty slaves. So also
the very great majority of large landholders and of large public security holders were Federalists. Once again McDonald's
conclusions are contrary to the evidence.

Chapter six closes with a discussion of the ratification in
New Hampshire. The shortage of biographical information
prevents any confident generalizations. McDonald concedes
that public securities were held mainly by the Federalists. All
of the merchants in the convention were Federalists; 60 per
cent of the Antifederalists and 53 per cent of the Federalists
were farmers or of unknown occupation. No summation is

made of the proportion of large property holders on either side. although such information as is provided makes it obvious that the Federalists had far more wealth, a conclusion which contemporaries shared.

To summarize the critique of this key chapter, the true situation is as follows: in all four of these states, among members of the conventions, (1) merchants and those connected with the commercial interest favored ratification by an overwhelming margin, (2) farmers took the opposite side, (3) public security holders were predominantly Federal, (4) the Federalists had far more property. This is precisely what Beard argued, yet McDonald, through the omission of pertinent data and the distortion, doubtless unconscious, of the facts he does give, arrives at an opposite conclusion.

The analysis which has been presented here could be extended through the third chapter on ratification, but enough has perhaps been said to prove the points at issue. A few additional remarks may be made. In Virginia, the delegates held properties in counties other than those which they represented, and these are not always noted—twenty-five Federalists and seventeen Antifederalists had more property than is shown. Some errors are made in regard to the professions of the delegates: among the Federalists, Simms, Z. Johnston, and Tomlin were merchants; T. Lewis, McClerry, and Bushrod Washington were lawyers; while Antifederalists R. Williams and R. Lawson were also lawyers. Federal delegates did have more slaves than the Antifederalists, and more of them were large public security holders, but it is true that the division of property among the delegates in the Virginia convention was more equal than was ordinarily the case. McDonald's concluding generalizations, as elsewhere, do not always follow from the evidence. The discussion of New York's ratification also contains some errors. His description of the convention delegates omits altogether the wealthy Federalist lawyer Richard Morris, while Philip Livingston was a merchant in addition to his other occupations. The impression is given that Federalist John Hobart was merely a debtor, but in fact he inherited a considerable estate. As usual the conclusion is drawn that the members were about equal in wealth and economic interest. No table is provided, so it is necessary to construct one:

	Federal	elected Anti, voted Fed.	elected Anti, did not vote	Antifederal
merchants	5	1	0	0
lawyers and large landowners	3	3	0	1
lawyers	5	0	4	7
large landowners	2	1	1	2
millers	0	1	0	1
obscure men	4	3	2	9
farmers	0	3	0	6

Obviously there was no such equality. It should also be noted that on the final alignment eleven Federalists and six Antifederalists held public securities worth over $500.

The last three chapters consider the economic origins of the Constitution from a more general point of view, and some more general criticisms are in order. In the first place, it can be seen from the foregoing that the attack upon Beard has been unsuccessful. The Federal Convention did not represent all or even most of the economic interests and political opinions. Analysis of the delegates to the ratifying conventions shows conclusively that the influence of the merchants, lawyers, and large landowners was pro-Constitution while most farmers were on the other side; that the Federalists held far more wealth than their opponents; and that the influence of public security holders was strongly on the side of ratification. The evidence upon which the final interpretative chapters is based therefore lacks validity and the conclusions themselves are of course invalid.

A second general criticism concerns the introductory paragraphs which precede the descriptions of the delegates in each state. These are designed to analyze some of the local factors which were involved in the ratification process. In some cases McDonald has uncovered new material, and parts of his introductions are very good, but they usually deal with only a few of the causative factors. Those which do not support his general thesis are omitted, although the reader is sometimes left with a different impression. Particular attention is given to the state paper money controversy, in discussing which McDonald tries to show that the Federalists were more deeply in debt than the Antifederalists and that they supported debtor bills. Several observations must be made here. The first is that by selecting particular votes and ignoring others, the evidence is "stacked." In the case of South Carolina, for example, all of the attention is concentrated on the debates in 1785. Yet it is conceded that two years later the planters had changed their minds (indeed the situation in 1785 was abnormal, not typical). It would seem pertinent therefore to examine a series of votes recorded on economic matters during 1787–88, in which the sectional division, correlating with the vote on the Constitution, is revealed. Secondly, the fact that men borrowed money, as did the South Carolina planters, does not make them debtors in the Beardian sense. The difference between the man of means, who borrows of his free will, or to avoid disposing of some of his less fluid wealth (as Washington borrowed £10,000), and the small property holder, who unwillingly falls into debt, or is forced to borrow from one creditor in order to pay another, is fundamental; and to treat them alike is as absurd as it would be to condemn United States Steel because its indebtedness is greater than that of a corner filling station. Thirdly, McDonald's anxiety to prove that Federalists were debtors leads him into some misstatements. We are informed for example that "virtually all of the fourteen delegates" from the Shenandoah Valley were debtors, but according to his source only five were in debt. Fourthly, in spite of what McDonald says, paper money advocates did tend to oppose the Constitution: (1) most of the Antifederal strength in Connecticut came from paper money districts, (2) the correlation in Massachusetts exceeds 80 per cent, (3) the correlation in New Hampshire is not high, but it exists, (4) the paper money forces in Rhode Island were Antifederal, (5) the alignment in New York is well known, (6) the correlation in North Carolina is very high (the situation there is not described by McDonald), and (7) paper money supporters in both Maryland and Virginia usually opposed ratification. There are certainly many cases in which the generalization does *not* hold, but it cannot be denied altogether. To do so, finally, is also to ignore a great deal of contemporary testimony. If the debtors did not, on the whole, oppose, and the creditors did not, by and large, support the Constitution, it would come as a great surprise to informed observers on both sides.[9]

Another general critical observation stems from what is in many ways an excellent suggestion: namely, that the economic aspects of the Constitution be studied by classifying Americans in terms of their occupations, of which McDonald distinguishes four major categories and over two dozen subgroups. Beyond doubt this kind of an investigation is needed and will be most rewarding. However, American society in 1787–88 can be structured in other ways than by occupation, of which one of the most important is by class, or (if the eixstence of classes be denied) at least by relative income or property held. It is not sufficient to distinguish, for example, between the occupations of subsistence farmers and merchants unless it is recognized also that the former were poor by comparison with the latter. Despite McDonald, it can be maintained that the Constitution was written by large property owners and that the division over its acceptance followed, to some extent, class lines. There is much evidence that this was

[9]Incidentally it should be added that if, as McDonald maintains, the Constitution did not prevent the states from issuing paper, makers and opponents alike thought that it did.

the case, and the thesis is stated explicitly in many contemporary letters and newspaper articles. At the very least the subject warrants investigation, and no program for research can be successful which ignores it.

A final point: the procedure adopted by McDonald and others of conducting their research with the intent of disproving someone's thesis is not likely to reveal the truth, because one's conclusions are prejudiced in advance. The facts of history do not, as a rule, all point inescapably in a single direction; interpretations are made by balancing the evidence. When one sets out deliberately to gather evidence on only one side the desired result can generally be achieved, for along the way first the "facts" and then the judgment are unconsciously distorted. McDonald has done much valuable research, and his errors are doubtless honest errors; yet no better example can be found of the pitfalls inherent in this methodology. (Beard, of course, can be criticized on the same basis, but this does not justify the method.) The full story of the Constitution and its ratification remains to be written. Until this is done, the historian seeking an interim interpretation will be better advised to follow Beard than McDonald.

THE PUBLIC DEBT AND THE POWER OF THE PURSE

E. James Ferguson

EDITOR'S NOTE Central to the Beard thesis and to McDonald's critique of it is the issue whether the holders of public securities were substantially united in their support of the Constitution and were, in Beard's phrase, "the dynamic element" behind the movement for it. No one knows more about that subject than E. James Ferguson of Queen's College, City University of New York, nor has anyone discussed it as sensibly as he in the final pages, reprinted below, of his masterly book, *The Power of the Purse: A History of American Public Finance, 1776–1790* (1961). Like Main, Ferguson was a student of Merrill Jensen and addressed himself to the relationship between economics and politics. *Power of the Purse* is an interpretation of constitutional history in the context of public finance. Ferguson argued that the power to tax was, to eighteenth century Americans, the determinant of sovereignty, and upon its location and extent depended the power of government and the right of self-government. The Continental Congress and the state governments incurred large debts as a result of the Revolution. The crucial issue in the relations between the states and the nascent central government during the years of the Confedera-

From E. James Ferguson, *The Power of the Purse: A History of American Public Finance, 1776–1790*, pp. 337–43. (Published for The Institute of Early American History and Culture by The University of North Carolina Press, 1961.) Reprinted by permission of The University of North Carolina Press.

tion was the debt—who should pay it, how, and when? "The broadest ‚cleavage in American society," wrote Ferguson, was "that which ranged mercantile capitalists and their allies against agrarians both great and small." On the issue of the debt, the former supported the nationalist cause by seeking to vest the debt in Congress and by giving Congress the taxing power to support it. The "power of the purse" would make the national government sovereign, rather than the states. Public finance, under agrarian control, was state oriented during the Confederation period, but the mercantile interests succeeded when the Constitution was adopted and Congress enacted Hamilton's funding program in 1790.

The Power of the Purse, wrote its author, was not intended to support or refute Beard. The book did not in fact support Beard on a number of important points. "The treatment of state assumption of federal securities during the Confederation might be employed," said Ferguson,

> to cast doubt on the unity of the creditor interest. The role of public creditors in the adoption of the Constitution is projected far below the implications of the Beard thesis. According to several reviewers, Hamiltonian funding is described in terms downright favorable to Hamilton. I might add that in some ways the book sustains the distinctly old-fashioned notion that the Confederation was a critical period.

Notwithstanding Ferguson's disclaimers and qualifications, the thrust of his book supports the Beard thesis that the drive for a strong central government was closely connected to the holders of public securities. As Ferguson observes in the following extract, "It seems indisputable that as a group the creditors supported the Constitution."

o o o o

THE FAILURE of constitutional revision in 1786 reflected less a division of opinion—all the states had endorsed a federal impost in principle—than the inherent difficulty of securing unanimous agreement to any proposal. It appeared that the Articles of Confederation could not by constitutional procedure be amended to give Congress the limited accretion of power which majority opinion already sanctioned. The difficulty was surmounted in the end by recourse to extra-legal procedures.

That the crisis of the Union inspired the calling of the Federal Convention indicates such a level of agreement as to suggest that there was no crisis at all; however, the movement for constitutional revision derived much of its impetus from conservative fear of social radicalism. Conservatives in New York and Pennsylvania had long regarded central government as a refuge against majority rule. The events of 1786 spread their convictions to the extremes of the nation. Paper money and Shays' Rebellion were enough to convince New England merchants and Virginia planters of the dangers of democracy. In a climate of opinion already favorable to reform, a national alliance of conservatives drove constitutional revision beyond its original goals.

The larger story of the Constitution lies outside the scope of this study. Neither the document itself nor the circumstances that led to its adoption are wholly explained by the train of events and conditions discussed here. In view of the current revision of the Beard thesis, however, the role of the public creditors deserves some consideration. Recent studies have attacked Beard's conclusions and have even raised a doubt as to whether creditors as a group supported the Constitution. One's impulse is to avoid the question: it is often a false issue the way it is argued; it is unprovable by the methods employed to investigate it; it is not an essential point, and to emphasize it constitutes a distortion.

Beard's major thesis that the Constitution was the handiwork of the classes of American society possessing status and property cannot be ascribed to him alone. It is a theme of historical interpretation supported by the testimony of the founding fathers and sustained on the whole by historical scholarship. It does not contradict the assumption that general considerations of national welfare weighed with the men who made the Constitution, and it is not incompatible with the idea—which one of Beard's critics very aptly suggests—that state interests were instrumental in forming the attitudes of political leaders and the views of their constituents.[1] What shocked Beard's contemporaries and still provokes the most criticism was his purported demonstration that many of the founding fathers held securities and stood to profit from their work.

Beard's method of proof was to search through accounts in the federal archives and list what he discovered of the holdings of members of the Constitutional Convention. Although his declared object was merely to identify the founders as members of an economic class, the implication was that they had a profit motive. A recent critic of the Beard thesis, Forrest McDonald, has re-examined the accounts, not only for members of the Constitutional Convention, but also the ratifying conventions. He concludes that ownership of securities was sufficiently distributed between those who upheld and those who opposed the Constitution as to rule out profit motive as a general determining factor.

[1]McDonald, *We the People*, 357. McDonald's provocative study explores an economic approach to the formation of the Union in terms of categories different from those of Beard. For an interesting critique of McDonald's work, see Jackson T. Main, "Charles A. Beard and the Constitution: A Critical Review of Forrest McDonald's *We the People*," *Wm. and Mary Qtly.*, 3rd ser., 17 (1960), 88–102, and "Forrest McDonald's Rebuttal," *ibid.*, 102–10.

Although the dispute has borne fruit in stimulating new research, it will probably be inconclusive unless argued on other ground. In what relates to securities, the proof on both sides is defective. The accounts upon which the case depends relate to subscriptions to the federal loan beginning in October 1790 and continuing for several years. Few of the documents indicate whether securities were originally issued to the subscribers or acquired by purchase—in any event, the parties to the controversy have made no effort to establish ownership of securities as early as 1787. On the basis of their findings for the 1790's, it is gratuitous to assume anything about individual holdings at the time of the Constitutional Convention.[2]

The securities held by particular persons, including former members of the Constitutional and ratifying conventions, cannot be determined with certainty even after 1790. Lacking the central Treasury records, which have been almost entirely destroyed, existing documents are so incomplete that fifty of the greatest holders in the country would not necessarily appear. A thousand big holders might escape detection.[3] Especially in the case of wealthy or professional men likely to engage in interstate speculation, it is impossible to prove that they did not own more securities than the records disclose. On the other hand, a moderate holding of securities in 1790 implies little, for whatever a man's attitude toward the Constitution, he must have been careless of his interest not to have seized the opportunity to profit in the rising market that

[2] There is material for several states which shows security holdings at various times from 1786 on—records of indent payments, and the subscriptions in Pennsylvania to the "new loan" of 1786. These have not been exploited. The material is incomplete and in most cases unrepresentative of the body of the public debt in particular states; therefore I have not used it in this study, except in the case of Virginia, where the record is full.

[3] The almost complete absence of documents relating to the enormous sums subscribed or registered at the Treasury conceals many millions of the holdings most likely to be speculative.

followed its adoption. The really surprising thing is that any man prominent enough to have taken part in either the Constitutional or the ratifying conventions had not gathered at least a hatful by 1790.

The analysis of individual motive on the basis of security holdings would remain uncertain even if holdings could be exactly determined, for it would require a close knowledge of private circumstances and personal judgment that is probably irrecoverable. If, for example, a creditor was primarily interested in purchasing state lands but had not acquired the securities with which to pay for them, he would suffer a loss from the rising values which attended the formation of the new government. He would be in the same predicament if he were a member of the Ohio Company, although it would occur to him that a stronger government would foster his western enterprise. If he was not concerned with land speculation, but was a citizen of Pennsylvania, Maryland, New York, or even New Jersey, and was receiving interest from the state, he could not be entirely certain in 1787 whether the new government would promote the value of his securities.

The discussion of state assumption set forth in this study may add something to the literature of the Beard controversy. That some of the states adopted public securities and paid good interest on them might be presumed to have weakened a creditor interest in a national government. Certainly the creditors in several middle states had an alternative, and a person with decided Antifederalist views might have felt free to follow his convictions. The Philadelphia merchant, Blair McClenachan, owned $74,000 in public securities, yet presided over the Harrisburg Convention. He may have regarded his state as better security than an unfledged central government; his fortune, at least, was not staked on the Constitutional Convention.[4] But McClenachan seems to have been exceptional.

[4]McClenachan, or McClenaghan, owned his securities in 1787. Nearly all were originally issued in his name.

Even in the states that gave most to them, it would appear
that the creditors hoped for an increment from the national
government, particularly as successive steps were taken to
establish it.[5] The proof is that in 1789 securities rose above
all previous levels. In many of the states, of course, there was
never any question that creditors preferred the federal government. Those in Georgia, South Carolina, North Carolina, and
in New England, could expect little from their state governments—a fact quite evident by the time of the Constitutional
Convention.

It seems indisputable that as a group the creditors supported the Constitution. This writer has never seen them represented in a formal statement or petition that did not endorse
stronger central government. In the writings of the times they
are uniformly described as adherents of the Constitution, but
one should not make the mistake of imputing to them a conspiratorial role or at least of attaching any great importance
to their conspiracies. Speculations were continuous throughout
the Confederation. Merchants and men of property acquired
securities in the normal course of business or for marginal
profits, without reference to Congressional funding. The prospect of a national government promised additional returns,
and as the Constitution was adopted the prospect became
solid enough to warrant speculation on the basis of renewed
possibilities. To eliminate entirely the role of economic motive
in the political affairs of the time is as doctrinaire and as unnecessary as Beard's overstatement of it. A creditor interest
certainly existed—yet it was no more than ancillary to the
political development that culminated in the founding of the
new government. Constitutional reform had always involved

[5]State creditors, on the other hand, could be expected to oppose the
establishment of a national government which would invade state
revenue sources—unless they hoped for federal assumption of state
debts. McDonald, in *We the People*, lumps subscribers to the federal loan
of 1790 in one category whether they subscribed state or federal securities, implying thereby that they had similar interests in 1787.

public finance. The decision to establish a national government entailed federal taxation and the payment of the debt, irrespective of the designs of creditors, who assisted the process, reaped its benefits, but did not create it. Proceeding rigidly by the axiom that related sovereignty with revenue power, the founding fathers crowned the new government with unlimited power of taxation.

By the time the public debt was funded it had become the property of a relative few. Figures covering millions in securities suggest a transfer rate of 80 per cent. The degree to which the debt had concentrated into major holdings can only be inferred, since most large subscribers were brokers or acting in partnership. However the fact speaks for itself that of $12,300,000 examined in this study, 280 individuals held $7,880,000, nearly two-thirds. The increase in securities which were registered or subscribed directly at the Treasury, amounting to $18,000,000 by October 1791, suggests the magnitude of interstate and foreign speculation. As the Constitution was ratified, foreign capital poured into the domestic debt, channeled largely through New York brokers. Foreign investment drove security prices up to prohibitive levels late in 1789 and then, in some degree inspired by foreknowledge of Hamilton's proposals, spilled over into the purchase of state debts.

Funding the public debt was the economic counterpart of the adoption of the Constitution. How one regards Hamilton's specific proposals depends somewhat upon the angle from which they are viewed. Seen as the arch of the emerging Federalist system, they are partisan, partial to wealth, commercial capitalism, the north as against the south, and denotative of the extremism which begat political parties. Considered on their merits, apart from their integral relation to other measures, and as a formula for dealing with the political as well as the financial legacy of the Confederation, they appear as a reasonable compromise of varying shades of the conservative opinion which the new government represented.

The essential feature of Hamilton's program for funding the public debt was specie payment. Rejecting agrarian modes, he pledged the central government to high finance, and in this he had the overwhelming approval of Congress. In terms of the political realities of the moment, it is hard to see how he could have done otherwise. The only real challenge in Congress was Madison's motion to discriminate between original and present holders of securities, but the proposal did not offer a true alternative, had little support, and was probably no more than a political maneuver. From all that one can gather, the people at large dissented from both Madison and Hamilton—they wanted to scale down the debt, or fund and pay it at its depreciated value. They were, however, but distantly represented in a Congress determined to ground the new order in financial orthodoxy.

Popular opposition was not effective because most of the country's leaders agreed that funding on something like Hamilton's terms was necessary to complete the federal structure. It was otherwise with the assumption of state debts, which was not clearly essential to the Union, needlessly increased the federal debt, and divided the nation's leaders along lines of state interests. Assumption passed only as a result of the famous trade that gave Virginia the permanent capital. What is not generally recognized is that there was another feature of the negotiation; the compromise of 1790 also conceded southern demands in the settlement of state accounts.

Class interests were scarcely at issue in the Congressional debate over financial legislation. The views of the masses were represented in about the same degree as at the Constitutional Convention. Madison's motion kindled the popular animus against rich men and speculators, but it did not implement the popular desire to pay debts at their depreciated value. Any such idea was heresy to the overwhelming majority of Congress, whose members differed only over the separate interests of the states they represented. Assumption provoked these differences, but it reconciled Massachusetts and South Carolina to the Union, and the onus was in part removed by its incorporation into the compromise of 1790. After the first Congress had finished its work, the future adversary of the regime, Thomas Jefferson, could still declare: "It is not foreseen that anything so generative of dissensions can arise again, & therefore the friends of the government hope that, this difficulty once surmounted in the states, everything will work well."

THE CONVENTION AS A CASE STUDY IN DEMOCRATIC POLITICS

John P. Roche

EDITOR'S NOTE The following article by John P. Roche of Brandeis University seems destined to become a minor classic of historical writing on the making of the Constitution. Since its publication in 1961 it has been reprinted a score of times, is widely used in courses, and has consistently drawn rave notices in annotated bibliographies. Doubtless Roche's crackling prose helps account for the popularity of his piece, but substance outweighs style. Despite his antecedents on the libertarian left, he avoids the socio-economic analysis that has kept the Beard thesis at the center of scholarly controversy; he hews instead to a political narrative that is an off-beat reflection of the consensus approach so common in contemporary historical writing. The focus is on the agreement on fundamentals rather than on differences, with class conflict being kicked out of even the rumble seat.

In a way Roche revives the approach of the older constitutional scholars like McLaughlin, Corwin, and Warren who saw the Constitutional Convention in essentially political terms. But where they stressed the triumph of nationalist politics, Roche, revealing the influence of Robert E. Brown whom he accepts too uncritically, stresses the dominance of democratic politics. As a sophisticated student

From John P. Roche, "The Founding Fathers: A Reform Caucus in Action," *The American Political Science Review*, December 1961, Vol. LV, No. 4, pp. 799–816. Reprinted without footnotes by permission.

of the psychology of politics and human behavior, he writes from the political perspective with a full knowledge of the seamy side of political conduct, the ambiguity of political rhetoric (on both the nationalist and antinationalist sides), and the knowledge that political leaders may sometimes rise above considerations of purse and status but rarely above the need to keep in touch with the electoral majorities. Roche also writes from the political perspective without the conservative bias or anti-majoritarianism, and without the faint filiopietism, of earlier scholars who similarly scorned the economic interpretation.

In the article that follows Roche is chiefly concerned with the political process at work in the Constitutional Convention. He has, he said, analyzed the Convention "as a case study in democratic politics." He sees the framers as "first and foremost superb democratic politicians," masterful professionals who pursued the task of radically reconstructing the American constitutional system in accordance with the prevailing rules of the game. That is, like the Warren-McLaughlin school, Roche depicts the framers as nationalists striving to build a strong, unified nation, and thus he calls the Convention a *"nationalist* reform caucus." But he emphasizes, above all, that they were acutely aware of the necessity of receiving popular approbation if their reforms were to succeed. Their only weapon, he observes, was the "effective mobilization of public opinion." Political realities forced them to water down their nationalist objectives and settle for the best that they could get. Thus they were responsible and responsive leaders operating in "a democratic society"—a Brownian hyperbole—who kept uppermost in mind the views of their respective constituents. The necessity of popular approval via ratification, "a democratic process," dominated the making of the Constitution. This thesis is especially striking in the light of the traditional view of the framers as men who feared and despised democracy.

With respect to the predominance of nationalist sentiment in the Convention, Roche describes the Virginia Plan as envisioning a "unitary" national government—another hyperbole?—effectively freed from and dominant over the states; he interprets the Paterson Plan as distinctly within the nationalist framework. He sees no clear-cut ideological divisions in the working majority of the Convention. He goes too far, however, in alleging that the Paterson Plan, which did not include the most fundamental power, that of the purse, provided for the same scope of national powers as the Virginia Plan. Readers may also question whether Roche has not mistakenly equated political realism or political pragmatism with democratic politics. His suggestive asides are sometimes overstated, as in that description of America as a democratic society in 1787, or in his references to the Constitution as a "makeshift" or "patchwork" document, or in his assertion that federalism was merely an "improvision which was later promoted into a political theory."

Federalism is a system of government in which powers are divided among a central government and several local ones, each with a fairly distinct sphere of authority, relatively sovereign within its sphere, and operating directly on people who are simultaneously citizens of both governments. As Andrew C. McLaughlin demonstrated, the federal system had its roots in the British empire before the Revolution. The improvisation of a political theory of federalism was the result not of *The Federalist* but of the American Revolution. The Articles of Confederation established a federal system with respect to the distribution of powers; the Constitutional Convention, benefiting from the experience of the Confederation, simply reallocated powers (chiefly tax and commerce) by building on an already familiar concept and practice. Nevertheless, even with its enlivening warts, Roche's article is without peer for illuminating the politics of the Convention. His major works include *The Quest for the Dream: the Development of Civil Rights and Human Relations in America* (1963), *Shadow and Substance: Essays on the Theory and Structure of Politics* (1964), and *Courts and Rights* (2nd ed., 1966).

o   o   o   o

OVER the last century and a half, the work of the Constitutional Convention and the motives of the Founding Fathers have been analyzed under a number of different ideological auspices. To one generation of historians, the hand of God was moving in the assembly; under a later dispensation, the dialectic (at various levels of philosophical sophistication) replaced the Deity: "relationships of production" moved into the niche previously reserved for Love of Country. Thus, in counterpoint to the Zeitgeist, the Framers have undergone miraculous metamorphoses: at one time acclaimed as liberals and bold social engineers, today they appear in the guise of sound Burkean conservatives, men who in our time would subscribe to *Fortune*, look to Walter Lippmann for political theory, and chuckle patronizingly at the antics of Barry Goldwater. The implicit assumption is that if James Madison were among us, he would be President of the Ford Foundation, while Alexander Hamilton would chair the Committee for Economic Development.

178

The "Fathers" have thus been admitted to our best circles; the revolutionary ferocity which confiscated all Tory property in reach and populated New Brunswick with outlaws has been converted by the "Miltown School" of American historians into a benign dedication to "consensus" and "prescriptive rights." The Daughters of the American Revolution have, through the ministrations of Professors Boorstin, Hartz, and Rossiter, at last found ancestors worthy of their descendants. It is not my purpose here to argue that the "Fathers" were, in fact, radical revolutionaries; that proposition has been brilliantly demonstrated by Robert R. Palmer in his *Age of the Democratic Revolution*. My concern is with the further position that not only were they revolutionaries; they were also democrats. Indeed, in my view, there is one fundamental truth about the Founding Fathers that *every* generation of Zeitgeisters has done its best to obscure: they were first and foremost superb democratic politicians. I suspect that in a contemporary setting, James Madison would be Speaker of the House of Representatives and Hamilton would be the *éminence grise* dominating (*pace* Theodore Sorensen or Sherman Adams) the Executive Office of the President. They were, with their colleagues, *political men*—not metaphysicians, disembodied conservatives or Agents of History—and as recent research into the nature of American politics in the 1780's confirms, they were committed (perhaps willy-nilly) to working within the democratic framework, within a universe of public approval. Charles Beard *and* the filiopietists to the contrary notwithstanding, the Philadelphia Convention was not a College of Cardinals or a council of Platonic guardians working within a manipulative, predemocratic framework; it was a *nationalist* reform caucus which had to operate with great delicacy and skill in a political cosmos full of enemies to achieve the one definitive goal—popular approbation.

Perhaps the time has come, to borrow Walton Hamilton's

fine phrase, to raise the Framers from immortality to mortality, to give them credit for their magnificent demonstration of the art of democratic politics. The point must be reemphasized; they *made* history, and did it within the limits of consensus. There was nothing inevitable about the future in 1787; the *Zeitgeist*, that fine Hegelian technique of begging causal questions, could be discerned only in retrospect. What they did was to hammer out a pragmatic compromise which would both bolster the "national interest" and be acceptable to the people. What inspiration they got came from their collective experience as professional politicians in a democratic society. As John Dickinson put it to his fellow delegates on August 13th: "Experience must be our guide. Reason may mislead us."

In this context, let us examine the problems they confronted and the solutions they evolved. The Convention has been described picturesquely as a counterrevolutionary junta and the Constitution as a *coup d'état*, but this has been accomplished by withdrawing the whole history of the movement for constitutional reform from its true context. No doubt the goals of the constitutional elite were "subversive" to the existing political order, but it is overlooked that their subversion could have succeeded only if the people of the United States endorsed it by regularized procedures. Indubitably they were "plotting" to establish a much stronger central government than existed under the Articles, but only in the sense in which one could argue equally well that John F. Kennedy was, from 1956 to 1960, "plotting" to become President. In short, on the fundamental *procedural* level, the Constitutionalists had to work according to the prevailing rules of the game. Whether they liked it or not is a topic for spiritualists—and is irrelevant: one may be quite certain that had Washington agreed to play the De Gaulle (as the Cincinnati once urged), Hamilton would willingly have held his horse, but such fertile speculation in no way alters the actual context in which events took place.

I

When the Constitutionalists went forth to subvert the Confederation, they utilized the mechanisms of political legitimacy. And the roadblocks which confronted them were formidable. At the same time, they were endowed with certain potent political assets. The history of the United States from 1786 to 1790 was largely one of a masterful employment of political expertise by the Constitutionalists as against bumbling, erratic behavior by the opponents of reform. Effectively, the Constitutionalists had to induce the states, by democratic techniques of coercion, to emasculate themselves. To be specific, if New York had refused to join the new Union, the project was doomed; yet before New York was safely in, the reluctant state legislature had *sua sponte* to take the following steps: (1) agree to send delegates to the Philadelphia Convention; (2) provide maintenance for these delegates (these were distinct stages: New Hampshire was early in naming delegates, but did not provide for their maintenance until July); (3) set up the special *ad hoc* convention to decide on ratification; and (4) concede to the decision of the *ad hoc* convention that New York should participate. New York admittedly was a tricky state, with a strong interest in a *status quo* which permitted her to exploit New Jersey and Connecticut, but the same legal hurdles existed in every state. And at the risk of becoming boring, it must be reiterated that the *only* weapon in the Constitutionalist arsenal was an effective mobilization of public opinion.

The group which undertook this struggle was an interesting amalgam of a few dedicated nationalists with the self-interested spokesmen of various parochial bailiwicks. The Georgians, for example, wanted a strong central authority to provide military protection for their huge, underpopulated state against the Creek Confederacy; Jerseymen and Connecticuters wanted to escape from economic bondage to New York; the Virginians hoped to establish a system which would give that great state its rightful place in the councils of the republic. The dominant figures in the politics of these states therefore co-operated in the call for the Convention. In other states, the thrust toward national reform was taken up by opposition groups who added the "national interest" to their weapons system; in Pennsylvania, for instance, the group fighting to revise the Constitution of 1776 came out foursquare behind the Constitutionalists, and in New York, Hamilton and the Schuyler ambience took the same tack against George Clinton. There was, of course, a large element of personality in the affair: there is reason to suspect that Patrick Henry's opposition to the Convention and the Constitution was founded on his conviction that Jefferson was behind both, and a close study of local politics elsewhere would surely reveal that others supported the Constitution for the simple (and politically quite sufficient) reason that the "wrong" people were against it.

To say this is not to suggest that the Constitution rested on a foundation of impure or base motives. It is rather to argue that in politics there are no immaculate conceptions and that in the drive for a stronger general government, motives of all sorts played a part. Few men in the history of mankind have espoused a view of the "common good" or "public interest" that militated against their private status; even Plato with all his reverence for disembodied reason managed to put philosophers on top of the pile. Thus it is not surprising that a number of diversified private interests joined to push the nationalist public interest; what would have been surprising was the absence of such a pragmatic united front. And the fact remains that, however motivated, these men did demonstrate a willingness to compromise their parochial interests in behalf of an ideal which took shape before their eyes and under their ministrations.

As Stanley Elkins and Eric McKitrick have suggested in a perceptive essay, what distinguished the leaders of the Constitutionalist caucus from their enemies was a "Continental" approach to political, economic, and military issues. To the extent that they shared an institutional base of operations, it was the Continental Congress (thirty-nine of the delegates to the Federal Convention had served in Congress), and this was hardly a locale which inspired respect for the state governments. Robert de Jouvenal observed French politics half a century ago and noted that a revolutionary deputy had more in common with a nonrevolutionary deputy than he had with a revolutionary nondeputy; similarly one can surmise that membership in the Congress under the Articles of Confederation worked to establish a Continental frame of reference, that a congressman from Pennsylvania and one from South Carolina would share a universe of discourse which provided them with a conceptual common denominator *vis à vis* their respective state legislatures. This was particularly true with respect to external affairs: the average state legislator was probably about as concerned with foreign policy then as he is today, but congressmen were constantly forced to take the broad view of American prestige, were compelled to listen to the reports of Secretary John Jay and to the dispatches and pleas from their frustrated envoys in Britain, France, and Spain. From considerations such as these, a "Continental" ideology developed which seems to have demanded a revision of our domestic institutions primarily on the ground that only by invigorating our general government could we assume our rightful place in the international arena. Indeed, an argument with great force—particularly since Washington was its incarnation—urged that our very survival in the Hobbesian jungle of world politics depended upon a reordering and strengthening of our national sovereignty.

Note that I am not endorsing the "Critical Period" thesis; on the contrary, Merrill Jensen seems to me quite sound in his view that for most Americans, engaged as they were in self-sustaining agriculture, the "Critical Period" was not particularly critical. In fact, the great achievement of the Constitutionalists was their ultimate success in convincing the elected representatives of a majority of the white male population that change was imperative. A small group of political leaders with a Continental vision and essentially a consciousness of the United States' *international* impotence, provided the matrix of the movement. To their standard other leaders rallied with their own parallel ambitions. Their great assets were (1) the presence in their caucus of the one authentic American "father figure," George Washington, whose prestige was enormous, (2) the energy and talent of their leadership (in which one must include the towering intellectuals of this time, John Adams and Thomas Jefferson, despite their absence abroad); and their communications "network," which was far superior to anything on the opposition side, (3) the preemptive skill which made "their" issue The Issue and kept the locally oriented opposition permanently on the defensive; and (4) the subjective consideration that these men were spokesmen of a new and compelling credo: *American* nationalism, that ill-defined but nonetheless potent sense of collective purpose that emerged from the American Revolution.

Despite great institutional handicaps, the Constitutionalists managed in the mid-1780's to mount an offensive which gained momentum as years went by. Their greatest problem was lethargy, and paradoxically, the number of barriers in their path may have proved an advantage in the long run. Beginning with the initial battle to get the Constitutional Convention called and delegates appointed, they could never relax, never let up the pressure. In practical terms, this meant that the local "organizations" created by the Constitutionalists were perpetually in movement building up their cadres for the next fight. (The word "organization" has to be used with great caution: a political organization in the United States—as in contemporary England—generally consisted of a magnate and his following, or a coalition of magnates. This did not necessarily mean that it was "undemocratic" or "aristocratic," in the Aristotelian sense of the word: while a few magnates such as the Livingstons could draft their followings, most exercised their leadership without coercion on the basis of popular endorsement. The absence of organized opposition did not imply the impossibility of competition any more than low public participation in elections necessarily indicated an undemocratic suffrage.)

The Constitutionalists got the jump on the "opposition" (a collective noun: oppositions would be more correct) at the outset with the demand for a Convention. Their opponents were caught in an old political trap: they were not being asked to approve any specific program of reform, but only to endorse a meeting to discuss and recommend needed reforms. If they took a hard line at the first stage, they were put in the position of glorifying the *status quo* and of denying the need for *any* changes. Moreover, the Constitutionalists could go to the people with a persuasive argument for "fair play"—"How can you condemn reform before you know precisely what is involved?" Since the state legislatures obviously would have the final say on any proposals that might emerge from the Convention, the Constitutionalists were merely reasonable men asking for a chance. Besides, since they did not make any concrete proposals at that stage, they were in a position to capitalize on every sort of generalized discontent with the Confederation.

Perhaps because of their poor intelligence system, perhaps because of overconfidence generated by the failure of all previous efforts to alter the Articles, the opposition awoke too late to the dangers that confronted them in 1787. Not only did the Constitutionalists manage to get every state but Rhode Island (where politics was enlivened by a party system reminiscent of the "Blues" and the "Greens" in the Byzantine Empire) to appoint delegates to Philadelphia, but when the results were in, it appeared that they dominated the delegations. Given the apathy of the opposition, this was a natural phenomenon: in an ideologically nonpolarized political atmosphere, those who get appointed to a special committee are likely to be the men who supported the movement for its creation. Even George Clinton, who seems to have been the first opposition leader to awake to the possibility of trouble, could not prevent the New York Legislature from appointing Alexander Hamilton—though he did have the foresight to send two of his henchmen to dominate the delegation. Incidentally, much has been made of the fact that the delegates to Philadelphia were not elected by the people; some have adduced this fact as evidence of the "undemocratic" character of the gathering. But put in the context of the time, this argument is wholly specious: the central government under the Articles was considered a creature of the component states; and in all the states but Rhode Island, Connecticut, and New Hampshire, members of the national Congress were chosen by state legislatures. This was not a consequence of elitism or fear of the mob; it was a logical extension of states'-rights doctrine to guarantee that the national institution did not end-run the state legislatures and make direct contact with the people.

II

With delegations safely named, the focus shifted to Philadelphia. While waiting for a quorum to assemble, James Madison got busy and drafted the so-called Randolph or Virginia Plan with the aid of the Virginia delegation. This was a political masterstroke. Its consequence was that once business got under way, the framework of discussion was established on Madison's terms. There was no interminable argument over agenda; instead the delegates took the Virginia Resolutions—"just for purposes of discussion"—as their point of departure.

And along with Madison's proposals, many of which were buried in the course of the summer, went his major premise: a new start on a Constitution rather than piecemeal amendment. This was not necessarily revolutionary—a little exegesis could demonstrate that a new Constitution might be formulated as "amendments" to the Articles of Confederation—but Madison's proposal that this "lump sum" amendment go into effect after approval by nine states (the Articles required unanimous state approval for any amendment) was thoroughly subversive.

Standard treatments of the Convention divide the delegates into "nationalists" and "states'-righters," with various improvised shadings ("moderate nationalists," and so on), but these are *a posteriori* categories which obfuscate more than they clarify. What is striking to one who analyzes the Convention as a case study in democratic politics is the lack of clear-cut ideological divisions in the Convention. Indeed, I submit that the evidence—Madison's *Notes*, the correspondence of the delegates, and debates on ratification—indicates that this was a remarkably homogeneous body on the ideological level. Yates and Lansing, Clinton's two chaperons for Hamilton, left in disgust on July 10th. (Is there anything more tedious than sitting through endless disputes on matters one deems fundamentally misconceived? It takes an iron will to spend a hot summer as an ideological *agent provocateur*.) Luther Martin, Maryland's bibulous narcissist, left on September 4th in a huff when he discovered that others did not share his self-esteem; others went home for personal reasons. But the hard core of delegates accepted a grinding regimen throughout the attrition of a Philadelphia summer precisely because they shared the Constitutionalist goal.

Basic differences of opinion emerged, of course, but these were not ideological; they were *structural*. If the so-called "states'-rights" group had not accepted the fundamental purposes of the Convention, they could simply have pulled out and by doing so have aborted the whole enterprise. Instead of bolting, they returned day after day to argue and to compromise. An interesting symbol of this basic homogeneity was the initial agreement on secrecy: these professional politicians did not want to become prisoners of publicity; they wanted to retain that freedom of maneuver which is possible only when men are not forced to take public stands in the preliminary stages of negotiation. There was no legal means of binding the tongues of the delegates: at any stage in the game a delegate with basic principled objections to the emerging project could have taken the stump (as Luther Martin did after his exit) and denounced the Convention to the skies. Yet Madison did not even inform Thomas Jefferson in Paris of the course of the deliberations, and available correspondence indicates that the delegates generally observed the injunction. Secrecy is certainly uncharacteristic of any assembly marked by strong ideological polarization. This was noted at the time: the *New York Daily Advertiser*, August 14, 1787, commented that the ". . . profound secrecy hitherto observed by the Convention [we consider] a happy omen, as it demonstrates that the spirit of party on any great and essential point cannot have arisen to any height."

Commentators on the Constitution who have read *The Federalist* in lieu of reading the actual debates have credited the Fathers with the invention of a sublime concept called "Federalism." Unfortunately, *The Federalist* is probative evidence for only one proposition: that Hamilton and Madison were inspired propagandists with a genius for retrospective symmetry. Federalism, as the theory is generally defined, was an improvisation which was later promoted into a political theory. Experts on "Federalism" should take to heart the advice of David Hume, who warned in his *Of the Rise and Progress of the Arts and Sciences* that ". . . there is no subject in which we must proceed with more caution than in [history], lest we assign causes which never existed and reduce what is merely contingent to stable and universal principles." In any event, the final balance in the Constitution between the states and the nation must have come as a great disappointment to Madison, while Hamilton's unitary views are too well known to need elucidation.

It is indeed astonishing how those who have glibly designated James Madison the "father" of Federalism have overlooked the solid body of fact which indicates that he shared Hamilton's quest for a unitary central government. To be specific, they have avoided examining the clear import of the Madison-Virginia Plan, and have disregarded Madison's dogged inch-by-inch retreat from the bastions of centralization. The Virginia Plan envisioned a unitary national government effectively freed from and dominant over the states. The lower house of the national legislature was to be elected directly by the people of the states with membership proportional to population. The upper house was to be selected by the lower, and the two chambers would elect the executive and choose the judges. The national government would be thus cut completely loose from the states.

The structure of the general government was freed from state control in a truly radical fashion, but the scope of the authority of the national sovereign as Madison initially formulated it was breathtaking—it was a formulation worthy of the Sage of Malmesbury himself. The national legislature was to be empowered to disallow the acts of state legislatures, and the central government was vested, in addition to the powers of the nation under the Articles of Confederation, with plenary authority wherever ". . . the separate States are incompetent or in which the harmony of the United States may be interrupted by the exercise of individual legislation." Finally, just to lock the door against state intrusion, the national Congress was to be given the power to use military force on recalcitrant states. This was Madison's "model" of an ideal national government, though it later received little publicity in *The Federalist*.

The interesting thing was the reaction of the Convention to this militant program for a strong autonomous central government. Some delegates were startled, some obviously leery of so comprehensive a project of reform, but nobody set off any fireworks and nobody walked out. Moreover, in the two weeks that followed, the Virginia Plan received substantial endorsement *en principe*; the initial temper of the gathering can be deduced from the approval "without debate or dissent," on May 31st, of the Sixth Resolution, which granted Congress the authority to disallow state legislation ". . . contravening *in its opinion* the Articles of Union." Indeed, an amendment was included to bar states from contravening national treaties.

The Virginia Plan may therefore be considered, in ideological terms, as the delegates' Utopia, but as the discussions continued and became more specific, many of those present began to have second thoughts. After all, they were not residents of Utopia or guardians in Plato's Republic who could simply impose a philosophical ideal on subordinate strata of the population. They were practical politicians in a democratic society, and no matter what their private dreams might be, they had to take home an acceptable package and defend it— and their own political futures—against predictable attack. On June 14th the breaking point between dream and reality took place. Apparently realizing that under the Virginia Plan, Massachusetts, Virginia, and Pennsylvania could virtually dominate the national government—and probably appreciating that to sell this program to the "folks back home" would be impossible—the delegates from the small states dug in their heels and demanded time for a consideration of alternatives. One gets a graphic sense of the inner politics from John Dickinson's reproach to Madison: "You see the consequences of pushing things too far. Some of the members from the small States wish for two branches in the General Legislature and are friends to a good National Government; but we would sooner submit to a foreign power than . . . be deprived of an equality of suffrage in both branches of the Legislature, and thereby be thrown under the domination of the large States."

The bare outline of the *Journal* entry for Tuesday, June 14th, is suggestive to anyone with extensive experience in deliberative bodies. "It was moved by Mr. Patterson [*sic*, Paterson's name was one of those consistently misspelled by Madison and everybody else] seconded by Mr. Randolph that the further consideration of the report from the Committee of the whole House [endorsing the Virginia Plan] be postponed til tomorrow, and before the question for postponement was taken. It was moved by Mr. Randolph seconded by Mr. Patterson that the House adjourn." The House adjourned by obvious prearrangement of the two principals: since the preceding Saturday when David Brearley and Paterson of New Jersey had announced their fundamental discontent with the representational features of the Virginia Plan, the informal pressure had certainly been building up to slow down the steamroller. Doubtless there were extended arguments at the Indian Queen between Madison and Paterson, the latter insisting that events were moving rapidly toward a probably disastrous conclusion, toward a political suicide pact. Now the process of accommodation was put into action smoothly—and wisely, given the character and strength of the doubters. Madison had the votes, but this was one of those situations where the enforcement of mechanical majoritarianism could easily have destroyed the objectives of the majority: the Constitutionalists were in quest of a qualitative as well as quantitative consensus. This was hardly from deference to local Quaker custom; it was a political imperative if they were to attain ratification.

ESSAYS ON THE MAKING OF THE CONSTITUTION

III

According to the standard script, at this point the "states'-rights" group intervened in force behind the New Jersey Plan, which has been characteristically portrayed as a reversion to the *status quo* under the Articles of Confederation with but minor modifications. A careful examination of the evidence indicates that only in a marginal sense is this an accurate description. It is true that the New Jersey Plan put the states back into the institutional picture, but one could argue that to do so was a recognition of political reality rather than an affirmation of states' rights. A serious case can be made that the advocates of the New Jersey Plan, far from being ideological addicts of states' rights, intended to substitute for the Virginia Plan a system which would both retain strong national power and have a chance of adoption in the states. The leading spokesman for the project asserted quite clearly that his views were based more on counsels of expediency than on principle; said Paterson on June 16th: "I came here not to speak my own sentiments, but the sentiments of those who sent me. Our object is not such a Governmt. as may be best in itself, but such a one as our Constituents have authorized us to prepare, and as they will approve." This is Madison's version; in Yates's transcription, there is a crucial sentence following the remarks above: "I believe that a little practical virtue is to be preferred to the finest theoretical principles, which cannot be carried into effect." In his preliminary speech on June 9th, Paterson had stated ". . . to the public mind we must accommodate ourselves," and in his notes for this and his later effort as well, the emphasis is the same. The *structure* of government under the Articles should be retained:

2. Because it accords with the Sentiments of the People
   [Proof:] 1. Coms. [Commissions from state legislatures defining the jurisdiction of the delegates]

> 2. News-papers—Political Barometer. Jersey
> never would have sent Delegates under the
> first [Virginia] Plan—
> Not here to sport Opinions of my own. Wt. [What] can be
> done. A little practical Virtue preferrable to Theory.

This was a defense of political acumen, not of states' rights. In fact, Paterson's notes of his speech can easily be construed as an argument for attaining the substantive objectives of the Virginia Plan by a sound political route, that is, pouring the new wine into the old bottles. With a shrewd eye, Paterson queried:

> Will the Operation and Force of the [central] Govt. de-
> pend upon the mode of Representn.—No—it will depend
> upon the Quantum of Power lodged in the leg. ex. and
> judy. Departments—Give [the existing] Congress the same
> Powers that you intend to give the two Branches, [under
> the Virginia Plan] and I apprehend they will act with as
> much Propriety and more Energy. . .

In other words, the advocates of the New Jersey Plan concentrated their fire on what they held to be the *political liabilities* of the Virginia Plan—which were matters of institutional structure—rather than on the proposed scope of national authority. Indeed, the Supremacy Cause of the Constitution first saw the light of day in Paterson's Sixth Resolution; the New Jersey Plan contemplated the use of military force to secure compliance with national law; and finally Paterson made clear his view that under either the Virginia or the New Jersey systems, the general government would ". . . act on individuals and not on states." From the states'-rights viewpoint, this was heresy: the fundament of that doctrine was the proposition that any central government had as its constituents the states, not the people, and could reach the people only through the agency of the state government.

Paterson then reopened the agenda of the Convention, but

he did so within a distinctly nationalist framework. Paterson's position was one of favoring a strong central government in principle, but opposing one which in fact *put the big states in the saddle*. (The Virginia Plan, for all its abstract merits, did very well by Virginia.) As evidence for this speculation, there is a curious and intriguing proposal among Paterson's preliminary drafts of the New Jersey Plan:

> Whereas it is necessary in Order to form the People of the U.S. of America in to a Nation, that the States should be consolidated, by which means all the Citizens thereof will become equally intitled to and will equally participate in the same Privileges and Rights. . . it is therefore resolved, that all the Lands contained within the Limits of each state individually, and of the U.S. generally be considered as constituting one Body or Mass, and be divided into thirteen or more integral parts.
>
> Resolved, That such Divisions or integral Parts shall be styled Districts.

This makes it sound as though Paterson was prepared to accept a strong unified central government along the lines of the Virginia Plan if the existing states were eliminated. He may have got the idea from his New Jersey colleague Judge David Brearley, who on June 9th had commented that the only remedy to the dilemma over representation was ". . . that a map of the U.S. be spread out, that all the existing boundaries be erased, and that a new partition of the whole be made into 13 equal parts." According to Yates, Brearley added at this point, ". . . then a government on the present [Virginia Plan] system will be just."

This proposition was never pushed—it was patently unrealistic—but one can appreciate its purpose: it would have separated the men from the boys in the large-state delegations. How attached would the Virginians have been to their reform principles if Virginia were to disappear as a component geo-

graphical unit (the largest) for representational purposes? Up
to this point, the Virginians had been in the happy position of
supporting high ideals with that inner confidence born of
knowledge that the "public interest" they endorsed would
nourish their private interest. Worse, they had shown little
willingness to compromise. Now the delegates from the small
states announced that they were unprepared to be offered up
as sacrificial victims to a "national interest" which reflected
Virginia's parochial ambition. Caustic Charles Pinckney was
not far off when he remarked sardonically that ". . . the whole
[conflict] comes to this: Give N. Jersey an equal vote, and she
will dismiss her scruples, and concur in the Natil. system."
What he rather unfairly did not add was that the Jersey
delegates were not free agents who could adhere to their
private convictions; they had to take back, sponsor, and risk
their reputations on the reforms approved by the Convention
—and in New Jersey, not in Virginia.

Paterson spoke on Saturday, and one can surmise that over
the weekend there was a good deal of consultation, argument,
and caucusing among the delegates. One member at least prepared a full-length address: on Monday, Alexander Hamilton,
previously mute, rose and delivered a six-hour oration. It was
a remarkably apolitical speech; the gist of his position was that
both the Virginia and New Jersey plans were inadequately
centralist, and he detailed a reform program which was
reminiscent of the Protectorate under the Cromwellian *Instrument of Government* of 1653. It has been suggested that
Hamilton did this in the best political tradition to emphasize
the moderate character of the Virginia Plan, to give the
cautious delegates something *really* to worry about; but this
interpretation seems somehow too clever, particularly since the
sentiments Hamilton expressed happened to be completely
consistent with those he privately—and sometimes publicly—
expressed throughout his life. He wanted, to take a striking
phrase from a letter to George Washington, a "strong well

mounted government"; in essence, the Hamilton Plan contemplated an elected life monarch, virtually free of public control, on the Hobbesian ground that only in this fashion could strength and stability be achieved. The other alternatives, he argued, would put policy-making at the mercy of the passions of the mob; only if the sovereign was beyond the reach of selfish influence would it be possible to have government in the interests of the whole community.

From all accounts, this was a masterful and compelling speech, but (aside from furnishing John Lansing and Luther Martin with ammunition for later use against the Constitution) it made little impact. Hamilton was simply transmitting on a different wavelength from the rest of the delegates; the latter adjourned after his great effort, admired his rhetoric, and then returned to business. It was rather as if they had taken a day off to attend the opera. Hamilton, never a particularly patient man or much of a negotiator, stayed for another ten days, and then left, in considerable disgust, for New York. Although he came back to Philadelphia sporadically and attended the last two weeks of the Convention, Hamilton played no part in the laborious task of hammering out the Constitution. His day came later when he led the New York Constitutionalists into the savage imbroglio over ratification—an arena in which his unmatched talent for dirty political infighting may well have won the day. For instance, in the New York Ratifying Convention, Lansing threw back into Hamilton's teeth the sentiments the latter had expressed in his June 18th oration in the Convention. However, having since retreated to the fine defensive positions immortalized in *The Federalist*, the Colonel flatly denied that he had ever been an enemy of the states, or had believed that conflict between states and nation was inexorable! As Madison's authoritative *Notes* did not appear until 1840, and there had been no press coverage, there was no way to verify his assertions, so in the words of the reporter, ". . . a warm personal altercation between [Lansing and Hamilton] engrossed the remainder of the day [June 28, 1788]."

IV

On Tuesday morning, June 19th, the vacation was over. James Madison led off with a long, carefully reasoned speech analyzing the New Jersey Plan which, while intellectually vigorous in its criticisms, was quite conciliatory in mood. "The great difficulty," he observed, "lies in the affair of Representation; and if this could be adjusted, all others would be surmountable." (As events were to demonstrate, this diagnosis was correct.) When he finished, a vote was taken on whether to continue with the Virginia Plan as the nucleus for a new constitution: seven states voted "Yes"; New York, New Jersey, and Delaware voted "No"; and Maryland, whose position often depended on which delegates happened to be on the floor, divided. Paterson, it seems, lost decisively; yet in a fundamental sense he and his allies had achieved their purpose: from that day onward, it could never be forgotten that the state governments loomed ominously in the background and that no verbal incantations could exorcise their power. Moreover, nobody bolted the convention: Paterson and his colleagues took their defeat in stride and set to work to modify the Virginia Plan, particularly with respect to its provisions on representation in the National Legislature. Indeed, they won an immediate rhetorical bonus; when Oliver Ellsworth of Connecticut rose to move that the word "national" be expunged from the Third Virginia Resolution ("Resolved that a *national* Government ought to be established consisting of a *supreme* Legislative, Executive and Judiciary"), Randolph agreed, and the motion passed unanimously. The process of compromise had begun.

For the next two weeks, the delegates circled around the problem of legislative representation. The Connecticut delegation appears to have evolved a possible compromise quite early in the debates, but the Virginians and particularly Madison (unaware that he would later be acclaimed as the prophet of "Federalism") fought obdurately against providing for equal representation of states in the second chamber. There was a good deal of acrimony, and at one point Benjamin Franklin—of all people—proposed the institution of a daily prayer; practical politicians in the gathering, however, were meditating more on the merits of a good committee than on the utility of divine intervention. On July 2nd, the ice began to break when through a number of fortuitous events—and one that seems deliberate—the majority against equality of representation was converted into a dead tie. The Convention had reached the stage where it was "ripe" for a solution (presumably all the therapeutic speeches had been made), and the South Carolinians proposed a committee. Madison and James Wilson wanted none of it, but with only Pennsylvania dissenting, the body voted to establish a working party on the problem of representation.

The members of this committee, one from each state, were elected by the delegates—and a very interesting committee it was. Despite the fact that the Virginia Plan had held majority support up to that date, neither Madison nor Randolph was selected (Mason was the Virginian), and Baldwin of Georgia, whose shift in position had resulted in the tie, was chosen. From the composition, it was clear that this was not to be a "fighting" committee: the emphasis in membership was on what might be described as "second-level political entrepreneurs." On the basis of the discussions up to that time, only Luther Martin of Maryland could be described as a "bitter-ender." Admittedly, some divination enters into this sort of analysis, but one does get a sense of the mood of the delegates from these choices—including the interesting selection of Benjamin Franklin, despite his age and intellectual wobbliness, over the brilliant and incisive Wilson or the sharp, polemical

Gouverneur Morris, to represent Pennsylvania. His passion for conciliation was more valuable at this juncture than Wilson's logical genius, or Morris's acerbic wit.

There is a common rumor that the Framers divided their time between philosophical discussions of government and reading the classics in political theory. Perhaps this is as good a time as any to note that their concerns were highly practical, that they spent little time canvassing abstractions. A number of them had some acquaintance with the history of political theory (probably gained from reading John Adams's monumental compilation *A Defence of the Constitutions of Government*, the first volume of which appeared in 1786), and it was a poor rhetorician indeed who could not cite Locke, Montesquieu, or Harrington *in support* of a desired goal. Yet up to this point in the deliberations, no one had expounded a defense of states' rights or the "separation of powers" on anything resembling a theoretical basis. It should be reiterated that the Madison model had no room either for the states or for the "separation of powers": effectively *all* governmental power was vested in the national legislature. The merits of Montesquieu did not turn up until *The Federalist;* and although a perverse argument could be made that Madison's ideal was truly in the tradition of John Locke's *Second Treatise of Government*, the Locke whom the American rebels treated as an honorary president was a pluralistic defender of vested rights, not of parliamentary supremacy.

It would be tedious to continue a blow-by-blow analysis of the work of the delegates; the critical fight was over representation of the states, and once the Connecticut Compromise was adopted, on July 17th, the Convention was over the hump. Madison, James Wilson, and Gouverneur Morris of New York (who was there representing Pennsylvania!) fought the compromise all the way in a last-ditch effort to get a unitary state with parliamentary supremacy. But their allies deserted them, and they demonstrated after their defeat the essentially opportunist character of their objections—using "opportunist" here in a nonpejorative sense, to indicate a willingness to swallow their objections and get on with the business. Moreover, once the compromise had carried (by five states to four, with one state divided), its advocates threw themselves vigorously into the job of strengthening the general government's substantive powers—as might have been predicted, indeed, from Paterson's early statements. It nourishes an increased respect for Madison's devotion to the art of politics, to realize that this dogged fighter could sit down six months later and prepare essays for *The Federalist* in contradiction to his basic convictions about the true course the Convention should have taken.

V

Two tricky issues will serve to illustrate the later process of accommodation. The first was the institutional position of the executive. Madison argued for an executive chosen by the National Legislature, and on May 29th this had been adopted with a provision that after his seven-year term was concluded, the chief magistrate should not be eligible for re-election. In late July this was reopened, and for a week the matter was argued from several different points of view. A good deal of desultory speechmaking ensued, but the gist of the problem was the opposition from two sources to election by the legislature. One group felt that the states should have a hand in the process; another small but influential circle urged direct election by the people, election by state governors, by electors chosen by state legislatures, by the National Legislature (James Wilson, perhaps ironically, proposed at one point that an electoral college be chosen by lot from the National Legislature!), and there was some resemblance to three-dimensional chess in the dispute because of the presence of two other variables, length of tenure and re-eligibility. Finally, after opening, reopening, and re-reopening the debate, the thorny problem was consigned to a committee for resolution.

The Brearley Committee on Postponed Matters was a superb aggregation of talent, and its compromise on the executive was a masterpiece of political improvisation. (The Electoral College, its creation, however, had little in its favor as an *institution*—as the delegates well appreciated.) The point of departure for all discussion about the Presidency in the Convention was that in immediate terms, the problem was non-existent; in other words, everybody present knew that under any system devised, George Washington would be President. Thus they were dealing in the future tense, and to a body of working politicians the merits of the Brearley proposal were obvious: everybody got a piece of cake. (Or, to put it more academically, each viewpoint could leave the Convention and argue to its constituents that it had *really* won the day.) First, the state legislatures had the right to determine the mode of selection of the electors; second, the small states received a bonus in the Electoral College in the form of a guaranteed minimum of three votes, while the big states got acceptance of the principle of proportional power; third, if the state legislatures agreed (as six did in the first presidential election), the people could be involved directly in the choice of electors; and finally, if no candidate received a majority in the College, the right of decision passed on to the National Legislature, with each state exercising equal strength. (In the Brearley recommendation, the election went to the Senate, but a motion from the floor substituted the House; this was accepted on the ground that the Senate already had enough authority over the executive in its treaty and appointment powers.)

This compromise was almost too good to be true, and the Framers snapped it up with little debate or controversy, No one seemed to think well of the College as an *institution*; indeed, what evidence there is suggests that there was an assumption that once Washington had finished his tenure as President, the electors would cease to produce majorities and that the Chief Executive would usually be chosen in the House. George Mason observed casually that the selection would be made in the House nineteen times in twenty, and no one seriously disputed this point. The vital aspect of the Electoral College was that it got the Convention over the hurdle and protected everybody's interests. The future was left to cope with the problem of what to do with this Rube Goldberg mechanism.

In short, the Framers did not in their wisdom endow the United States with a College of Cardinals—the Electoral College was neither an exercise in applied Platonism nor an experiment in indirect government based on elitist distrust of the masses. It was merely a jerry-rigged improvisation which has subsequently been endowed with a high theoretical content. When an elector from Oklahoma in 1960 refused to cast his vote for Nixon (naming Byrd and Goldwater instead) on the ground that the Founding Fathers intended him to exercise his great independent wisdom, he was indulging in historical fantasy. If one were to indulge in counterfantasy, he would be tempted to suggest that the Fathers would be startled to find the College still in operation—and perhaps even dismayed at their descendants' lack of judgment or inventiveness.

The second issue on which some substantial practical bargaining took place was slavery. The morality of slavery was, by design, not at issue; but in its other concrete aspects, slavery colored the arguments over taxation, commerce, and representation. The "Three-Fifths Compromise," that three-fifths of the slaves would be counted both for representation and for purposes of direct taxation (which was drawn from the past—it was a formula of Madison's utilized by Congress in 1783 to establish the basis of state contributions to the Confederation treasury), had allayed some northern fears about southern over-representation (no one then foresaw the trivial role that direct taxation would play in later federal financial policy), but doubts still remained. The Southerners, on the other hand, were afraid that congressional control over commerce would lead to the exclusion of slaves or to their excessive taxation as imports. Moreover, the Southerners were disturbed over "navigation acts," that is, tariffs, or special legislation providing, for example, the exports be carried only in American ships; as a section depending upon exports, they wanted protection from the potential voracity of their commercial brethren of the eastern states. To achieve this end, Mason and others urged that the Constitution include a proviso that navigation and commercial laws should require a two-thirds vote in Congress.

These problems came to a head in late August and, as usual, were handed to a committee in the hope that, in Gouverneur Morris's words, ". . . these things may form a bargain among the Northern and Southern states." The committee reported its measures of reconciliation on August 25th, and on August 29th the package was wrapped up and delivered. What occurred can best be described in George Mason's dour version (he anticipated Calhoun in his conviction that permitting navigation acts to pass by majority vote would put the South in economic bondage to the North—it was mainly on this ground that he refused to sign the Constitution):

> The Constitution as agreed to till a fortnight before the Convention rose was such a one as he would have set his hand and heart to. . . . [Until that time] The 3 New England States were constantly with us in all questions . . . so that it was these three States with the 5 Southern ones against Pennsylvania, Jersey and Delaware. With respect to the importation of slaves, [decision-making] was left to Congress. This disturbed the two Southernmost States who knew that Congress would immediately suppress the importation of slaves. Those two States therefore

struck up a bargain with the three New England States. If they would join to admit slaves for some years, the two Southern-most States would join in changing the clause which required the 2/3 of the Legislature in any vote [on navigation acts]. It was done.

On the floor of the Convention there was a virtual love feast on this happy occasion. Charles Pinckney, of South Carolina, attempted to overturn the committee's decision, when the compromise was reported to the Convention, by insisting that the South needed protection from the imperialism of the northern states. But his southern colleagues were not prepared to rock the boat, and General C. C. Pinckney arose to spread oil on the suddenly ruffled waters; he admitted that:

It was in the true interest of the S[outhern] States to have no regulation of commerce; but considering the loss brought on the commerce of the Eastern States by the Revolution, their liberal conduct towards the views of South Carolina [on the regulation of the slave trade] and the interests the weak Southn. States had in being united with the strong Eastern states, he thought it proper that no fetters should be imposed on the power of making commercial regulations; *and that his constituents, though prejudiced against the Eastern States, would be reconciled to this liberality.* He had himself prejudices agst the Eastern States before he came here, but would acknowledge that he had found them as liberal and candid as any men whatever. [Italics added]

Pierce Butler took the same tack, essentially arguing that he was not too happy about the possible consequences but that a deal was a deal. Many southern leaders were later—in the wake of the "Tariff of Abominations"—to rue this day of reconciliation; Calhoun's *A Disquisition on Government* was little more than an extension of the argument in the Convention against permitting a congressional majority to enact navigation acts.

VI

Drawing on their vast collective political experience, utilizing every weapon in the politician's arsenal, looking constantly over their shoulders at their constituents, the delegates put together a Constitution. It was a makeshift affair; some sticky issues (for example, the qualification of voters) they ducked entirely; others they mastered with that ancient instrument of political sagacity, studied ambiguity (for example, citizenship), and some they just overlooked. In this last category, I suspect, fell the matter of the power of the federal courts to determine the constitutionality of acts of Congress. When the judicial article was formulated (Article III of the Constitution), deliberations were still in the stage where the legislature was endowed with broad power under the Randolph formulation, authority which by its own terms was scarcely amenable to judicial review. In essence, courts could hardly determine when ". . . the separate States are incompetent or . . . the harmony of the United States may be interrupted"; the National Legislature, as critics pointed out, was free to define its own jurisdiction. Later the definition of legislative authority was changed into the form we know, a series of stipulated powers, *but the delegates never seriously reexamined the jurisdiction of the judiciary under this new limited formulation.* All arguments on the intention of the Framers in this matter are thus deductive and *a posteriori*, though some obviously make more sense than others.

The Framers were busy and distinguished men, anxious to get back to their families, their positions, and their constituents, not members of the French Academy devoting a lifetime to a dictionary. They were trying to do an important job, and do it in such fashion that their handiwork would be acceptable to very diverse constituencies. No one was rhapsodic about the final document, but it was a beginning, a move in the right direction, and one they had reason to believe the people would endorse. In addition, since they had modified the impossible amendment provisions of the Articles (the requirement of unanimity which could always be frustrated by "Rogues Island") to one demanding approval by only three-quarters of the states, they seemed confident that gaps in the fabric which experience would reveal could be rewoven without undue difficulty.

So with a neat phrase introduced by Benjamin Franklin (but devised by Gouverneur Morris) which made their decision sound unanimous, and an inspired benediction by the Old Doctor urging doubters to doubt their own infallibility, the Constitution was accepted and signed. Curiously, Edmund Randolph, who had played so vital a role throughout, refused to sign, as did his fellow Virginian George Mason and Elbridge Gerry of Massachusetts. Randolph's behavior was eccentric, to say the least—his excuses for refusing his signature have a factitious ring even at this late date; the best explanation seems to be that he was afraid that the Constitution would prove to be a liability in Virginia politics, where Patrick Henry was burning up the countryside with impassioned denunciations. Presumably, Randolph wanted to check the temper of the populace before he risked his reputation, and perhaps his job, in a fight with both Henry and Richard Henry Lee. Events lend some justification to this speculation: after much temporizing and use of the conditional subjunctive tense, Randolph endorsed ratification in Virginia and ended by getting the best of both worlds.

Madison, despite his reservations about the Constitution, was the campaign manager in ratification. His first task was to get the Congress in New York to light its own funeral pyre by approving the "amendments" to the Articles and sending them on to the state legislatures. Above all, momentum had to be maintained. The anti-Constitutionalists, now thoroughly alarmed and no novices in politics realized that their best tactic was attrition rather than direct opposition. Thus they settled on a position expressing qualified approval but calling for a second Convention to remedy various defects (the one with the most demagogic appeal was the lack of a Bill of Rights). Madison knew that to accede to this demand would be equivalent to losing the battle, nor would he agree to conditional approval (despite wavering even by Hamilton). This was an all-or-nothing proposition: national salvation or national impotence with no intermediate positions possible. Unable to get congressional approval, he settled for second best: a unanimous resolution of Congress transmitting the Constitution to the states for whatever action they saw fit to take. The opponents then moved from New York and the Congress, where they had attempted to attach amendments and conditions, to the states for the final battle.

At first the campaign for ratification went beautifully: within eight months after the delegates set their names to the document, eight states had ratified. Only in Massachusetts had the result been close (187–168). Theoretically, a ratification by one more state convention would set the new government in motion, but in fact until Virginia and New York acceded to the new Union, the latter was a fiction. New Hampshire was the next to ratify; Rhode Island was involved in its characteristic political convulsions (the legislature there sent the Constitution out to the towns for decision by popular vote and it got lost among a series of local issues); North Carolina's convention did not meet until July, and then postponed a final decision. This is hardly the place for an extensive analysis of the conventions of New York and Virginia. Suffice it to say that the Constitutionalists clearly outmaneuvered their opponents, forced them into impossible political positions, and won both states narrowly. The Virginia Convention could serve as a classic study in effective floor management: Patrick Henry had to be contained, and a reading of the debates discloses a standard two-stage technique. Henry would give a four- or five-hour speech denouncing some section of the Constitution on every conceivable ground (the federal district, he averred at one point, would become a haven for convicts escaping from state authority!). When Henry subsided, "Mr. Lee of Westmoreland" would rise and poleax him with sardonic invective. (When Henry complained about the militia power, "Lighthorse Harry" really punched below the belt: observing that while the former governor had been sitting in Richmond during the Revolution, *he* had been out in the trenches with the troops and thus felt better qualified to discuss military affairs.) Then the gentlemanly Constitutionalists (Madison, Pendleton, and Marshall) would pick up the matters at issue and examine them in the light of reason.

Indeed, modern Americans who tend to think of James Madison as a rather desiccated character should spend some time with this transcript. Probably Madison put on his most spectacular demonstration of nimble rhetoric in what might be called the "Battle of the Absent Authorities." Patrick Henry in the course of one of his harangues alleged that Jefferson was known to be opposed to Virginia's approving the Constitution. This was clever: Henry hated Jefferson, but was prepared to use any weapon that came to hand. Madison's riposte was superb: First, he said that with all due respect to the great reputation of Jefferson, he was not in the country and therefore could not formulate an adequate judgment; second, no one should utilize the reputation of an outsider—the Virginia Convention was there to think for itself; third, if there were to be recourse to outsiders, the opinions of George Washington should certainly be taken into consideration; and, finally, he knew from privileged personal communications from Jefferson that in fact the latter *strongly favored* the Constitution. To devise an assault route into this rhetorical fortress was literally impossible.

VII

The fight was over; all that remained now was to establish the new frame of government in the spirit of its Framers. And who were better qualified for this task than the Framers themselves? Thus victory for the Constitution meant simultaneous victory for the Constitutionalists; the anti-Constitutionalists either capitulated or vanished into limbo—soon Patrick Henry would be offered a seat on the Supreme Court and Luther Martin would be known as the Federalist "bull-dog." And, irony of ironies, Alexander Hamilton and James Madison would shortly accumulate a reputation as the formulators of what is often alleged to be our political theory, the concept of "Federalism." Also, on the other side of the ledger, the arguments would soon appear over what the Framers "really meant"; while these disputes have assumed the proportions of a big scholarly business in the last century, they began almost before the ink on the Constitution was dry. One of the best early ones featured Hamilton versus Madison on the scope of presidential power, and other Framers characteristically assumed positions in this and other disputes on the basis of their political convictions.

Probably our greatest difficulty is that we know so much more about what the Framers *should have meant* than they themselves did. We are intimately acquainted with the problems that their Constitution should have been designed to master; in short, we have read the mystery story backward. If we are to get the right "feel" for their time and their circumstances, we must, in Maitland's phrase, ". . . think ourselves back into a twilight." Obviously, no one can pretend completely to escape from the solipsistic web of his own environment, but if the effort is made, it is possible to appreciate the past roughly on its own terms. The first step in this process is to abandon the academic premise that because we can ask a question, there must be an answer.

Thus we can ask what the Framers meant when they gave Congress the power to regulate interstate and foreign commerce, and we emerge, reluctantly perhaps, with the reply that (Professor Crosskey to the contrary notwithstanding) they may not have known what they meant, that there may not have been any semantic consensus. The Convention was not a seminar in analytic philosophy or linguistic analysis. Commerce was *commerce*—and if different interpretations of the word arose, later generations could worry about the problem of definition. The delegates were in a hurry to get a new government established; when definitional arguments arose, they characteristically took refuge in ambiguity. If different men voted for the same proposition for varying reasons, that was politics (and still is); if later generations were unsettled by this lack of precision, that would be their problem.

There was a good deal of definitional pluralism with respect to the problems the delegates did discuss, but when we move to the question of extrapolated intentions we enter the realm of spiritualism. When men in our time, for instance, launch into elaborate talmudic exegesis to demonstrate that federal aid to parochial schools is (or is not) in accord with the intentions of the men who established the Republic and endorsed the Bill of Rights, they are engaging in historical extrasensory perception. (If one were to join this E.S.P. contingent for a minute, he might suggest that the hard-boiled politicians who wrote the Constitution and Bill of Rights would chuckle scornfully at such an invocation of authority: obviously a politician would chart his course on the intentions of the living, not of the dead, and count the number of Catholics in his constituency.)

The Constitution, then, was not an apotheosis of "constitutionalism," a triumph of architectonic genius; it was a patchwork sewn together under the pressure of both time and events by a group of extremely talented democratic politicians. They refused to attempt the establishment of a strong, centralized sovereignty on the principle of legislative supremacy, for the excellent reason that the people would not accept it. They risked their political fortunes by opposing the established doctrines of state sovereignty because they were convinced that the existing system was leading to national impotence and probably foreign domination. For two years they worked to get a convention established. For over three months, in what must have seemed to the faithful participants an endless process of give-and-take, they reasoned, cajoled, threatened, and bargained amongst themselves. The result was a Constitution which the people, in fact, by democratic processes, did accept, and a new and far better national government was established.

Beginning with the inspired propaganda of Hamilton, Madison, and Jay, the ideological buildup got under way. *The Federalist* had little impact on the ratification of the Constitution, except perhaps in New York, but this volume had enormous influence on the image of the Constitution in the minds of future generations, particularly on historians and political scientists who have an innate fondness for theoretical symmetry. Yet, while the shades of Locke and Montesquieu *may* have been hovering in the background and the delegates *may* have been unconscious instruments of a transcendent *telos,* the careful observer of the day-to-day work of the Convention finds no overarching principles. The "separation of powers" to him seems to be a by-product of suspicion, and "Federalism" he views as a *pis aller,* as the farthest point the delegates felt they could go in the destruction of state power without themselves inviting repudiation.

To conclude, the Constitution was neither a victory for abstract theory nor a great practical success. Well over half a million men had to die on the battlefields of the Civil War before certain constitutional principles could be defined—a baleful consideration which is somehow overlooked in our customary tributes to the farsighted genius of the Framers and to the supposed American talent for "constitutionalism."

The Constitution was, however, a vivid demonstration of effective democratic political action, and of the forging of a national elite which literally persuaded its countrymen to hoist themselves by their own boot straps. American pro-consuls would be wise not to translate the Constitution into Japanese, or Swahili, or treat it as a work of semi-Divine origin; but when students of comparative politics examine the process of nation-building in countries newly freed from colonial rule, they may find the American experience instructive as a classic example of the potentialities of a democratic elite.

YOUTH AND THE CONTINENTAL VISION

Stanley M. Elkins and Eric McKitrick

EDITOR'S NOTE Stanley M. Elkins of Smith College and Eric McKitrick of Columbia University have teamed up to write a series of brilliant articles on various aspects and periods of American politics. Independently, Elkins has published an intellectually dazzling book, *Slavery* (1959), and McKitrick's book, *Andrew Johnson and Reconstruction* is easily the best on that equally controversial subject. Their article on the making of the Constitution might have served as the introduction to this anthology, rather than its conclusion, but for the fact that their achievement is so lucid, systematic, and judicious that they leave too little for the student to think for himself. The first half of their article is historiographic, a critical evaluation of the principal historical writings on the making of the Constitution from the nineteenth-century classics to the successive revisionist interpretations of Beard, Jensen, Brown, and McDonald. Elkins and McKitrick show that the reconstruction of the past through written history is, to a considerable extent, contemporary history. Each generation, that is, forms its own conceptions of the past in accordance with its own values and needs, so that events frozen in time are reflected through the looking glass of the present's predilections and presuppositions. Historians' history is to a large degree a source for the study of the varying and successive images which

From Stanley M. Elkins and Eric McKitrick, "The Founding Fathers: Young Men of the Revolution," *Political Science Quarterly*, June 1961, Vol. LXXVI, pp. 181–216. Copyright by the authors. Reprinted by permission.

the past has had of itself—and which the present too has of itself. At the hands of Elkins and Mc-Kitrick the critical evaluation of written history as a battleground of ideas and interests as well as of events becomes an illuminating excursion into intellectual history.

In the second half of their article they advance their own, essentially political, interpretation of the making of the Constitution. Their theme, reflected in their subtitle, "Young Men of the Revolution," was suggested by Charles Warren in the concluding section of his great book, the introduction to which is reprinted in this anthology. Warren observed that the men of 1787 were removed from the Stamp Act by less than a quarter of the century. Having fought for the liberty of the individual and of their states, the older men naturally were alarmed at the semblance of a return to a centralized authority. "It is in connection with this phase of the situation," Warren wrote, "that a line of division between Antifederalists and Federalists should be noted which has been little commented upon— the line of age." The former, Warren observed, were generally the older men, "the patriots of '75" as they were called in the press. The Federalists, on the whole, had been too young to be on the forefront of the pre-war fight against King and Parliament; their careers were fashioned during the Revolution and the Confederation.

Elkins and McKitrick substantially expand Warren's suggestion, not only by associating energy, will, and a desire for change with youth; they also stress that the younger men tended to be shaped by a "continental" outlook fostered by the war and by association with the government of the nascent union, rather than with the state governments. The Anti-Federalists tended to be state-centered in their careers, while their opponents tended to become more nationalistic as their experience and political commitment transcended provincial boundaries. Elkins and McKitrick conclude with the point that the Convention framed a Constitution that was congenial to the culture's basic values, republicanism and capitalism, and quite naturally protected property, both real and personal. Like John P. Roche they believe that the issue of constitutional reform was not fought on economic or ideological grounds. They even downgrade the conflict as a struggle between nationalism and localism, focusing, rather, on the struggle between inertia (age) and energy (youth).

o   o   o   o

THE INTELLIGENT American of today may know a great deal about his history, but the chances are that he feels none too secure about the Founding Fathers and the framing and ratification of the Federal Constitution. He is no longer certain what the "enlightened" version of that story is, or even whether there is one. This is because, in the century and three quarters since the Constitution was written, our best thinking on that subject has gone through two dramatically different phases and is at this moment about to enter a third.

Americans in the nineteenth century, whenever they reviewed the events of the founding, made reference to an Olympian gathering of wise and virtuous men who stood splendidly above all faction, ignored petty self-interest, and concerned themselves only with the freedom and well-being of their fellow-countrymen. This attitude toward the Fathers has actually never died out; it still tends to prevail in American history curricula right up through most of the secondary schools. But bright young people arriving at college have been regularly discovering, for nearly the last fifty years, that in the innermost circle this was regarded as an old-fashioned, immensely oversimplified, and rather dewy-eyed view of the Founding Fathers and their work. Ever since J. Allen Smith and Charles Beard wrote in the early years of the twentieth century, the "educated" picture of the Fathers has been that of a group not of disinterested patriots but of hardfisted conservatives who were looking out for their own interests and those of their class. According to this worldlier view, the document which they wrote—and in which they embodied these interests—was hardly intended as a thrust toward popular and democratic government. On the contrary, its centralizing tendencies all reflected the Fathers' distrust of the local and popular rule which had been too little restrained under the Articles of Confederation. The authors of the Constitution represented the privileged part of society. Naturally, then, their desire for a strong central government was, among other things, an effort to achieve solid national guarantees for the rights of property—rights not adequately protected under the Articles—and to obtain for the propertied class (their own) a favored position under the new government.

This "revisionist" point of view—that of the Founding Fathers as self-interested conservatives—has had immeasurable influence in the upper reaches of American historical thought. Much of what at first seemed audacious to the point of lèse majesté came ultimately to be taken as commonplace. The Tory-like, almost backward-turning quality which this approach has imparted to the picture of constitution-making even renders it plausible to think of the Philadelphia Convention of 1787 as a counter-revolutionary conspiracy, which is just the way a number of writers have actually described it. That is, since the Articles of Confederation were the product of the Revolution, to overthrow the Articles was—at least symbolically—to repudiate the Revolution. The Declaration of Independence and the Constitution represented two very different, and in some ways opposing, sets of aspirations; and (so the reasoning goes) the Philadelphia Convention was thus a significant turning-away from, rather than an adherence to, the spirit of the Declaration.

In very recent years, however, a whole new cycle of writing and thinking and research has been under way; the revisionists of the previous generation are themselves being revised. The economic ideas of the late Professor Beard, which dominated this field for so long, have been partially if not wholly discredited. And yet many of the old impressions, intermingled with still older ones, persist. Much of the new work, moreover, though excellent and systematic, is still in progress. Consequently the entire subject of the Constitution and its creation has become a little murky; new notions having the clarity and assuredness of the old have not as yet fully emerged; and meanwhile one is not altogether certain what to think.

Before the significance of all this new work can be justly assessed, and before consistent themes in it may be identified with any assurance, an effort should be made to retrace somewhat the psychology of previous conceptions. At the same time, it should be recognized that any amount of fresh writing on this subject will continue to lack something until it can present us with a clear new symbolic image of the Fathers themselves. The importance of this point lies in the function that symbols have for organizing the historical imagination, and the old ones are a little tired. The "father" image is well and good, and so also in certain respects is the "conservative" one. But we may suppose that these men saw themselves at the time as playing other rôles too, rôles that did not partake so much of retrospection, age, and restraint as those which would come to be assigned to them in after years. The Republic is now very old, as republics go, yet it *was* young once, and so were its founders. With youth goes energy, and the "energy" principle may be more suggestive now, in reviewing the experience of the founding, than the principle of paternal conservatism.

I

Charles A. Beard, who in 1913 published *An Economic Interpretation of the Constitution of the United States*, did more than any single figure to make of the Constitution something other than a topic for ceremonial praise. By calling it a product of economic forces, Beard established an alternative position and enabled the entire subject to become one for serious historical debate. He thus created the first real dialectic on the Constitution and Founding Fathers, and for that reason Beard's work must still be taken as the point of departure for any historical treatment of that subject.

For Beard, the reality behind the movement for a constitution in the 1780's was economic interest. The animating surge came from holders of depreciated Continental securities who were demanding that their bonds be paid at par, and from conservative elements throughout the Confederation who wanted a national bulwark against agrarian-debtor radicalism. Beard thus identified the Federalists as those who wanted protection for property, especially personal property. The Anti-Federalists, on the other hand, were the great mass of agrarian debtors agitating for schemes of confiscation and paper money inflation in the state legislatures. Their hard-earned taxes would go to support any new bonds that a stronger United States government might issue; conversely, further fiscal experimentation on their part would be checked by national power. The Anti-Federalists, those who opposed a new constitution, were therefore the radicals; the Federalists, who favored it, were the conservatives.

Beard's argument was immediately challenged and kept on being challenged, which helped it to retain the fresh attractiveness of an avant-garde position for many years. But the man's influence grew, and his work played a vital part in historical thinking until well after the Second World War. Historical thinking, however, has its own historical setting. Why should such a statement as Beard's not have been made until the twentieth century, more than 125 years after the event?

In the nineteenth century the American Constitution had operated as the central myth of an entire political culture. While that culture was still in the tentative stages of its growth, still subject to all manner of unforeseen menaces, and with very little that was nationally sacred, there reigned everywhere the tacit understanding that here was the one unifying abstraction, the one symbol that might command all loyalties and survive all strife. The Constitution thus served multiple functions for a society that lacked tradition, folk-memory, a sovereign, and a body of legend. The need to keep the symbol inviolate seems to have been felt more instinctively during its earlier history than later on. Public controversy of the bitterest kind might occur over the charter's true meaning; enemies might accuse each other of miconstruing the document; but one did not challenge the myth itself. Americans even fought a civil war with both sides claiming to be the true upholders of the Constitution. Thus it was natural that when the historians of the nineteenth century—Bancroft, Hildreth, Frothingham, Fiske, McMaster—came to describe the origins of the Constitution, they should reach for the non-controversial idiom and imagery of a Golden Age. The Supreme Law had been fashioned and given to the people by a race of classic heroes.[1]

America's veneration for its Constitution became steadily more intense in the years that followed the Civil War. Now it was the symbol not only of the Union, for which that generation had made such heavy sacrifices, but also of the un-

[1] Richard B. Morris has pointed out that in Henry Dawson there was at least one exception to this universal veneration for the Constitution. Dawson in 1871 published an article wherein he deplored the ancestor-worship which already wreathed the Fathers and their work. See Morris, "The Confederation and the American Historian," *William and Mary Quarterly*, XIII, 3rd ser. (April 1956), pp. 139–56; Dawson, "The Motley Letter," *Historical Magazine*, IX, 2nd ser. (March 1871), pp. 157 *et seq.*

fettered capitalism which was turning the United States into one of the richest and most powerful nations in the world. The new material order—wasteful, disorderly, already acquainted with labor disturbances, yet immensely productive—was watched over by the benevolent and solicitous eye of the Constitution.

In 1888, in a setting darkened by portents of industrial warfare, John Fiske published *The Critical Period of American History*, an account of the events leading to the Philadelphia Convention of 1787. It was an instant success; the notion of the Confederation interlude as a "critical period" was dramatically perfect. A time of trouble, political drift, threatening disunity, and irresponsible agitation provided the occasion at Philadelphia for a supreme act of disinterested statesmanship. There, an intrepid conclave of Old Romans rose above personal and local concerns and presented their countrymen with an instrument of vigorous and effective government.

By the opening of the twentieth century, the state of mind in which men could uncritically ascribe a sort of immaculateness to their political and legal arrangements had altered sharply. By then a profound economic and social crisis had been met and overcome, but with remnants of psychological crisis left unresolved in its wake. The ending of the depression and hard times of the 1890's, the defeat of Populism and Bryanism, the election of McKinley and return of Republican rule —these things were not enough to restore the old complacent innocence. The American public, now full of guilty misgivings, had begun to ask itself searching questions about the evils of the existing order and about the price it had allowed itself to pay for material progress. The answer which was hit upon by publicists and civic spokesmen was *vested interest*. The formula was not exactly new, but after the experience of the 1890's, when public rhetoric had abounded in sinister allusions to "Wall Street" and "the monopolies," it was no more than natural that the "vested interest" concept should have taken on an immensely new and widened range of application. The "interests" were the shadowy powers that manipulated things and made them run the way they did. Thus vested interest came to be seen in the Progressive Era—those years roughly from the turn of the century through the First World War— as the ultimate reality behind the life of affairs.

It was in that era, moreover, that "reality" itself first came to be a synonym for all the equivocal, seamy, and downright evil facts of life from which innocent and respectable people are normally sheltered. Few periods in American history have been so strikingly noted for civic awareness and the reforming spirit—and reform meant getting to the bottom of things. The most efficacious step in exorcising an evil was exposing it. Thus the literature of exposure, which claimed an enormous amount of journalistic and literary energy, did much to whet and sustain that generation's relish for reform. "Muckraking" meant dredging up heaps of grubby "reality" for all to behold. "Reality," as Richard Hofstadter has said,

> was the bribe, the rebate, the bought franchise, the sale of adulterated food. It was what one found in *The Jungle, The Octopus, Wealth against Commonwealth,* or *The Shame of the Cities.* . . . Reality was a series of unspeakable plots, personal iniquities, moral failures, which, in their totality, had come to govern American society. . . .

The sheer excitement of discovery tended to leave people's perceptions of appearance and reality somewhat unbalanced. It is perhaps too much to say that anything hidden was taken as bad (though there were certainly strong presumptions); yet one of the great unspoken dogmas of American thought, implanted in this period, was that the "facts of life" had to be hidden in order to qualify as "real."

In academic precincts, meanwhile, such thinkers as Roscoe Pound, John Dewey, Thorstein Veblen, Arthur Bentley, and J. Allen Smith had begun to challenge the older static and formalist theories of law, philosophy, economics, and government. They were no longer so interested in the formal outlines which enclosed, say, government or the law; they were much more concerned to locate the dynamic forces inside these realms—to identify the powers that made them really work. Thus "economic interest" as a kind of *élan vital*, a basic prime mover, came to be given greater and greater emphasis. "Wherever we turn," wrote E. R. A. Seligman as early as 1902, " . . . we are confronted by the overwhelming importance attached by the younger and abler scholars to the economic factor in political and social progress." Here was "reality" being given an intellectual and scholarly sanction.

In view of this mounting preoccupation with "interests," one might be led to conclude that significant numbers of intelligent people were approaching a "class" theory of society not unlike that of Marx—a theory in which classes and class interests contended more or less frankly with each other for advantage. Yet by and large this did not happen; these were not the terms in which most people thought about society. For one reason, there was very little evidence to support such a theory. But a more important reason was that, to a people saturated in democratic prejudices, "class" habits of thought were fantastically difficult to understand, let alone imitate. To the Progressive mind, the way vested interest worked was not so much through class as through *conspiracy*.

Vested interest and conspiracy were concepts so closely related that they were almost synonymous. The interests worked in secret; their power rested on stealthy understandings and was exercised through the pulling of invisible strings. Hidden from view, they might freely circumvent the law and gain their ends by corrupting and manipulating the agencies of government. The Marxian view that a man openly and automatically reflected the interests of his class, doing this even in the name of ideals and justice, was incomprehensible to most Americans. The mediating term between economic interest and political action had to be something both simpler and more disreputable, and the techniques such as could not bear daylight. One important source of this attitude was the Progressive faith in the essential honesty of the people. Only the few, acting in secret, would set their interests against those of the nation. They achieved their aims not by consulting the majority will but by thwarting and evading it. Thus when writers of the Progressive period tried to weigh the importance of economic factors in any political development, the imagery they slipped into was almost invariably that of a conspiracy against the people. Such a mode of conceiving reality would even be brought to bear upon the origins of the United States Constitution.

Two of Charles Beard's immediate precursors in that realm were J. Allen Smith and Algie Simons. They were, for their own purposes, innovators; yet in a broader sense their minds followed a typical Progressive pattern. In J. Allen Smith's *Spirit of American Government, A Study of the Constitution* (1907), the myth of the Philadelphia convention as a forum of disinterested statesmen came under sharp attack. Claiming that "it was the property-owning class that framed and secured the adoption of the Constitution," Smith seemed to be feeling his way toward an economic interpretation based on class. But this tentative theme was quickly overshadowed by the central idea, that of a conspiracy against democratic rule:

> Democracy . . . was not the object which the framers of the American Constitution had in view, but the very thing they wished to avoid. . . . Accordingly the efforts of the Constitutional Convention were directed to the task of devising a system of government which was just popular enough not to excite popular opposition and which at the same time gave the people as little as possible of the substance of political power.

Algie Simons, who was a convinced socialist and should therefore have hewed more consistently to the doctrine of class interest, fell into much the same sort of reasoning. In

Social Forces in American History (1912), Simons' words seemed at first full of cool detachment when he said that it was not necessarily bad for the Constitutional Convention to have been virtually a committee of the propertied class, because that class "represented progress." But the lures of "conspiracy" in the end proved too much for him. Simons' closing rhetoric almost sweats with rural superstition as he tells his readers that

> the organic law of this nation was formulated in secret session by a body called into existence through a conspiratory trick, and was forced upon a disfranchised people by means of dishonest apportionment in order that the interests of a small body of wealthy rulers might be served.

But it was Charles A. Beard, taking up the "class interest" formula in his famous *Economic Interpretation* the following year, who succeeded to all intents and purposes in making it stick. Whereas neither Smith nor Simons had made any secret of their reforming passions (they denied that the Constitution was a sacred document, so their fellow-citizens should feel free to change it if they wished), Beard disclaimed any intention of writing a political tract. He would simply be the observer of historical events, impassively examining the facts. All he wanted to do was discover whether in fact economic forces had played a significant part in the drafting and ratification of the Constitution. Early in his book Beard insisted that it was not his purpose "to show that the Constitution was made for the personal benefit of the members of the Convention," but merely to determine whether the Fathers represented "distinct groups whose economic interests they understood and felt in concrete, definite form, through their own personal experience with identical property rights. . . ." Then, setting in motion an impressive system of scholarly apparatus, he proceeded to answer his own questions.

Beard's ostensible argument—that the Fathers were pursuing class rather than personal interests and that there was a real distinction between them—had a certain Marxian subtlety, but he would not have made his case with very many Progressive readers if he had actually stuck to it. Instead, in the course of his book that side of the case, the "class" side, slipped entirely out of sight while the personal side, the one that really engaged Beard's mind, just grew and grew. The distinction was impossible to maintain; even to him it was probably not very serious. At any rate, the reason he was able to create his sensation was that the things he showed the Fathers doing were of exactly the sort that the muckraking magazines had, in other connections, made all too familiar.

Beard's basic research materials were a batch of old Treasury records which had never previously been opened ("reality"), and in them he found the names of a number of the Federalist leaders, members of the Philadelphia Convention as well as delegates to ratifying conventions in the various states. These men held substantial amounts of Continental securities which—Beard reasoned from later developments—would rise sharply in value with the establishment of a strong central government. This seemed to explain the energy with which they worked to bring such a government into being, and this was just the sort of evidence that impressed Beard's contemporaries most. Beard himself, for all his disclaimers, sums up his argument in language whose dominant theme is *direct personal interest*. Here, three of his thirteen conclusions are quite explicit:

(1) The first firm steps toward the formation of the Constitution were taken by a small and active group of men immediately interested through their personal possessions in the outcome of their labors.

(2) The members of the Philadelphia Convention who drafted the Constitution were, with a few exceptions,

immediately, directly, and personally interested in, and derived economic advantages from, the establishment of the new system.

(3) The leaders who supported the Constitution in the ratifying conventions represented the same economic groups as the members of the Philadelphia Convention; and in a large number of instances they were also directly and personally interested in the outcome of their efforts.

Accompanying the principal theme of personal interest were several sub-themes:

(1) The Constitution was essentially an economic document based upon the concept that the fundamental private rights of property are anterior to government and morally beyond the reach of popular majorities.

(2) [The entire process, from the calling of the Philadelphia Convention to the ratifying of the Constitution, was unrepresentative and undemocratic; there was no popular vote on calling the convention; a large propertyless (and therefore disfranchised) mass was not represented at Philadelphia; and only a small minority in each state voted for delegates to the ratifying conventions.][2]

(3) [Where battles did occur over ratification], the line of cleavage . . . was between substantial personalty interests on the one hand and the small farmers and debtor interests on the other.

Beard thus managed in the end to have it both ways; he charged the Fathers, as members of a class, with things of which he had said he was not going to accuse them as individuals. But the distinction was too fine to matter a great deal; the response to the book, both favorable and hostile, was based on the secrets Beard had unearthed about the Fathers as individuals. Few of his readers had paid much attention to the subtle relationship which he had tried to establish between class interest and political ideology, so few could have

[2]Not a direct quotation but a summary of four of the thirteen conclusions.

noticed when the relationship began to dissolve. Actually, few had had any real quarrel with capitalism in the first place; the Progressive mentality was simply frightened by *big* capitalism—that is, by the vested interests. Beard himself was nothing if not a Progressive, fully immersed in his times. It was the interests and their inside doings that caught the Progressive imagination; it was this that the Progressives longed to befool and discomfit by public exposure. If Beard was to show that the Federal Constitution was not a product of abstract political theory but of concrete economic drives, there was no happier way of doing it than to paint the Founding Fathers in the familiar image of the vested interests—the small group of wealthy conspirators hostile to, even contemptuous of, the majority will, and acting for clear, "practical" reasons such as rigging the value of public securities.

Despite the bursts of pained protests which *An Economic Interpretation* initially drew from many older academics (who either thought that Beard could comprehend no motives other than base ones, or else concluded that he must be a socialist), it also drew plenty of praise from academic as well as nonacademic quarters. Not only did the book do well for a scholarly monograph, it did better and better as time went on. In the 1920's the reforming side of Progressivism had lost its popularity, but this was not true of the debunking side. Meanwhile the success of Vernon L. Parrington's *Main Currents in American Thought* (which owed much to Beardian influences), as well as of Beard's own *Rise of American Civilization,* served to keep Beard's views before the public.

The *Economic Interpretation* came fully into its own in the New Deal era. The times by then required a conception of the Constitution that would stress the flexible, rather than the rigid and immutable aspects of the document. Former President Hoover, and even the Supreme Court, were apparently insisting in the face of all enlightened opinion that social and economic experimentation of any kind was ruled out by the spirit of the Constitution. Yet it would be reasonable enough to expect that the Constitution should respond to the economic needs of the present, if there were convincing historical proof that its very birth had been in response to the economic needs of its framers. American intellectuals, moreover, had by this time become a good deal more accustomed to ideas of class conflict than formerly. To significant numbers of them the image of class struggle was now appealing enough that they had begun applying it in a spirit of experimentation to a great variety of problems. Business groups of every sort had fallen into bad odor. This was the setting in which prophetic insights came to be ascribed to the writings of Charles A. Beard. Those writings by the late 1930's had become voluminous, and the Master had acquired a legion of followers.

And the Master himself could still have it both ways. Marxist and quasi-Marxist interpretations of society could, and did for a season, draw much historical sanction from his pages. At the same time Beard had bequeathed to American historical method something far more pervasive, a technique of explanation which could take "class" interpretations or leave them alone. This was the "reality" technique, which assumes that the most significant aspects of any event are those concealed from the eye. Men's true intentions are to be judged neither from the words we hear them speak nor the deeds we see them do, and the "real" forces behind historical change will turn out, more often than not, to be those of conspiracy.

II

In 1940 certain new and interesting corollaries were added to the mode of approach which, due so largely to Beard's example, had come to influence historical thinking on the formation of the Constitution. In that year Merrill Jensen published *The Articles of Confederation: An Interpretation of*

*the Social-Constitutional History of the American Revolution,
1774–1781.* Jensen's own approach was consistent with most
of the general principles which had been laid down by Beard.
But whereas Beard's primary interest had been with the Federalists—the men who led and supported the campaign for a
new constitution—Jensen turned his attention to the Anti-
Federalists, those who had opposed the constitutional movement. What, he asked, was the nature of the political system
which the Constitution displaced, and what were the aims
and intentions of the men who had created that system?

In the face of most prior opinion to the contrary, Jensen
found in the Confederation just the sort of loose arrangement
most favorable to democratic self-rule on the local and state
level, inasmuch as the primary authority was located in the
state legislatures. It was for achieving exactly this object, he
thought, that the Confederation's strongest supporters—such
leaders as Samuel Adams, Patrick Henry, Thomas Burke, and
Richard Henry Lee—had pushed the Colonies into the Revolution in the first place. Conversely, those who opposed the Confederation were the men who had at first been reluctant to
support the Revolution. They had feared the consequences of
a break with England because that would remove the one
central power strong enough to restrain the forces of local
democracy. These men did, to be sure, join the Patriot forces
after the break had become inevitable. Yet almost at once
they began working for a continental government which might
supply the stabilizing and conservative force previously maintained by the Crown. Their eventual triumph would come,
of course, at Philadelphia in 1787.

In a second book, *The New Nation* (1950), Jensen considered the accomplishments of the Confederation, together with
the social and economic conditions of the period from 1781
to 1789. He concluded that the "critical period" was really
not so critical after all. American ships were not excluded
from many foreign ports; tariff wars between states were the

exception rather than the rule; the Confederation government had solved the problem of western lands and was well on the way to settling the outstanding boundary disputes. By 1786 the economic depression which had struck the country in 1784 was coming to an end. Even the problem of national credit was not so serious as the Federalists wanted people to believe, since a number of the states had assumed responsibility for portions of the Continental debt held by their own citizens. Had the states been brought to accept a national impost—a tariff duty on incoming foreign goods levied solely and exclusively by Congress, the revenue of which would be reserved for the support of the government—the Confederation would have been fully capable of surviving and functioning as a true federal establishment.

The collapse of the Confederation, Jensen argued, was not the logical outcome of weakness or inefficiency. It was the result of a determined effort by a small but tightly-organized group of nationalists to impose a centralized government upon the entire country despite the contrary desires of great majorities everywhere:

> Most of these men were by temperament or economic interest believers in executive and judicial rather than legislative control of state and central governments, in the rigorous collection of taxes, and, as creditors, in strict payment of public and private debts. . . . They deplored the fact that there was no check upon the actions of majorities in state legislatures; that there was no central government to which minorities could appeal from the decisions of such majorities, as they had done before the Revolution.

These were the men who conspired to overthrow the Confederation and who masterminded the triumph of the Constitution.

There were points at which Jensen had not seen eye to eye with Beard. He was more impressed, for instance, by the

Fathers' general outlook and ideology than by their property holdings; unlike Beard, moreover, he denied that the Confederation era was a time of serious economic difficulty. Yet he had actually strengthened the Beardian logic at more than one point, and the differences were minor in the light of the convictions which united the two in spirit and intention. The work of Merrill Jensen, like that of Beard and Parrington and J. Allen Smith before him, still balanced on the assumption that the energy behind the American Constitution was conspiratorial energy, and that the Constitution came into being by means of a coup d'état—through the plotting of a well-disciplined Toryish few against the interests of an unvigilant democratic majority.

Indeed, Merrill Jensen's *The New Nation*—published two years after the death of Charles Beard—was the last major piece of Constitution scholarship to be done in the Progressive tradition, and represented the end of an era. By that time, 1950, Beard's own notions had begun to arouse not the admiration, but the suspicion, of a new generation of postwar intellectuals.

III

A few modest little articles, case studies of ratifying conventions held in individual states in 1788, had begun appearing here and there in the regional quarterlies. In 1947 there was one by Philip Crowl on Maryland, another on North Carolina by William Pool in 1950, still another on Virginia by Robert Thomas in 1953. Such fragments, of course, could not be expected to cause much immediate stir. But these studies carried implications, similar in each case, that would prove in the long run profoundly damaging to the whole structure of Beardian scholarship and Beardian reasoning.

A major item in that reasoning had been Beard's assumption that the principle which differentiated Federalists from

Anti-Federalists was the principle of class and property interests—that the Federalists as a group were upholding one kind of class interest and defending one form of property while the Anti-Federalists, presumably, represented something else, something basically opposed. For some reason, Beard had never taken the trouble to check the Anti-Federalist side of his equation. Thomas, in his study of the delegates to the Virginia ratifying convention (where the fight had been unusually bitter), discovered that the members of both sides held property of essentially the same kind, in approximately the same amounts, and represented the same social class—the planting gentry. The other studies showed a similar pattern. In short, the conflict over ratification was apparently fought out not between classes, but between cliques of the same ruling class within these states, and whatever the conflict's "real" basis, it was not a struggle over property rights as such. Beard's "class" and "property" formula was simply indeterminate; the story had to be found elsewhere.

By 1956, Beard's *Economic Interpretation* had been set up for the *coup de grâce*. The executioner was Robert E. Brown, a professor at Michigan State who had been at work for some time implacably compiling a catalogue of the Master's offenses. In his *Charles Beard and the Constitution*, published that year, Brown tracked Beard through every page of the latter's masterpiece and laid the ax to virtually every statement of importance that Beard had made in it. There was absolutely no correlation between the Philadelphia delegates' property holdings and the way they behaved on the question of a constitution. It was not true that large numbers of adult males were disfranchised; the suffrage was remarkably liberal everywhere. Farmers as a class were by no means chronically debtors; many were creditors and many others were both. The supporters of Shays' Rebellion (the debtors' uprising in western Massachusetts which occurred during the fall and winter of 1786–1787) were certainly not united against the

Constitution; if they had been, it could never have been ratified, since the Shaysites had a clear majority at the time of the Massachusetts convention. Nor did the Philadelphia delegates know that the Continental debt would be funded at par. If they had, the banker Robert Morris, for one, would never have speculated in western lands with the thought of paying for them in depreciated Continental paper.

Not only was Beard's evidence inconclusive at all points, Brown insisted, but there were even occasions when the Master had not been above doctoring it. He edited Madison's Federalist No. 10 to eliminate all but its economic emphasis; he quoted only those passages of the Philadelphia debates that made the Fathers look least democratic; he arranged his treatment of the ratification process in an order that violated chronology, centered unjustified attention on states where hard struggles did occur, overlooked the ease with which ratification was achieved in other states, and thus created a wildly exaggerated picture of the opposition at large.

Brown's book was respectfully received; there was little inclination to dispute his arguments; no champions arose to do serious battle for the departed Beard. Some of the reviewers were a little dismayed at Brown's tone; they thought it need not have been quite so ferocious. And the book did seem to bear out the principle that any work of destruction in the realm of discourse, however necessary, must be executed within restrictions that make for a certain stultification. Richard Hofstadter remarked in this connection that Brown was "locked in such intimate embrace with his adversary that his categories are entirely dictated by Beard's assertions." Even Brown, in his way, had toyed with the "reality" theme. He had exonerated the Fathers of conspiratorial intentions but convicted Charles Beard in their place: Beard had cooked the evidence, had conspired to hide the truth.

The first effort in recent years to view the Constitution all over again in a major way, shaking off the Beardian categories and starting as it were from scratch, has been undertaken by Forrest McDonald. *We The People*, published in 1958, was the first of a planned trilogy whose design was to survey anew the entire story of how the Constitution was brought into existence. Although McDonald, like Brown, felt it necessary to show the inadequacy of Beard's conclusions, his strategy was quite different from Brown's; it was undertaken less to discredit Beard than to clear the way for his own projected treatment of the great subject. In the *Economic Interpretation*, Beard had made a number of proposals for research which he himself had not performed—and never did perform—but which would, Beard felt, further corroborate his own "frankly fragmentary" work. McDonald began by undertaking the very research which Beard had suggested, and its results convinced him that Beard had simply asked all the wrong questions.

One of the things McDonald investigated in *We The People* was an assumption upon which Beard had put a great deal of stress, the notion of a fundamental antagonism between "personalty" and "realty" interests at the time of the Philadelphia Convention. ("Personalty" was wealth based on securities, money, commerce, or manufacturing; "realty" was landed property whose owners' outlook tended to be primarily agrarian.) He found that there was no such split in the Convention. The seven men who either walked out of the Convention or else refused to sign the completed document were among the heaviest security-holders there, and represented "an all-star team of personalty interests." In state after state, moreover, there was no appreciable difference between the property holdings of Federalists and Anti-Federalists. Finally, the three states that ratified the Constitution unanimously—Delaware, New Jersey, and Georgia—were overwhelmingly dominated by agrarian interests.

Unlike Brown, McDonald was quite unwilling to write off the possibility of an economic analysis (his book's subtitle was *The Economic Origins of the Constitution*); it was just that Beard's particular economic categories led nowhere. Beard's sweeping "personalty" and "realty" classifications were meaningless, and he had deceived himself profoundly in supposing that the Federalists' property interests "knew no state boundaries" but were "truly national in scope." On these two points of difference McDonald set up an entirely new and original research scheme, and in so doing effected a really impressive conceptual maneuver. He was quite ready, in the first place, to find "economic forces" behind the movement for a constitution, but these must be sought not in "classes" or in broad categories of property but rather in the specific business interests of specific groups in specific places. The other organizing category would be the individual states themselves. The political framework within which any group had to operate was still that imposed by the state; the states were, after all, still sovereign units, and the precise relationship between economic forces and political action depended almost entirely on the special conditions within those states, conditions which varied from one to the other.

By abandoning Beard's "national" framework and recasting the entire problem on a state-by-state basis, McDonald made it possible to see with a sudden clarity things which ought to have been obvious all along. The states where ratification was achieved most readily were those that were convinced, for one reason or another, that they could not survive and prosper as independent entities; those holding out the longest were the ones most convinced that they could go it alone. The reasons for supporting ratification might vary considerably from state to state. For Georgia, an impending Indian war and the need for military protection could transcend any possible economic issue; New York, at one time imagining for itself an independent political and economic future, would finally ratify for fear of being isolated from a system which already included ten states and which might soon be joined by a seceded New York City.

The single problem of the Continental debt took different

forms in different states. New Jersey, Massachusetts, and New York had each assumed portions of the debt held by their own citizens, but New Jersey and Massachusetts found their obligations intolerably burdensome while New York did not. Massachusetts had put an excessively heavy load on its direct property and poll-tax system; thus any possibility of the debt's being funded by a new Federal government should have found both the Boston security-holder and the Shaysite debtor more than willing to support such a government—and this, it appears, is about what happened. In New York and New Jersey an additional key to the debt issue was the question of a national tariff. New York had a state tariff, which was part of a financial system worked out to service the debt, and for that reason the state had been reluctant to accept a national impost in 1786. New Jersey, on the other hand, with no ocean trade of any account and having to receive most of its imports through New York, had no such revenue, was hard pressed to maintain interest payments on its debt, and thus had everything to gain from both a national impost and a national funding system. New Jersey was one of the first to ratify, and did so unanimously.

Recognizing the importance of specific location made it also easier and more natural to appreciate the way in which particular interests in particular places might be affected by the question of a stronger national government. Boston shipping interests, for example, seem to have been less concerned in the 1780's over class ideology or general economic philosophy than over those conditions of the times which were especially bad for business. The British would not let them into the West Indies, the French were excluding their fish, and their large vessels were no longer profitable. A strong national government could create a navy whose very existence would reduce high insurance rates; it could guarantee an orderly tariff system that would remove all pressure for higher and higher state tariffs; and it could counter British and French discrimination by means of an effective navigation act. Manufacturing interests would also tend to favor the Constitution, though not necessarily on principle; the vigor of their support would depend on the size of their establishments and the extent to which they competed with England. Support from Pennsylvania iron and Connecticut textiles would be particularly energetic. So also with the wheat and tobacco farmers of the Connecticut Valley, though not for the same reason. They had to pay import taxes to New York for the goods they bought (their crops were sold there); they were heavily taxed, at the same time, to support a state-funded debt which they would be only too glad to see removed by a central government. Farmers in the Kentucky area, on the other hand, could be very suspicious of a Constitution under which northeastern shipping interests might influence the government to surrender free navigation on the Mississippi in return for a favorable trade treaty with Spain.

Forrest McDonald's work, according to him, has only just begun; years of it still lie ahead. But already a remarkable precision of detail has been brought to the subject, together with a degree of sophistication which makes the older economic approach—"tough-minded" as it once imagined itself—seem now a little wan and misty. The special internal conditions of the several states now seem fully valid as clues to the ratification policies of those states, each in its separate turn. And there is a credibility about the immediate needs and aspirations of particular groups, and the way they varied from place to place, that Beard's "interests" never quite possessed—or if they did, they had long since lost their hold on the modern mind.

And yet there are overtones in McDonald's work—for all its precise excellence, perhaps partly because of it—that have already succeeded in creating a new kind of "reality" spell. McDonald is very open-minded about all the manifold and complex and contradictory forces that converged upon the movement for a constitution. But somehow the ones he takes most seriously—the "real" forces behind the movement—were specific, particular, circumscribed, hard, and immediate. They were to be looked for mostly on the local level, because that is where one really finds things. A state—the largest permissible "reality" unit—was an agglomeration of specific, particular, immediate localities. There were interests to be served, political or economic, and they were *hard*. They were pursued rationally and without sentimentality; men came down where they did because their hard, immediate, specific interests brought them there. But are we prepared to say that the final result was just the sum—or extension—of these interests?

No doubt large enough numbers of people were convinced of the economic advantages they would gain under a new federal government that we may, thanks to Professor Mc-Donald, account for a considerable measure of the support which the Constitution received. In places where there was a balance to tip, we have a much better idea of just how it happened. Still, Merrill Jensen pointed out some time ago that the economic situation was already somewhat on the mend by 1786. There were, moreover, certain powerful states such as Virginia and New York that might very well have thrived either as independent units or in coalitions with their immediate neighbors. And conditions in general could not have been so desperate that a national government was absolutely required for solving economic problems, let alone for staving off economic collapse. The steps actually taken were not the only ones possible; there were certainly alternatives, and it is hard to believe that they would all have led to disaster.

The new approach is extremely enlightening and useful. But has it yet taken on life? When will it fully engage the question of initiative and energy? How do we account for the dedication, the force and éclat, of Federalist leadership? When all is said and done, we do not exactly refer to the "interests" of a James Madison. We wonder, instead, about the terms in which he conceives of personal fulfillment, which is not at all the same. What animates him? The nationalist movement *did* have a mystique that somehow transfigured a substantial number of its leaders. What was it like, what were its origins?

IV

The work of Merrill Jensen, done in the 1930's and 1940's, has suffered somewhat in reputation due to the sweep and vehemence of the anti-Beardian reaction. Yet that work contains perceptions which ought not to be written off in the general shuffle. They derive not so much from the over-all Beardian traditions and influences amid which Jensen wrote, as from that particular sector of the subject which he marked off and preëmpted for his own. Simply by committing himself —alone among Beardians and non-Beardians—to presenting the Confederation era as a legitimate phase of American history, entitled to be taken seriously like any other and having a positive side as well as a negative one, he has forced upon us a peculiar point of view which, by the same token, yields its own special budget of insights. For example, Jensen has been profoundly impressed by the sheer force, determination, and drive of such nationalist leaders as Hamilton, Madison, Jay, Knox, and the Morrises. This energy, he feels, created the central problem of the Confederation and was the major cause of its collapse. He deplores this, seeing in the Confederation "democratic" virtues which it probably never had, finding in the Federalists an "aristocratic" character which in actual fact was as much or more to be found in the Anti-Federalists, smelling plots everywhere, and in general shaping his nomenclature to fit his own values and preferences. But if Professor Jensen seems to have called everything by the wrong name, it is well to remember that nomenclature is not everything. The important thing—what does ring true—is that this driving "nationalist" energy was, in all probability, central to the movement that gave the United States a new government.

The other side of the picture, which does not seem to have engaged Jensen's mind half so much, was the peculiar sloth and inertia of the Anti-Federalists. Cecelia Kenyon, in a brilliant essay on these men,[3] has shown them as an amazingly reactionary lot. They were transfixed by the specter of power. It was not the power of the aristocracy that they feared, but power of any kind, democratic or otherwise, that they could not control for themselves. Their chief concern was to keep governments as limited and as closely tied to local interests as possible. Their minds could not embrace the concept of a national interest which they themselves might share and which could transcend their own parochial concerns. Republican government that went beyond the compass of state boundaries was something they could not imagine. Thus the chief difference between Federalists and Anti-Federalists had little to do with "democracy" (George Clinton and Patrick Henry were no more willing than Gouverneur Morris to trust the innate virtue of the people), but rather in the Federalists' conviction that there was such a thing as national interest and that a government could be established to care for it which was fully in keeping with republican principles. To the Federalists this was not only possible but absolutely necessary, if the nation was to avoid a future of political impotence, internal discord, and in the end foreign intervention. So far so good. But still, exactly how did such convictions get themselves generated?

Merrill Jensen has argued that the Federalists, by and large, were reluctant revolutionaries who had feared the consequences of a break with England and had joined the Revolution only when it was clear that independence was inevitable. The argument is plausible; few of the men most prominent later on as Federalists had been quite so hot for revolution

[3]"Men of Little Faith: The Anti-Federalists on the Nature of Representative Government," *William and Mary Quarterly*, XII, 3rd ser. (January 1955), pp. 3–43.

in the very beginning as Patrick Henry and Samuel Adams. But this may not be altogether fair; Adams and Henry were already veteran political campaigners at the outbreak of hostilities, while the most vigorous of the future Federalists were still mere youngsters. The argument, indeed, could be turned entirely around: the source of Federalist, or nationalist, energy was not any "distaste" for the Revolution on these men's part, but rather their profound and growing involvement in it.

Much depends here on the way one pictures the Revolution. In the beginning it simply consisted of a number of state revolts loosely directed by the Continental Congress; and for many men, absorbed in their effort to preserve the independence of their own states, it never progressed much beyond that stage even in the face of invasion. But the Revolution had another aspect, one which developed with time and left a deep imprint on those connected with it, and this was its character as a continental war effort. If there is any one feature that most unites the future leading supporters of the Constitution, it was their close engagement with this continental aspect of the Revolution. A remarkably large number of these someday Federalists were in the Continental Army, served as diplomats or key administrative officers of the Confederation government, or, as members of Congress, played leading rôles on those committees primarily responsible for the conduct of the war.

Merrill Jensen has compiled two lists, with nine names in each, of the men whom he considers to have been the leading spirits of the Federalists and Anti-Federalists respectively. It would be well to have a good look at this sample. The Federalists—Jensen calls them "nationalists"—were Robert Morris, John Jay, James Wilson, Alexander Hamilton, Henry Knox, James Duane, George Washington, James Madison, and Gouverneur Morris. Washington, Knox, and Hamilton were deeply involved in Continental military affairs; Robert Morris was Superintendent of Finance; Jay was president of the Continental Congress and minister plenipotentiary to Spain (he would later be appointed Secretary for Foreign Affairs); Wilson, Duane, and Gouverneur Morris were members of Congress, all three being active members of the war committees. The Anti-Federalist group presents a very different picture. It consisted of Samuel Adams, Patrick Henry, Richard Henry Lee, George Clinton, James Warren, Samuel Bryan, George Bryan, George Mason, and Elbridge Gerry. Only three of these—Gerry, Lee, and Adams—served in Congress, and the latter two fought consistently against any effort to give Congress executive powers. Their constant preoccupation was state sovereignty rather than national efficiency. Henry and Clinton were active war governors, concerned primarily with state rather than national problems, while Warren, Mason, and the two Bryans were essentially state politicians.

The age difference between these two groups is especially striking. The Federalists were on the average ten to twelve years younger than the Anti-Federalists. At the outbreak of the Revolution George Washington, at 44, was the oldest of the lot; six were under 35 and four were in their twenties. Of the Anti-Federalists, only three were under 40 in 1776, and one of these, Samuel Bryan, the son of George Bryan, was a boy of 16.

This age differential takes on a special significance when it is related to the career profiles of the men concerned. Nearly half of the Federalist group—Gouverneur Morris, Madison, Hamilton, and Knox—quite literally saw their careers launched in the Revolution. The remaining five—Washington, Jay, Duane, Wilson, and Robert Morris—though established in public affairs beforehand, became nationally known after 1776 and the wide public recognition which they subsequently achieved came first and foremost through their identification with the continental war effort. All of them had been united in an experience, and had formed commitments, which dissolved provincial boundaries; they had come to full public maturity in a setting which enabled ambition, public service, leadership, and self-fulfillment to be conceived, for each in his way, with a grandeur of scope unknown to any previous generation. The careers of the Anti-Federalists, on the other hand, were not only state-centered but—aside from those of Clinton, Gerry, and the young Bryan—rested heavily on events that preceded rather than followed 1776.

As exemplars of nationalist energy, two names in Professor Jensen's sample that come most readily to mind are those of Madison and Hamilton. The story of each shows a wonderfully pure line of consistency. James Madison, of an influential Virginia family but with no apparent career plans prior to 1774, assumed his first public role as a member of the Orange County Revolutionary Committee, of which his father was chairman. As a delegate from Orange County he went to the Virginia convention in 1776 and served on the committee that drafted Virginia's new constitution and bill of rights. He served in the Virginia Assembly in 1776 and 1777 but failed of reelection partly because he refused to treat his constituents to whisky. (He obviously did not have the right talents for a state politician.) In recognition of Madison's services, however, the Assembly elected him to the Governor's Council, where he served from 1778 to 1780. Patrick Henry was then Governor; the two men did not get on well and in time became bitter political enemies. At this period Madison's primary concern was with supplying and equipping the Continental Army, a concern not shared to his satisfaction by enough of his colleagues. It was then, too, that he had his first experience with finance and the problems of paper money. He was elected to the Continental Congress in 1780, and as a member of the Southern Committee was constantly preoccupied with the military operations of Nathanael Greene. The inefficiency and impotence of Congress pained him unbearably. The Virginia Assembly took a strong stand against federal taxation which Madison ignored, joining Hamilton in the unsuccessful effort to persuade the states to accept the impost of 1783. From the day he entered politics up to that time, the energies of James Madison were involved in continental rather than state problems—problems of supply, enlistment, and finance—and at every point his chief difficulties came from state parochialism, selfishness, and lack of imagination. His nationalism was hardly accidental.

The career line of Alexander Hamilton, *mutatis mutandis*, is functionally interchangeable with that of James Madison. Ambitious, full of ability, but a young man of no family and no money, Hamilton arrived in New York from the provinces at the age of 17 and in only two years would be catapulted into a brilliant career by the Revolution. At 19 he became a highly effective pamphleteer while still a student at King's College, was captain of an artillery company at 21, serving with distinction in the New York and New Jersey campaigns, and in 1777 was invited to join Washington's staff as a lieutenant-colonel. He was quickly accepted by as brilliant and aristocratic a set of youths as could be found in the country. As a staff officer he became all too familiar with the endless difficulties of keeping the Continental Army in the field from 1777 to 1780. With his marriage to Elizabeth Schuyler in 1780 he was delightedly welcomed into one of New York's leading families, and his sage advice to his father-in-law and Robert Morris on matters of finance and paper money won him the reputation of a financial expert with men who knew an expert when they saw one. He had an independent command at Yorktown. He became Treasury representative in New York in 1781, was elected to Congress in 1782, and worked closely with Madison in the fruitless and discouraging effort to create a national revenue in the face of state particularism. In the summer of 1783 he quit in despair and went back to New York. Never once throughout all this period had Alexander Hamilton been involved in purely state affairs. His career had been a continental one, and as long as the state-centered

George Clinton remained a power in New York, it was clear that this was the only kind that could have any real meaning for him. As with James Madison, Hamilton's nationalism was fully consistent with all the experience he had ever had in public life, experience whose sole meaning had been derived from the Revolution. The experience of the others—for instance that of John Jay and Henry Knox—had had much the same quality; Knox had moved from his bookstore to the command of Washington's artillery in little more than a year, while Jay's public career began with the agitation just prior to the Revolution and was a story of steady advancement in continental affairs from that time forward.

The logic of these careers, then, was in large measure tied to a chronology which did not apply in the same way to all the men in public life during the two decades of the 1770's and 1780's. A significant proportion of relative newcomers, with prospects initially modest, happened to have their careers opened up at a particular time and in such a way that their very public personalities came to be staked upon the national quality of the experience which had formed them. In a number of outstanding cases energy, initiative, talent, and ambition had combined with a conception of affairs which had grown immense in scope and promise by the close of the Revolution. There is every reason to think that a contraction of this scope, in the years that immediately followed, operated as a powerful challenge.

V

The stages through which the constitutional movement proceeded in the 1780's add up to a fascinating story in political management, marked by no little élan and dash. That movement, viewed in the light of the Federalist leaders' commitment to the Revolution, raises some nice points as to who were the "conservatives" and who were the "radicals." The spirit of unity generated by the struggle for independence had, in the eyes of those most closely involved in coördinating the effort, lapsed; provincial factions were reverting to the old provincial ways. The impulse to arrest disorder and to revive the flame of revolutionary unity may be pictured in "conservative" terms, but this becomes quite awkward when we look for terms with which to picture the other impulse, so different in nature: the urge to rest, to drift, to turn back the clock.

Various writers have said that the activities of the Federalists during this period had in them a clear element of the conspiratorial. Insofar as this refers to a strong line of political strategy, it correctly locates a key element in the movement. Yet without a growing base of popular dissatisfaction with the status quo, the Federalists could have skulked and plotted forever without accomplishing anything. We now know, thanks to recent scholarship, that numerous elements of the public were only too ripe for change. But the work of organizing such a sentiment was quite another matter; it took an immense effort of will just to get it off the ground. Though it would be wrong to think of the Constitution as something that had to be carried in the face of deep and basic popular opposition, it certainly required a series of brilliant maneuvers to escape the deadening clutch of particularism and inertia. An Anti-Federalist "no" could register on exactly the same plane as a Federalist "yes" while requiring a fraction of the energy. It was for this reason that the Federalists, even though they cannot be said to have circumvented the popular will, did have to use techniques which in their sustained drive, tactical mobility and risk-taking smacked more than a little of the revolutionary.

By 1781, nearly five years of intimate experience with the war effort had already convinced such men as Washington, Madison, Hamilton, Duane, and Wilson that something had to be done to strengthen the Continental government, at least to the point of providing it with an independent income. The ratification of the Articles of Confederation early in the year (before Yorktown) seemed to offer a new chance, and several promising steps were taken at that time. Congress organized executive departments of war, foreign affairs, and finance to replace unwieldy and inefficient committees; Robert Morris was appointed Superintendent of Finance; and a 5 per cent impost was passed which Congress urged the states to accept.

By the fall of 1782, however, the surge for increased efficiency had lost the greater part of its momentum. Virginia had changed its mind about accepting the impost, Rhode Island having been flatly opposed all along, and it became apparent that as soon as the treaty with England (then being completed) was ratified, the sense of common purpose which the war had created would be drained of its urgency. At this point Hamilton and the Morrises, desperate for a solution, would have been quite willing to use the discontent of an unpaid army as a threat to coerce the states out of their obstructionism, had not Washington refused to lend himself to any such scheme. Madison and Hamilton thereupon joined forces in Congress to work out a revenue bill whose subsidiary benefits would be sufficiently diffuse to gain it general support among the states. But in the end the best that could be managed was a new plan for a 5 per cent impost, the revenues of which would be collected by state-appointed officials. Once more an appeal, drafted by Madison was sent to the states urging them to accept the new impost, and Washington wrote a circular in support of it. The effort was in vain. The army, given one month's pay in cash and three in certificates, reluctantly dispersed, and the Confederation government, with no sanctions of coercion and no assured revenues, now reached a new level of impotence. In June, 1783, Alexander Hamilton, preparing to leave Congress to go back to private life, wrote in discouragement and humiliation to Nathanael Greene:

There is so little disposition either in or out of Congress
to give solidity to our national system that there is no

motive to a man to lose his time in the public service, who has no other view than to promote its welfare. Experience must convince us that our present establishments are Utopian before we shall be ready to part with them for better.

Whether or not the years between 1783 and 1786 should be viewed as a "critical period" depends very much on whose angle they are viewed from. Although it was a time of economic depression, the depressed conditions were not felt in all areas of economic life with the same force, nor were they nearly as damaging in some localities as in others; the interdependence of economic enterprise was not then what it would become later on, and a depression in Massachusetts did not necessarily imply one in Virginia, or even in New York. Moreover, there were definite signs of improvement by 1786. Nor can it necessarily be said that government on the state level lacked vitality. Most of the states were addressing their problems with energy and decision. There were problems everywhere, of course, many of them very grave, and in some cases (those of New Jersey and Connecticut in particular) solutions seemed almost beyond the individual state's resources. Yet it would be wrong, as Merrill Jensen points out, to assume that no solutions were possible within the framework which then existed. It is especially important to remember that when most people thought of "the government" they were not thinking of Congress at all, but of their own state legislature. For them, therefore, it was by no means self-evident that the period through which they were living was one of drift and governmental impotence.

But through the eyes of men who had come to view the states collectively as a "country" and to think in continental terms, things looked altogether different. From their viewpoint the Confederation was fast approaching the point of ruin. Fewer and fewer states were meeting their requisition payments, and Congress could not even pay its bills. The states refused to accept any impost which they themselves could not control, and even if all the rest accepted, the continued refusal of New York (which was not likely to change) would render any impost all but valueless. Local fears and jealousies blocked all efforts to establish uniform regulation of commerce, even though some such regulation seemed indispensable. A number of the states, New York in particular, openly ignored the peace treaty with England and passed discriminatory legislation against former Loyalists; consequently England, using as a pretext Congress' inability to enforce the treaty, refused to surrender the northwest posts. Morale in Congress was very low as members complained that lack of a quorum prevented them most of the time from transacting any business; even when a quorum was present, a few negative votes could block important legislation indefinitely. Any significant change, or any substantial increase in the power of Congress, required unanimous approval by the states, and as things then stood this had become very remote. Finally, major states such as New York and Virginia were simply paying less and less attention to Congress. The danger was not so much that of a split with the Confederation—Congress lacked the strength that would make any such "split" seem very urgent—but rather a policy of neglect that would just allow Congress to wither away from inactivity.

These were the conditions that set the stage for a fresh effort—the Annapolis Convention of 1786—to strengthen the continental government. The year before, Madison had arranged a conference between Maryland and Virginia for the regulation of commerce on the Potomac, and its success had led John Tyler and Madison to propose a measure in the Virginia Assembly that would give Congress power to regulate commerce throughout the Confederation. Though nothing came of it, a plan was devised in its place whereby the several states would be invited to take part in a convention to be held at Annapolis in September, 1786, for the purpose of discussing commercial problems. The snapping-point came when delegates from only five states appeared. The rest either distrusted one another's intentions (the northeastern states doubted the southerners' interest in commerce) or else suspected a trick to strengthen the Confederation government at their expense. It was apparent that no serious action could be taken at that time. But the dozen delegates who did come (Hamilton and Madison being in their forefront) were by definition those most concerned over the state of the national government, and they soon concluded that their only hope of saving it lay in some audacious plenary gesture. It was at this meeting, amid the mortification of still another failure, that they planned the Philadelphia Convention.

The revolutionary character of this move—though some writers have correctly perceived it—has been obscured both by the stateliness of historical retrospection and by certain legal peculiarities which allowed the proceeding to appear a good deal less subversive than it actually was. The "report" of the Annapolis meeting was actually a call, drafted by Hamilton and carefully edited by Madison, for delegates of all the states to meet in convention at Philadelphia the following May for the purpose of revising the Articles of Confederation. Congress itself transmitted the call, and in so doing was in effect being brought to by-pass its own constituted limits. On the one hand, any effort to change the government within the rules laid down by the Articles would have required a unanimous approval which could never be obtained. But on the other hand, the very helplessness which the several states had imposed upon the central government meant in practice that the states were sovereign and could do anything they pleased with it. It was precisely this that the nationalists now prepared to exploit: this legal paradox had hitherto prevented the growth of strong loyalty to the existing Confederation and could presently allow that same Confederation, through the action of the states, to be undermined in the deceptive odor of legitimacy. Thus the Beardian school of constitutional thought, for all its errors of economic analysis and its transposing of ideological semantics, has called attention to one element— the element of subversion—that is actually entitled to some consideration.

But if the movement had its plotters, balance requires us to add that the "plot" now had a considerable measure of potential support, and that the authority against which the plot was aimed had become little more than a husk. Up to this time every nationalist move, including the Annapolis Convention, had been easily blocked. But things were now happening in such a way as to tip the balance and to offer the nationalists for the first time a better-than-even chance of success. There had been a marked improvement in business, but shippers in Boston, New York, and Philadelphia were still in serious trouble. Retaliatory measures against Great Britain through state legislation had proved ineffective and useless; there was danger, at the same time, that local manufacturing interests might be successful in pushing through high state tariffs. In the second place, New York's refusal to reconsider a national impost, except on terms that would have removed its effectiveness, cut the ground from under the moderates who had argued that, given only a little time, everything could be worked out. This did not leave much alternative to a major revision of the national government. Then there were Rhode Island's difficulties with inflationary paper money. Although that state's financial schemes actually made a certain amount of sense, they provided the nationalists with wonderful propaganda and helped to create an image of parochial irresponsibility.

The most decisive event of all was Shays' Rebellion in the fall and winter of 1786–1787. It was this uprising of hard-pressed rural debtors in western Massachusetts that frightened moderate people everywhere and convinced them of the need for drastic remedies against what looked like anarchy. The important thing was not so much the facts of the case as the impression which it created outside Massachusetts. The Shaysites had no intention of destroying legitimate government or of redistributing property, but the fact that large numbers of people could very well imagine them doing such things added a note of crisis which was all to the Federalists' advantage. Even the levelheaded Washington was disturbed, and his apprehensions were played upon quite knowingly by Madison, Hamilton, and Knox in persuading him to attend the Philadelphia Convention. Actually the Federalists and Shaysites had been driven to action by much the same conditions; in Massachusetts their concern with the depressed state of trade and the tax burden placed them for all practical purposes on the same side, and there they remained from first to last.

Once the balance had been tipped in enough states, to the point of a working consensus on the desirability of change, a second principle came into effect. Unless a state were absolutely opposed—as in the extreme case of Rhode Island—to any change in the Articles of Confederation, it was difficult to ignore the approaching Philadelphia Convention as had been done with the Annapolis Convention: the occasion was taking on too much importance. There was thus the danger, for such a state, of seeing significant decisions made without having its interests consulted. New York, with strong Anti-Federalist biases but also with a strong nationalist undercurrent, was not quite willing to boycott the convention. Governor Clinton's solution was to send as delegates two rigid state particularists, John Yates and Robert Lansing, along with the nationalist Hamilton, to make sure that Hamilton would not accomplish anything.

We have already seen that nineteenth century habits of thought created a ponderous array of stereotypes around the historic Philadelphia conclave of 1787. Twentieth century thought and scholarship, on the other hand, had the task of breaking free from them, and to have done so is a noteworthy achievement. And yet one must return to the point that stereotypes themselves require some form of explanation. The legend of a transcendent effort of statesmanship, issuing forth in a miraculously perfect instrument of government, emerges again and again despite all efforts either to conjure it out of existence or to give it some sort of rational linkage with mortal affairs. Why should the legend be so extraordinarily durable, and was there anything so special about the circumstances that set it on its way so unerringly and so soon?

The circumstances *were*, in fact, special; given a set of delegates of well over average ability, the Philadelphia meeting provides a really classic study in the sociology of intellect. Divine accident, though in some measure present in men's doings always, is not required as a part of this particular equation. The key conditions were all present in a pattern that virtually guaranteed for the meeting an optimum of effectiveness. A sufficient number of states were represented so that the delegates could, without strain, realistically picture themselves as thinking, acting, and making decisions in the name of the entire nation. They themselves, moreover, represented interests throughout the country that were diverse enough, and they had enough personal prestige at home, that they could act in the assurance of having their decisions treated at least with respectful attention. There had also been at work a remarkably effective process of self-selection, as to both men and states. Rhode Island ignored the convention, and as a result its position was not even considered there. There were leading state particularists such as Patrick Henry and Richard Henry Lee who were elected as delegates but refused to serve. The Anti-Federalist position, indeed, was hardly represented at all, and the few men who did represent it had surprisingly little to say. Yates and Lansing simply left before the convention was over. Thus a group already predisposed in a national direction could proceed unhampered by the friction of basic opposition in its midst. This made it possible for the delegates to "try on" various alternatives without having to remain accountable for everything they said. At the same time, being relieved from all outside pressures meant that the only way a man could expect to make a real difference in the convention's deliberations was to reach, through main persuasion, other men *or* considerable ability and experience. Participants and audience were therefore one, and this in itself imposed standards of debate which were quite exacting. In such a setting the best minds in the convention were accorded an authority which they would not have had in political debates aimed at an indiscriminate public.

Thus the elements of secrecy, the general inclination for a national government, and the process whereby the delegates came to terms with their colleagues—appreciating their requirements and adjusting to their interests—all combined to produce a growing esprit de corps. As initial agreements were worked out, it became exceedingly difficult for the Philadelphia delegates not to grow more and more committed to the product of their joint efforts. Indeed, this was in all likelihood the key mechanism, more important than any other in explaining not only the peculiar genius of the main compromises but also the general fitness of the document as a whole. That is, a group of two or more intelligent men who are subject to no cross-pressures and whose principal commitment is to the success of an idea, are perfectly capable—as in our scientific communities of today—of performing what appear to be prodigies of intellect. Moving, as it were, in the same direction with a specific purpose, they can function at maximum efficiency. It was this that the historians of the nineteenth century did in their way see, and celebrated with sweeping rhetorical flourishes, when they took for granted that if an occasion of this sort could not call forth the highest level of statesmanship available, then it was impossible to imagine another that could.

Once the Philadelphia Convention had been allowed to meet and the delegates had managed, after more than three months of work, to hammer out a document that the great majority of them could sign, the political position of the Federalists changed dramatically. Despite the major battles still impending, for practical purposes they now had the initiative. The principal weapon of the Anti-Federalists—inertia—had greatly declined in effectiveness, for with the new program in motion it was no longer enough simply to argue that a new federal government was unnecessary. They would have to take positive steps in blocking it; they would have to arouse the people and convince them that the Constitution represented a positive danger.

Moreover, the Federalists had set the terms of ratification in such a way as to give the maximum advantage to energy and purpose; the key choices, this time, had been so arranged that they would fall right. Only nine states had to ratify before the Constitution would go into effect. Not only would this rule out the possibility of one or two states holding up the entire effort, but it meant that the Confederation would be automatically destroyed as an alternative before the difficult battles in New York and Virginia had to be faced. (By then, Patrick Henry in Virginia would have nothing but a vague alliance with North Carolina to offer as a counter-choice.) Besides, there was good reason to believe that at least four or five states, and possibly as many as seven, could be counted as safe, which meant that serious fighting in the first phase would be limited to two or three states. And finally, conditions were so set that the "snowball" principle would at each successive point favor the Federalists.

As for the actual process of acceptance, ratification would be done through state conventions elected for the purpose. Not only would this circumvent the vested interests of the legislatures and the ruling coteries that frequented the state capitals, but it gave the Federalists two separate chances to make their case—once to the people and once to the conventions. If the elected delegates were not initially disposed to do the desired thing, there was still a chance, after the convention met, of persuading them. Due partly to the hampering factor of transportation and distance, delegates had to have considerable leeway of choice and what amounted to quasi-plenipotentiary powers. Thus there could be no such thing as a fully "instructed" delegation, and members might meanwhile remain susceptible to argument and conversion. The convention device, moreover, enabled the Federalists to run as delegates men who would not normally take part in state politics.

The revolutionary verve and ardor of the Federalists, their resources of will and energy, their willingness to scheme tirelessly, campaign everywhere, and sweat and agonize over every vote meant in effect that despite all the hairbreadth squeezes and rigors of the struggle, the Anti-Federalists would lose every crucial test. There was, to be sure, an Anti-Federalist effort. But with no program, no really viable commitments, and little purposeful organization, the Anti-Federalists somehow always managed to move too late and with too little. They would sit and watch their great stronghold, New York, being snatched away from them despite a two-to-one Anti-Federalists majority in a convention presided over by their own chief, George Clinton. To them, the New York Federalists must have seemed possessed of the devil. The Federalists' convention men included Alexander Hamilton, James Duane, John Jay, and Robert Livingston—who knew, as did everyone else, that the new government was doomed unless Virginia and New York joined it. They insisted on debating the Constitution section by section instead of as a whole, which meant that they could out-argue the Anti-Federalists on every substantive issue and meanwhile delay the vote until New Hampshire and Virginia had had a chance to ratify. (Madison and Hamilton had a horse relay system in readiness to rush the Virginia news northward as quickly as possible.) By the time the New York convention was ready to act, ten others had ratified, and at the final moment Hamilton and his allies spread the chilling rumor that New York City was about to secede from the state. The Anti-Federalists, who had had enough, directed a chosen number of their delegates to cross over, and solemnly capitulated.

In the end, of course, everyone "crossed over." The speed with which this occurred once the continental revolutionists had made their point, and the ease with which the Constitution so soon became an object of universal veneration, still stands as one of the minor marvels of American history. But the document did contain certain implications, of a quasi-philosophical nature, that make the reasons for this ready consensus not so very difficult to find. It established a national government whose basic outlines were sufficiently congenial to the underlying commitments of the whole culture—republicanism and capitalism—that the likelihood of its being the subject of a true ideological clash was never very real. That the Constitution should mount guard over the rights of property —"realty," "personalty," or any other kind—was questioned by nobody. There had certainly been a struggle, a long and exhausting one, but we should not be deceived as to its nature. It was not fought on economic grounds; it was not a matter of ideology; it was not, in the fullest and most fundamental sense, even a struggle between nationalism and localism. The key struggle was between inertia and energy; with inertia overcome, everything changed.

There were, of course, lingering objections and misgivings; many of the problems involved had been genuinely puzzling and difficult; and there remained doubters who had to be converted. But then the perfect bridge whereby all could become Federalists within a year was the addition of a Bill of Rights. After the French Revolution, anti-constitutionalism in France would be a burning issue for generations; in America, an anti-constitutional party was undreamed of after 1789. With the Bill of Rights, the remaining opponents of the new system could say that, ever watchful of tyranny, they had now got what they wanted. Moreover, the Young Men of the Revolution might at last imagine, after a dozen years of anxiety, that *their* Revolution had been a success.

BILL OF RIGHTS

Leonard W. Levy

THE BILL OF RIGHTS consists of the first ten amendments to
the Constitution of the United States. Congress submitted
those amendments to the states for ratification on September
25, 1789, and the requisite number of state legislatures had
ratified them by December 15, 1791. The triumph of individual
liberty against government power, as epitomized by the Bill
of Rights, is one of our history's noblest and most enduringly
important themes. Yet James Madison, justly remembered as
the "father" of the Bill of Rights, privately referred on August
19, 1789 to the "nauseous project of amendments." He had
proposed the Bill of Rights, in part, because "It will kill the
opposition everywhere. . . ." In this attitude lies a suggestion
that party politics saturated the making of the first ten amendments. Thomas Jefferson, who must have been profoundly
gratified by the ratification of the amendments, which he had
urged, was the secretary of state who officially notified the
governors of the states that ratification was an accomplished
fact; he had the honor, he wrote, of enclosing copies of an
act "concerning certain fisheries," another establishing the post
office, and "the ratifications by three fourths of the . . . States,
of certain articles in addition and amendment of the Constitution. . . ." The history of the Bill of Rights from its rejection
by the Constitutional Convention in Philadelphia to its belated
ratification is not as passionless, because the omission of a
bill of rights in the original Constitution had been the most
important obstacle in the way of its adoption by the states.

The omission of a bill of rights was a deliberate act of the

From *Encyclopedia of American Political History*, ed. Jack P. Greene
(New York: Charles Scribner's Sons, 1984), vol. 2, pp. 104–25.

Constitutional Convention. The Convention's work was almost done when it received from the Committee on Style copies of the proposed Constitution and the letter by which the Convention would submit it to Congress. The major task that remained was to adopt, engross, and sign the finished document. The weary delegates, after a hot summer's work in Philadelphia, were eager to return home. At that point, on September 12, 1787, George Mason of Virginia remarked that he "wished the plan had been prefaced by a Bill of Rights," because it would "give great quiet" to the people. Mason thought that with the states' bills of rights as models, "a bill might be prepared in a few hours." He made no stirring speech for civil liberties in general or any rights in particular. He did not even argue the need for a bill of rights or move the adoption of one, although he offered to second a motion if one were made. Elbridge Gerry of Massachusetts then moved for a committee to prepare a bill of rights, and Mason seconded the motion. Roger Sherman of Connecticut observed that the rights of the people should be secured if necessary, but because the Constitution did not repeal the bills of rights of the states, the Convention need not do anything. Without further debate the delegates, voting by states, defeated the motion 10–0. Two days later, after the states unanimously defeated a motion by Mason to delete from the Constitution a ban on ex post facto laws by Congress, Charles Pinckney of South Carolina, seconded by Gerry, moved to insert a declaration "that the liberty of the Press should be inviolably observed." Sherman laconically replied, "It is unnecessary. The power of Congress does not extend to the Press," and the motion lost 7–4. Three days later the Convention adjourned.

In the Congress of the Confederation, Richard Henry Lee of Virginia moved that a bill of rights, which he had adapted from his own state's constitution, be added to the federal Constitution. Lee was less interested in the adoption of a bill of rights than in defeating the Constitution. Amendments recommended by Congress required ratification by all the state legislatures, not just nine state ratifying conventions. Lee's motion was defeated, but it showed that, from the start of the ratification controversy, the omission of a bill of rights became an Antifederalist mace with which to smash the Constitution. Its opponents sought to prevent ratification and exaggerated the bill-of-rights issue because it was one with which they could enlist public support. Their prime loyalty belonged to states' rights, not civil rights.

Mason, the author of the celebrated Virginia Declaration of Rights of 1776, soon wrote his influential "Objections to the Constitution," which began, "There is no Declaration of Rights. . . ." The sincerity of Mason's desire for a bill of rights is beyond question, but he had many other reasons for opposing the Constitution. Almost two weeks before, on September 12, when he raised the issue of a bill of rights, he had declared "that he would sooner chop off his right hand than put it to the Constitution as it now stands." A bill of rights might protect individuals against the national government, but it would not protect the states. He believed that the new government would diminish state powers and by the exercise of its commerce power could "ruin" the southern states; the control of commerce by a mere majority vote of Congress was, to Mason, "an insuperable objection." But the lack of a bill of rights proved to be the most powerful argument against ratification of the Constitution in the Antifederalist armory.

Why did the Constitutional Convention omit a bill of rights? No delegate opposed one in principle. As George Washington informed Lafayette, "there was not a member of the Convention, I believe, who had the least objection to what is contended for by the advocates for a Bill of Rights. . . ." All the framers were civil libertarians as well as experienced politicians who had the confidence of their constituents and the state legislatures that elected them. Even the foremost opponents of ratification praised the make-up of the Convention.

Mason himself, for example, wrote that "America has certainly upon this occasion drawn forth her first characters . . . of the purest intentions"; and Patrick Henry, who led the Antifederalists in Virginia, conceded that the states had trusted the "object of revising the Confederation to the greatest, the best, and most enlightened of our citizens." Their liberality of spirit is suggested by the fact that many—Protestants all and including the entire Virginia delegation—made a point of attending divine service at the Roman Catholic St. Mary's Chapel. As Washington recorded in his diary, "Went to the Romish church to high mass." How could such an "assembly of demigods," as Jefferson called them, neglect the liberties of the people?

On July 26 the Convention had adjourned until August 6 to permit a Committee of Detail to frame a "constitution conformable to the Resolutions passed by the Convention." The committee, consisting of six men including Edmund Randolph of Virginia, James Wilson of Pennsylvania, and Oliver Ellsworth of Connecticut, generously construed its charge by acting as a miniature convention. Introducing a number of significant changes, such as the explicit enumeration of the powers of Congress, the committee, without recommendations from the Convention, decided on a preamble. Randolph left a fragmentary record of the committee's decision that the preamble did not seem a proper place for a philosophic statement of the ends of government because "we are not working on the natural rights of men not yet gathered into society" but upon rights "modified by society and interwoven with what we call . . . the rights of states." According to American revolutionary theory, the natural rights to which Randolph referred were possessed by individuals in the state of nature, which existed before they voluntarily contracted with each other to establish a government in order to secure their rights. In the state of nature, when only the law of nature governed, the theory posited that—as the first section of the Virginia Declaration of Rights stated—"all men are by nature equally free and independent, and have certain inherent rights, of which, when they enter into a state of society, they cannot, by any compact, deprive or divest their posterity; namely, the enjoyment of life and liberty, with the means of acquiring and possessing property, and pursuing and obtaining happiness and safety." The adoption of the state constitutions having ended the state of nature, there was no need to enumerate the rights reserved to the people—or so the framers of the Constitution reasoned.

On the other hand they recognized that the existence of organized society and government required the affirmation of certain rights that did not exist in the state of nature but that served to protect natural rights. Trial by jury, for example, was unknown in the state of nature but necessary for the protection of one's life, liberty, and property. Accordingly the framers recognized a class of rights "modified by society," just as they recognized that the legitimate powers of government that did not belong to the central government of the Union could be called "the rights of the states." The principal task of the Convention was to provide for an effective national government by redistributing the powers of government. Thus the Committee of Detail, when enumerating the powers of Congress, began with the power to tax and the power to regulate commerce among the states and with foreign nations (the two great powers that the Articles of Confederation had withheld from Congress) and ended with an omnibus clause that granted implied powers: "And to make all laws that shall be necessary and proper for carrying into execution the foregoing powers, and all other powers vested, by this Constitution, in the government of the United States, or in any department thereof." That "necesary and proper" clause was the most formidable in the array of national powers, therefore the most controversial, and the one most responsible later for the demand for a bill of rights to ensure that the United States did not violate the rights of the people or of the states.

The Committee of Detail, again on its own initiative, recommended some rights ("modified by society"), among them trial by jury in criminal cases, a tight definition of treason to prevent improper convictions, a ban on titles of nobility (a way of guaranteeing against a privileged class), freedom of speech and debate for members of the legislature, and a guarantee that the citizens of each state should have the same privileges and immunities as citizens in other states. In addition, the committee introduced the clause guaranteeing to each state a republican form of government. In the minds of the framers, many provisions of the Constitution had a libertarian character—the election of public officials, the representative system, the separation of powers among three branches of government, and the requirement that revenue and appropriation measures originate in the House of Representatives, a protection of the natural right to property and a bar against taxation without representation. During the controversy over the ratification of the Constitution, when the omission of a bill of rights was the major issue, many framers argued, as did Hamilton in *The Federalist* number 84, "that the Constitution is itself, in every rational sense, and to every useful purpose, a Bill of Rights."

All the rights recommended by the Committee of Detail eventually found their way into the Constitution, but Charles Pinckney believed that the committee had neglected several others that also deserved constitutional recognition. On August 20 he recommended "sundry propositions," including a guarantee of the writ of habeas corpus, which protected citizens from arbitrary arrest; an injunction that the liberty of the press should be "inviolably preserved"; a ban on maintaining an army in time of peace except with the consent of Congress; an explicit subordination of the military to the civil power; a prohibition on the quartering of troops in private homes during peacetime; and a ban on religious tests as a qualification for any U.S. office.

None of these provisions secured what theoreticians re-

garded as natural rights. The freedoms of speech and conscience were natural rights, but the liberty of the press was
probably distinguishable as a right that did not exist in the
state of nature. If liberty of the press was a natural right the
Convention acted consistently when voting that its protection
was unnecessary. Similarly the ban on religious tests, though
protecting the right of conscience, was another example of
what Randolph had called a right "modified by society," not
preexisting it. Significantly Pinckney had not recommended
a protection of freedom or religion or of speech. Without debate or consideration the Convention referred his proposals
to the Committee of Detail, but it made no recommendations
on any of them.

On the floor of the Convention, Gerry moved that Congress
should be denied the power to pass bills of attainder and ex
post facto laws. The motion passed with hardly any discussion.
Bills of attainder were legislative declarations of the guilt of
individuals and legislative imposition of criminal penalties,
without the usual judicial proceedings. No instrument of the
criminal law was more dreaded or violative of the fair procedures associated with trial by jury than a bill of attainder,
the most expeditious way of condemning political opponents.
Ex post facto laws in the field of criminal law were nearly as
notorious and as unfair, for they were legislative acts that
made criminal any conduct that did not constitute a crime
at the time committed, or acts that retroactively increased the
penalty for a crime or changed the rules of evidence in order
to obtain a conviction. With little debate the Convention also
placed prohibitions on the power of the states to enact bills
of attainder and ex post facto laws. Some delegates, including
George Mason, opposed the ban on the latter because they did
not wish to limit the power of the states to enact retroactive
legislation in civil cases, and they insisted, against the authority of Sir William Blackstone's *Commentaries*, that ex post
facto laws included civil legislation as well as criminal. The

Supreme Court in 1798 would settle the matter in favor of the Blackstonian interpretation.

Bills of attainder and ex post facto laws, being legislative enactments, came into existence after the people had compacted to form a government. Banning such enactments, therefore, constituted means for the protection of natural rights, but the bans did not protect natural rights as such. The same may be said of protecting the cherished writ of habeas corpus as a device for ensuring the personal liberty of an individual wrongfully imprisoned. After the Convention unanimously adopted the Committee of Detail's recommendation for a clause on trial by jury in criminal cases, Pinckney urged the Convention to secure the benefit of the writ as well, and by a vote of 7–3 a habeas corpus clause was adopted. Pinckney also moved a prohibition on religious tests, which the Convention summarily adopted by unanimous vote. In so doing the Convention demonstrated a rare liberality of spirit, because all the framers but those who represented New York and Virginia came from states that had constitutions discriminating against some religious denominations by imposing as a qualification for public office some religious test. In Pennsylvania, for example, a state having a constitution that contained the broadest guarantee of religious freedom and a provision that no man acknowledging God should be deprived of any civil right on account of his religion, the oath of office required an acknowledgment of the divine inspiration of the New Testament. A Jew from Philadelphia petitioned the Constitutional Convention not to frame a similar oath of office imposing a civil disability upon him. Unitarians, Deists, and Roman Catholics suffered from various religious disabilities in many states. By prohibiting religious tests the Convention showed a greater regard for religious liberty than most states; yet the Convention did not protect religious liberty itself.

Thus, all the protections written into the Constitution were means of vindicating natural rights, but no natural rights were constitutionally protected. The overwhelming majority of the Convention believed, as Sherman succinctly declared, "It is unnecessary." Why was it unnecessary, given the fact that the Convention recommended a new and powerful national government that could operate directly on individuals? The framers believed that the national government could exercise only enumerated powers or powers necessary to carry out those enumerated, and no provision of the Constitution authorized the government to act on any natural rights. A bill of rights would restrict national powers; but, as Hamilton declared, such a bill would be "dangerous" as well as unnecessary because it "would contain various exceptions to powers not granted and, on this very account, would afford a colorable pretext to claim more than were granted. For why declare that things shall not be done which there is no power to do? Why, for instance, should it be said that the liberty of the press shall not be restrained, when no power is given by which restrictions may be imposed?"

Hamilton expressed a standard Federalist position, echoing other framers and advocates of ratification. Excluding a bill of rights from the Constitution was fundamental to the constitutional theory of the framers. James Wilson, whose influence at the Convention had been second only to that of Madison, led the ratificationist forces in Pennsylvania and several times sought to explain the omission of a bill of rights. The people of the states, he declared, had vested in their governments all powers and rights "which they did not in explicit terms reserve," but the case was different as to a federal government whose authority rested on positive grants of power expressed in the Constitution. For the federal government, "the reverse of the proposition prevails, and everything which is not given, is reserved" to the people or the states. That distinction, Wilson argued, answered those who believed that the omission of a bill of rights was a defect. Its inclusion would have been "absurd," because a bill of rights stipulated the reserved rights of the people, whereas the function of the Constitution was to provide for the existence of the federal government rather than enumerate rights not divested. Like Hamilton and other Federalists, Wilson believed that a formal declaration on freedom of the press or religion, over which Congress had no powers whatsoever, could "imply" that some degree of power had been granted because of the attempt to define its extent. Wilson also insisted on the impossibility of enumerating and reserving all the rights of the people. "A bill of rights annexed to a constitution," he added, "is an enumeration of the powers reserved. If we attempt an enumeration, everything that is not enumerated is presumed to be given. The consequence is, that an imperfect enumeration would throw all implied powers into the scale of the government; and the rights of the people would be rendered incomplete."

Civil liberties, the supporters of the Constitution believed, faced real dangers from the possibility of repressive state action, but that was a matter to be guarded against by state bills of rights. They also argued, inconsistently, that some states had no bills of rights but were as free as those with bills of rights. They were as free because personal liberty, to Federalist theoreticians, depended not on "parchment provisions," which Hamilton called inadequate in "a struggle with public necessity," but on public opinion, an extended republic, a pluralistic society of competing interests, and a free and limited government structured to prevent any interest from becoming an overbearing majority.

The fact that six states had no bills of rights, and that none had a comprehensive list of guarantees, provided the supporters of ratification with the argument, made by Wilson among others, that an imperfect bill of rights was worse than none at all because the omission of some rights might justify their infringement by implying an unintended grant of government power. The record was not reassuring; the states had very imperfect bills of rights, which proved to be ineffective when confronted by "public necessity," and the state governments did in fact abridge rights that had not been explicitly reserved.

Virginia's Declaration of Rights, for example, did not ban bills of attainder. In 1778 the Virginia assembly adopted a bill of attainder and outlawry, drafted by Jefferson at the instigation of Governor Patrick Henry, against a reputed cutthroat Tory, one Josiah Philips, and some fifty unnamed "associates." By legislative enactment they were condemned for treason and murder, and on failure to surrender were subject to being killed by anyone. At the Virginia ratifying convention, Edmund Randolph, irked beyond endurance by Henry's assaults on the Constitution as dangerous to personal liberties, recalled with "horror" the "shocking" attainder. When Henry defended the attainder, John Marshall, who supported ratification without a bill of rights, declared, "Can we pretend to the enjoyment of political freedom or security, when we are told that a man has been, by an act of Assembly, struck out of existence without a trial by jury, without examination, without being confronted with his accusers and witnesses, without the benefits of the law of the land?"

The framers of the Constitution tended to be skeptical about the value of "parchment barriers" against "overbearing majorities," as Madison said. He had seen repeated violations of bills of rights in every state. Experience proved the "inefficacy of a bill of rights to those occasions when its control is most needed," he said. In Virginia, for example, despite an explicit protection of the rights of conscience, the legislature had favored an establishment of religion, which was averted only because Madison turned the tide of opinion against the bill. As realists the framers believed that constitutional protections of rights meant little during times of popular hysteria; any member of the Constitutional Convention could have cited examples of gross abridgments of civil liberties in states that had bills of rights.

Virginia's bill was imperfect not just because it lacked a ban on bills of attainder. The much vaunted Declaration of Rights of Virginia also omitted the freedoms of speech, assembly, and petition; the right to the writ of habeas corpus; the right to grand jury proceedings; the right to counsel; separation of church and state; and freedom from double jeopardy and from ex post facto laws. The rights omitted were as numerous and important as those included. Twelve states, including Vermont, had framed constitutions, and the only right secured by all was trial by jury in criminal cases. Although all protected religious liberty, five either permitted or provided for an establishment of religion. Two states passed over a free press guarantee. Four neglected to ban excessive fines, excessive bail, compulsory self-incrimination, and general search warrants. Five ignored protections for the rights of assembly, petition, counsel, and trial by jury in civil cases. Seven omitted a prohibition of ex post facto laws. Nine failed to provide for grand jury proceedings, and nine failed to condemn bills of attainder. Ten said nothing about freedom of speech, while eleven were silent on double jeopardy. Whether omissions implied a power to violate, they seemed, in Federalist minds, to raise dangers that could be prevented by avoiding an unnecessary problem entirely: omit a bill of rights when forming a federal government of limited powers.

That the framers of the Constitution actually believed their own arguments purporting to justify the omission of a bill of rights is difficult to credit. Some of the points they made were patently absurd, like the insistence that the inclusion of a bill of rights would be dangerous and, on historical grounds, unsuitable. The last point most commonly turned up in the claim that bills of rights were appropriate in England but not in America. Magna Carta, the Petition of Right of 1628, and the Bill of Rights of 1689 had been grants wrested from kings to secure royal assent to certain liberties, and therefore had "no application to constitutions . . . founded upon the power of the people" who surrendered nothing and retained everything.

That argument, made in *Federalist* number 84 and by leading ratificationists as sophisticated as Wilson and Oliver Ellsworth of Connecticut, was so porous that it could persuade no one. Excepting Rhode Island and Connecticut, the two corporate colonies that retained their charters (with all royal references deleted), eleven states had framed written constitutions during the Revolution, and seven drew up bills of rights; even the four without such bills inserted in their constitutions provisions normally found in a bill of rights.

To imply that bills of rights were un-American or unnecessary merely because in America the people were the source of all power was unhistorical. Over a period of a century and a half America had become accustomed to the idea that government existed by consent of the governed; that people created government; that they created it by written compact; that the compact constituted fundamental law; that the government must be subject to such limitations as are necessary for the security of the rights of the people; and, usually, that the reserved rights of the people were enumerated in bills of rights. Counting Vermont (an independent republic from 1777 until its admission to the Union in 1791), eight states had bills of rights, notwithstanding any opinion that such bills properly belonged only in a compact between a king and his subjects. The dominant theory in the United States from the time of the Revolution was that the fundamental law limited all branches of the government, not just the crown as in England, where the great liberty documents did not limit the legislative power.

When Randolph for the Committee of Detail alluded to the fact that "we are not working on the natural rights of men not yet gathered into society," he was thinking of the framing of the state constitutions. The constitution of Wilson's state began with an elaborate preamble, the first words of which established the proposition that "all government ought to be instituted . . . to enable the individuals who compose [the commonwealth] to enjoy their natural rights . . ."; this preamble was followed by as comprehensive a "Declaration of the Rights of the Inhabitants" as existed in any state. Yet Wilson repeatedly informed Pennsylvania's ratifying convention that rights and liberties could be claimed only in a contract between king and subjects, not when "the fee simple of freedom and government is declared to be in the people." Governor Randolph at the Virginia ratifying convention merely exaggerated when claiming that the Virginia Declaration of Rights "has never secured us against any danger; it has been repeatedly disregarded and violated." But Randolph's rhetoric became unpardonable when he declared that although a bill of rights to limit the king's prerogative made sense in England, "Our situation is radically different from that of the people of England. What have we to do with bills of rights? . . . A bill of rights, therefore, accurately speaking, is quite useless, if not dangerous to a republic." But at the Constitutional Convention Randolph had been able to distinguish natural rights from some rights modified by society.

That supporters of the Constitution could ask, "What have we to do with a bill of rights?" suggests that they had made a colossal error of judgment, which they compounded by refusing to admit it. Their single-minded purpose of creating an effective national government had exhausted their energies and good sense, and when they found themselves on the defensive, accused of threatening the liberties of the people, their frayed nerves led them into indefensible positions. Any Antifederalist could have answered Randolph's question, Wilson's speeches, or Hamilton's number 84, and many did so capably without resorting to Patrick Henry's grating hysteria. "Centinel," who answered Wilson in a Philadelphia newspaper, declared that the explanation for the omission of a bill of rights "is an insult on the understanding of the people."

Abroad, two wise Americans serving their country in diplomatic missions coolly appraised the proposed Constitution without the obligation of having to support a party line. John Adams, having received a copy of the document in London, wrote a short letter to Jefferson in Paris. The Constitution seemed "admirably calculated to preserve the Union," Adams thought, and he hoped it would be ratified with amendments adopted later. "What think you," he asked, "of a Declaration of Rights? Should not such a Thing have preceded the Model?" Jefferson, in his first letter to Madison on the subject of the Constitution, began with praise but ended with what he did not like: "First the omission of a bill of rights. . . ." After listing rights he thought deserved special protection, starting with freedom of religion and of the press, Jefferson dismissed as campaign rhetoric Wilson's justification for the omission of a bill of rights and concluded, "Let me add that a bill of rights is what the people are entitled to against every government on earth, general or particular, and what no just government should refuse, or rest on inference."

Adams and Jefferson in Europe were much closer to popular opinion than the framers of the Constitution, who had worked secretly for almost four months and, with their supporters, became locked into a position that defied logic and experience. During the ratification controversy, some Federalists argued that the Constitution protected basic rights, exposing them to the reply that they had omitted the liberty of the press, religious freedom, security against general warrants, trial by jury in civil cases, and other basic rights. If the framers intended to protect only the rights arising from the existence of society and government and unknown in a state of nature, they were inconsistent. In the first place they protected only some of the non-natural rights; the first ten amendments are crowded with such rights, which the framers neglected. Second, any reader of John Locke would realize that the clause in Article I, section 10, prohibiting the states from impairing the obligation of contracts, protected a natural right. At the close of chapter two of *The Second Treatise of Goverment*, Locke wrote that the "promises and bargains" between two men on a desert island or between a Swiss and an Indian in the woods of America "are binding to them, though they are perfectly in a state of nature to one another. . . ." Oddly, the Convention had failed to adopt the contract clause when it was proposed; the Committee on Style inserted it into the Constitution, and the Convention, without discussion, agreed to the clause in its closing days. The inclusion of one natural right raises the question of why all others were excluded. The contract clause operates only against state infringement, raising the additional question of why the Convention failed to include a comparable prohibition on the United States.

Natural rights, in accordance with American theory and experience, required protection in any government made by compact. At the Convention, Madison declared that the delegates had assembled to frame "a compact by which an authority was created paramount to the parties, and making laws for the government of them." Some of the states, when formally ratifying the Constitution, considered themselves to be "entering into an explicit and solemn compact," as Massachusetts declared. During the ratification controversy, publicists on both sides referred to the Constitution as a compact. Chief Justice John Jay, who had been one of the authors of *The Federalist*, observed in *Chisholm v. Georgia* (1793) that "the Constitution of the United States is . . . a compact made by the people of the United States in order to govern themselves."

The new compact created a government whose powers seemed intimidating. Article VI, declaring the Constitution, laws made in its pursuance, and treaties of the United States to be the supreme law of the land, anything in the state constitutions to the contrary notwithstanding, seemed to many Antifederalists as superseding their state bills of rights and authorizing laws "repugnant to every article of your rights," as "The Impartial Examiner" wrote. Most believed that enumerated powers could be abused at the expense of fundamental liberties. Congress's power to tax, for example, might be aimed at the press and was thus, in the words of Richard Henry Lee, "a power to destroy or restrain the freedom of it." Others feared that taxes might be exacted from the people for the support of a religious denomination. Tax collectors, unrestrained by a ban on general warrants, Patrick Henry argued, might invade homes "and search, ransack, and measure, every thing you eat, drink, and wear."

The necessary-and-proper clause particularly enraged advocates of a bill of rights. They saw that clause as the source of undefined and unlimited powers to aggrandize the national government and victimize the people, unless, as "An Old Whig" declared, "we had a bill of rights to which we might appeal." "A Democratic Federalist" wrote, "I lay it down as a general rule that wherever the powers of government extend to the lives, the persons, and properties of the subject, all their rights ought to be clearly and expressly defined, otherwise they have but a poor security for their liberties." Henry warned that Congress might "extort a confession by the use of torture" in order to convict a violator of federal law. Numerous opponents of ratification contended that Congress could define as crimes the violation of any laws it might legitimately enact, and lacking a bill of rights, accused persons might be deprived of the rights to counsel, to indictment, to cross-examine witnesses against them, to produce evidence in their own behalf, to be free from compulsory self-incrimination, to be protected against double jeopardy or excessive bail, to be exempt from excessive fines or cruel and unusual punishments, and to enjoy other rights traditionally belonging to accused persons. Such an argument was invariably advanced as one among many refuting the Federalist claim that a bill of rights was unnecessary.

If it was unnecessary, Antifederalists asked, why did the Constitution protect some rights? The protection of some opened the Federalists to devastating rebuttal. They claimed that because no bill of rights could be complete, the omission of any particular right might imply a power to abridge it as unworthy of respect by the government. That argument, in effect that to include some would exclude all others, boomeranged. The protection of trial by jury in criminal cases, the bans on religious tests, ex post facto laws, and bills of attainder, the narrow definition of treason, and the provision for the writ of habeas corpus, by the Federalists' own reasoning, were turned against them. Robert Whitehall, answering Wilson on the floor of the Pennsylvania ratifying convention, noted that the writ of habeas corpus and trial by jury had been expressly reserved and in vain called on Wilson to reconcile the reservation with his "favorite proposition." "For, if there was danger in the attempt to enumerate the liberties of the people," Whitehall explained, "lest it should prove imperfect and defective, how happens it, that in the instances I have mentioned, that danger has been incurred? Have the people no other rights worth their attention, or is it to be inferred, agreeable to the maxim of our opponents that every other right is abandoned?" Stipulating a right, he concluded, destroyed the "argument of danger." Surely, Antifederalists said, their opponents might think of some rights in addition to those protected. The ban on religious tests could have reminded them of freedom of religion. Did not its omission, by their reasoning, necessarily mean that the government could attack freedom of religion?

Henry cleverly observed that the "fair implication" of the Federalist argument against a bill of rights was that the government could do anything not forbidden by the Constitution. Because the provision on the writ of habeas corpus allowed its suspension when the public safety required, Henry reasoned, "It results clearly that, if it had not said so, they could suspend it in all cases whatsoever. It reverses the position of the friends of this Constitution, that every thing is retained which is not given up; for, instead of this, every thing is given up which is not expressly reserved." In his influential *Letters of a Federal Farmer*, Lee observed that a clause of the Constitution prohibited Congress from granting titles of nobility. If the clause had been omitted, he wondered whether Congress would have the power to grant such titles and concluded that it would not under any provision of the Constitution. "Why then by a negative clause, restrain congress from doing what it had no power to do? This clause, then, must have no meaning, or imply, that were it omitted, congress would have the power in question . . . on the principle that congress possesses the powers not expressly reserved." Lee objected to leaving the rights of the people to "logical inferences," because Federalist principles led to the implication that all the rights not mentioned in the Constitution were intended to be relinquished.

Far from being dangerous, a bill of rights, as "A Federal Republican" stated in answer to Wilson, "could do no harm, but might do much good." Lee, discoursing on the good it might do, observed that having a bill of rights assisted popular "education," because it taught "truths" upon which freedom depends and which the people must believe as "sacred." James Winthrop of Massachusetts, writing as "Agrippa," explained another positive value of a bill of rights: it "serves to secure the minority against the usurpations and tyranny of the majority." History, he wrote, proved the "prevalence of a disposition to use power wantonly. It [a bill of rights] is therefore as necessary to defend an individual against the majority in a republick as against the king in a monarchy."

In sum, the usually masterful politicians who had dominated the Convention had blundered by botching constitutional theory and making a serious political error. Their arguments justifying the omission of a bill of rights were impolitic and unconvincing. Mason's point that a bill of rights would quiet the fears of the people was unanswerable. Alienating him and the many who agreed with him was bad politics and handed to the opposition a stirring cause around which they could muster sentiment against ratification. The single issue that united Antifederalists throughout the country was the lack of a bill of rights. No rational argument—and the lack of a bill of rights created an intensely emotional issue because people believed that their liberties were at stake—could possibly allay the fears generated by demagogues like Henry and principled opponents of ratification like Mason. Washington believed that even Mason's "Objections" were meant "to alarm the people." And, when Antifederalists in New York demanded a bill of rights, Hamilton alleged, "It is the plan of men of this stamp to frighten the people with ideal bugbears, in order to mould them to their own purposes. The unceasing cry of these designing croakers is, My friends, your liberty is invaded!" The Antifederalists capitalized on the Federalist blunder, hoping to defeat the Constitution or get a second convention that would revise it in order to hamstring the national government.

In Pennsylvania, the second state to ratify, the minority demanded a comprehensive bill of rights similar to that in their state constitution. Massachusetts, the sixth state to ratify, was the first to do so with recommended amendments. Only two of the recommended amendments, dealing with jury trial in civil suits and grand jury indictment, belonged in a bill of rights. Supporters of the Constitution in Massachusetts had withdrawn a proposed bill of rights on the supposition that Antifederalists would use it as proof that the Constitution endangered liberty. Maryland too would have recommended a bill of rights, but the Federalist majority jettisoned it when the Antifederalists tried to insert curbs on national powers to tax and regulate commerce. Nevertheless, Federalists grudgingly accepted ratification with recommended amendments to ward off conditional ratification or the defeat of the Constitution. New Hampshire, whose approval as the ninth state made ratification an accomplished fact, urged a comprehensive bill of rights for adoption by amendments after the new government went into operation. Virginia and New York, whose ratification was politically indispensable, followed suit. North Carolina was the fourth state to ratify with a model bill of rights among its recommendations. But the states also recommended crippling restrictions on delegated powers.

Thus, the Constitution was ratified only because crucial states, where ratification had been in doubt, were willing to accept the promise of a bill of rights in the form of subsequent amendments to the Constitution. State recommendations for amendments, including those of the Pennsylvania minority, received nationwide publicity, adding to the clamor for a bill of rights. Every right that became part of the first ten amendments was included in state recommendations except the clause in the Fifth Amendment requiring just compensation for private property taken for public use.

James Madison was one of the Federalists who finally realized that statecraft and political expediency dictated a switch in position. At the Virginia ratifying convention in June 1788 Madison had upheld the usual Federalist arguments for the omission of a bill of rights but finally voted to recommend such a bill in order to avoid previous amendments. He later conceded that the Constitution would have been defeated without a pledge from its supporters to back subsequent amendments. In Virginia, Madison's own political position deteriorated because he had opposed a bill of rights. The Antifederalists, who controlled the state legislature, elected two of their own, Richard Henry Lee and William Grayson, as the state's first United States senators. Madison faced a tough contest for election to the House of Representatives, and he feared that the Antifederalists might succeed in their call for a second constitutional convention. He needed to clarify his position on a bill of rights.

Although Madison had periodically apprised Jefferson, in Paris, on ratification developments, he had not answered Jefferson's letter of December 1787 supporting a bill of rights.

On October 17, 1788, the eve of his campaign for a House seat, Madison faced the issue. He favored a bill of rights, he wrote, but had "never thought the omission a material defect" and was not "anxious to supply it even by subsequent amendments"; he did not even think the matter important. Still agreeing with Wilson that the delegated powers did not extend to reserved rights, Madison also worried about the difficulty of adequately protecting the most important rights; experience proved that a bill of rights was a mere parchment barrier when most needed. Government, after all, was the instrument of the majority, which could endanger liberty. "What use then . . . can a bill of rights serve in popular Governments?" Its political truths, he conceded by way of answer, could educate the people, thereby inhibiting majority impulses.

Jefferson's reply of March 15, 1789, had a profound influence on Madison, as Madison's great speech of June 8 would show. An argument for a bill of rights that Madison had omitted, wrote Jefferson, was "the legal check which it puts into the hands of the judiciary." Jefferson believed that an independent court could withstand oppressive majority impulses by holding unconstitutional any acts violating a bill of rights. The point was not new to Madison, for he himself, when defending a ban on ex post facto laws at the Constitutional Convention, had declared that it would "oblige the Judges to declare [retrospective] interferences null and void." As for the point that the delegated powers did not reach the reserved rights of the people, Jefferson answered that because the Constitution protected some rights but ignored others, it raised implications against them, making a bill of rights "necessary by way of supplement." Moreover, he added, the Constitution "forms us into one state as to certain objects," requiring a bill of rights to guard against abuses of power. As for the point that a bill of rights could not be perfect, Jefferson replied with the adage that half a loaf is better than none; even if all rights could not be secured, "let us secure what we can." Madison had also argued that the limited powers of the federal government and the jealousy of the states afforded enough security, to which Jefferson answered that a bill of rights "will be the text whereby to try all the acts of the federal government." The argument that a bill of rights was inconvenient and not always efficacious did not impress Jefferson. Sometimes, he replied, it was effective, and if it inconveniently cramped the government, the effect was short-lived and remediable, whereas the inconveniences of not having a bill of rights could be "permanent, afflicting, and irreparable." Legislative tyranny, Jefferson explained, would be a formidable dread for a long time, and executive tyranny would likely follow.

Jefferson's arguments, however persuasive, would have been unproductive but for the dangerous political situation, which Madison meant to ameliorate. Four states, including his own and New York, had called for a second convention, whose purpose, Madison feared, would be to "mutilate the system," especially as to the power to tax. Omitting it "will be fatal" to the new federal government. Madison correctly believed that many Antifederalists favored an effective Union on condition that a bill of rights bridled the new government. His strategy was to win them over by persuading the first Congress to adopt protections of civil liberties, thereby alleviating the public's anxieties, providing popularity and stability for the government, and isolating those Antifederalists whose foremost objective was "subverting the fabric . . . if not the Union itself."

In the first Congress, Representative Madison sought to fulfill his pledge of subsequent amendments. His accomplishment in the face of opposition and apathy entitles him to be remembered as "father of the Bill of Rights" even more than as "father of the Constitution." Many Federalists thought that the House had more important tasks, like the passage of tonnage duties and a judiciary bill. The opposition party, which had previously exploited the lack of a bill of rights in the

Constitution, realized that its adoption would sink the movement for a second convention and make unlikely any additional amendments that would cripple the substantive powers
of the government. They had used the bill-of-rights issue as
a smokescreen for objections to the Constitution that could
not be dramatically popularized, and now they sought to scut-
tle Madison's proposals. They began by stalling, then tried
to annex amendments aggrandizing state powers, and finally
depreciated the importance of the very protections of individual liberty that they had formerly demanded as a guarantee
against impending tyranny. Madison meant to prove that the
new government was a friend of liberty; he also understood
that his amendments, if adopted, would thwart the passage
of proposals aggrandizing state powers and diminishing national ones. He would not be put off; he was insistent, compelling, unyielding, and, finally, triumphant.

On June 8, 1789, he made his long, memorable speech
before an apathetic House, introducing amendments culled
mainly from state constitutions and state ratifying convention
proposals, especially Virginia's. All power, he argued, is subject to abuse and should be guarded against by constitutionally
securing "the great rights of mankind." The government had
only limited powers, but it might, unless prohibited, abuse its
discretion as to its choice of means under the necessary-and-
proper clause; it might, for example, use general warrants in
the enforcement of its revenue laws. In Britain, bills of rights
merely erected barriers against the powers of the crown, leaving the powers of Parliament "altogether indefinite," and the
British constitution left unguarded the "choicest" rights of the
press and of conscience. The great objective he had in mind,
Madison declared, was to limit the powers of government, thus
preventing legislative as well as executive abuse, and above
all preventing abuses of power by "the body of the people,
operating by the majority against the minority." Mere "paper
barriers" might fail, but they raised a standard that might

educate the majority against acts to which they might be inclined.

To the argument that a bill of rights was not necessary because the states constitutionally protected freedom, Madison had two responses. One was that some states had no bills of rights, other "very defective ones," and the states constituted a greater danger to liberty than the new national government. The other was that the Constitution should, therefore, include an amendment, that "No State shall violate the equal rights of conscience, or the freedom of the press, or the trial by jury in criminal cases." This, Madison declared, was "the most valuable amendment in the whole list." To the contention that an enumeration of rights would disparage those not protected, Madison replied that the danger could be guarded against by adopting a proposal of his composition that became the Ninth Amendment. If his amendments were "incorporated" into the Constitution, Madison said, using another argument borrowed from Jefferson, "independent tribunals of justice will consider themselves in a peculiar manner the guardians of those rights; they will be an impenetrable bulwark against every assumption of power in the legislative or executive; they will be naturally led to resist every encroachment upon rights expressly stipulated for in the constitution."

Although many Federalists preferred to give the new government time to operate before amending the Constitution, supporters of Madison exulted, largely for political reasons. Hugh Williamson of North Carolina, a signer of the Constitution, informed Madison that the Antifederalists of that state did not really want a bill of rights; William R. Davie, who had been Williamson's colleague in the Convention, gleefully reported to Madison that his amendments had "confounded the Anties exceedingly. . . ." Edmund Pendleton of Virginia wrote of Madison's amendments that "nothing was further from the wish of some, who covered their Opposition to the Government under the masque of uncommon zeal for amendments. . . ." Tench Coxe of Pennsylvania praised Madison for having stripped the Constitution's opponents of every rationale "and most of the popular arguments they have heretofore used."

Notwithstanding the support of correspondents, Madison's speech stirred no immediate support in Congress. Indeed, every speaker who followed him, regardless of party affiliation, either opposed a bill of rights or believed that the House should attend to far more important duties. Six weeks later Madison "begged" for a consideration of his amendments, but the House assigned them to a special committee instead of debating them. That committee, which included Madison, reported in a week. It added freedom of speech to the rights protected against state abridgement, deleted Madison's reference to no "unreasonable searches and seizures," made some stylistic revisions, but otherwise recommended the amendments substantially as he had proposed them. The committee's report was tabled, impelling Madison on August 3 to implore its consideration.

On August 13 the House finally began to consider the reported amendments, and in the course of debate it made some significant changes. Madison had proposed to "incorporate" the amendments within the text of the Constitution at appropriate points. He did not recommend their adoption as a separate "bill of rights," although he had referred to them collectively by that phrase. Members objected that to incorporate the amendments would give the impression that the framers of the Constitution had signed a document that included provisions not of their composition. Another argument for lumping the amendments together was that the matter of form was so "trifling" that the House should not squander its time debating the placement of the various amendments. Ironically, Roger Sherman, who still believed that the amendments were unnecessary, deserves the credit for insistently arguing that they should be appended as a supplement to the

Constitution instead of being interspersed within it. Thus, what became the Bill of Rights achieved its significant collective form over the objections of its foremost proponent, Madison, and because of the desire of its opponents in both parties to downgrade its importance.

The House recast the free exercise of religion clause and its allied clause banning establishments of religion, improving Madison's original language. The House also confined to criminal cases Madison's broad phrasing that no person should be compelled to give evidence against himself. On the other hand the House restored the extremely important principle against unreasonable searches and seizures, dropped by the committee. In another major decision the House decisively defeated Gerry's motion, for the Antifederalists, to consider not just the committee's report but all amendments that the several states had proposed; the Antifederalists thus failed to intrude crippling political amendments. Finally the House added "or to the people" in the recommendation by Madison that the powers not delegated to the United States be reserved to the states. On the whole the House adopted Madison's amendments with few significant alterations during the course of its ten-day debate on the Bill of Rights.

In the midst of that debate Madison wrote a letter to a fellow Federalist explaining why he was so committed to "the nauseous project of amendments" that some of the party supported reluctantly. Protecting essential rights was "not improper," he coolly explained, and could be of some influence for good. He also felt honor-bound to redeem a campaign pledge to his constituents, mindful that the Constitution "would have been *certainly* rejected" by Virginia without assurances from its supporters to seek subsequent amendments. Politics, moreover, made proposing the amendments a necessity to beat the Antifederalists at their own game. If Federalists did not support the amendments, Antifederalists would claim that they had been right all along and gain support for a second convention. And, Madison wrote, the amendments "will kill the opposition everywhere, and by putting an end to disaffection to the Government itself, enable the administration to venture on measures not otherwise safe."

Madison had, in fact, upstaged and defeated the Antifederalists. That is why Congressman Aedanus Burke of South Carolina cried sour grapes. During the debate on what would become the First Amendment, he argued that the proposals before the House were "not those solid and substantial amendments which the people expect, they are little better than whip-syllabub, frothy and full of wind. . . . Upon the whole, I think . . . we have done nothing but lose our time, and that it will be better to drop the subject now, and proceed to the organization of the Government." The private correspondence of Senators Lee and Grayson of Virginia reveals the explanation for the attitude of their party toward a bill of rights. A few days after Madison had introduced his amendments, Grayson complained to his mentor Patrick Henry that the Federalists meant to enact "amendments which shall effect [*sic*] personal liberty alone, leaving the great points of the Judiciary, direct taxation, &c, to stand as they are." Lee and Grayson had failed in their effort to have the Senate amend the House's proposals by adopting the Virginia ratifying convention's recommendations on direct taxation and the treaty and commerce powers. Lee then regretted the original Antifederalist strategy of opposing the Constitution unless revised by the addition of a bill of rights and other amendments. He sorrowfully informed Henry that "the idea of subsequent amendments, was little better than putting oneself to death first, in expectation that the doctor, who wished our destruction, would afterwards restore us to life." Later, after the Senate had approved the amendments that became the Bill of Rights, Grayson reported, "they are good for nothing, and I believe, as many others do, that they will do more harm than benefit."

The Senate, which kept no record of its debates, had deliberated on seventeen amendments submitted by the House. One the Senate killed, the proposal Madison thought "the most valuable": protection against state infringement of speech, press, religion, or trial by jury. The motion to adopt failed to receive the necessary two-thirds vote, although by what margin is unknown. The Senate also weakened the House's ban on establishments of religion. Otherwise the Senate accepted the House proposals, although the Senate combined several, reducing the total number from seventeen to twelve. The first of the twelve dealt with the relation of population to the number of representatives from each state, and the second would have prevented any law going into effect that would have increased the salaries of members of Congress until after the next election.

The House adamantly refused to accept the Senate's version of its ban on establishments. A conference committee of both houses met to resolve differences. The committee, which included Madison, accepted the House's ban on establishments but otherwise accepted the Senate's version. On September 24, 1789, the House voted for the committee report; on the following day the Senate concurred, and the twelve amendments were submitted to the states for ratification.

Within six months nine states ratified the Bill of Rights, although of the twelve amendments submitted for approval, the first and second were rejected. The four recalcitrant states by mid-1790 were Virginia, Massachusetts, Connecticut, and Georgia. The admission of Vermont to the Union made necessary the ratification by eleven states. Connecticut and Georgia refused to ratify. Georgia's position was that amendments were superfluous until experience under the Constitution proved a need. Connecticut believed that any suggestion that the Constitution was not perfect would add to the strength of Antifederalism.

In Massachusetts, Federalist apathy to the Bill of Rights

was grounded on a satisfaction with the Constitution as it was, and the Antifederalists were more interested in amendments that would strengthen the states at the expense of the national government. Nevertheless the Massachusetts lower house adopted all but the first, second, and twelfth amendments, and the upper house adopted all but the first, second, and tenth. Thus both houses of the Massachusetts legislature actually approved what became the First through Seventh Amendments and the Ninth: but a special committee, dominated by Antifederalists, urged that all amendments recommended by Massachusetts should be adopted before the state concurred in any amendments. As a result the two houses never passed a bill promulgating ratification of eight amendments. Jefferson, the secretary of state, believed that Massachusetts, "having been the 10th state which has ratified, makes up the threefourth [sic] of the legislatures whose ratification was to suffice." He wrote to a Massachusetts official, asking for clarification. The reply was, "It does not appear that the Committee ever reported any bill." In 1939, Massachusetts joined Connecticut and Georgia when they belatedly ratified on the sesquicentennial anniversary of the Constitution.

Ratification of the Bill of Rights by Vermont, in November 1789, left Virginia the last state to act. Its ratification as the eleventh state was indispensable, although the hostility of its Antifederalist leaders presaged a doubtful outcome. Senators Grayson and Lee reported to the Virginia legislature that they transmitted the recommended amendments "with grief." They still hoped for a new constitutional convention that would devise "real and substantial Amendments" to "secure against the annihilation of the state governments. . . ." Patrick Henry vainly moved to postpone consideration of the Bill of Rights. The victims of a dilemma of their own making, the Antifederalists then sought to sabotage the Bill of Rights and finally, after delaying ratification for nearly two years, irresolutely acquiesced. The Federalists of Virginia, however, eagerly supported the Bill of Rights in the knowledge that its adoption would appease public fears and stymie the amendments supported by the Antifederalists. Virginia's lower house, controlled by the Federalists, acted quickly, but the opposition dominated the state senate. Not all Antifederalists were implacably opposed. Some respected George Mason's opinion. When he had first heard of Madison's amendments he called them "Milk and Water Propositions," not "important & substantial Amendments"; but Mason changed his mind, saying that they gave "much satisfaction," although he still wanted other amendments, including one that prevented commercial regulations by mere majority vote of Congress. Virginia's senate, as Edmund Randolph reported to Washington, postponed consideration of the amendments, "for a majority is unfriendly to the government." As a member of the lower house reported to Madison, the senate inclined to reject the Bill of Rights, not because of opposition to its guarantees, but from an apprehension "that the adoption of them at this time will be an obstacle to the chief object of their pursuit, the amendment on the subject of direct taxation." For that reason, Randolph reported to Washington, the Federalists meant to "push" the Bill of Rights; passage would "discountenance any future importunities for amendments."

Virginia's senate at the close of 1789 rejected what became the First, Sixth, Ninth, and Tenth Amendments, at least until the next session, thereby allowing time for the electorate to express itself. The Antifederalists still hoped to drum up support for "radical" amendments, as Lee called them. The senators in the majority also issued a statement grossly misrepresenting the First Amendment (then the third). Madison confidently expected that this Antifederalist tactic would backfire, and it did. For the senators' statement was not only inaccurate on its face; it came from men who with a single exception did not go before the electorate with clean hands. Like Henry and Lee, who planned the senators' statement, the senators had rcords of having voted against religious liberty and in favor of compulsory taxes for the support of religion. By contrast Madison had led the fight in Virginia against a state establishment of religion and for religious liberty, and his supporters in the Virginia senate had aided him. In the end Madison's confidence proved justified. Jefferson made his influence felt on behalf of the Bill of Rights, and the Antifederalists grudgingly gave ground before public opinion. On December 15, 1791, after two years of procrastination, the senate finally ratified without record vote, thereby completing the process of state ratification and making the Bill of Rights part of the Constitution.

The history of the framing and ratification of the Bill of Rights indicates slight passion on the part of anyone to enshrine personal liberties in the fundamental law of the land. We know almost nothing about what the state legislatures thought concerning the meanings of the various amendments, and the press was perfunctory in its reports, if not altogether silent. But for Madison's persistence the amendments would have died in Congress. Our precious Bill of Rights, at least in its immediate background, resulted from the reluctant necessity of certain Federalists to capitalize on a cause that had been originated, in vain, by the Antifederalists for ulterior purposes. The party that had first opposed the Bill of Rights inadvertently wound up with the responsibility for its framing and ratification, whereas the party that had at first professedly wanted it discovered too late that it was not only embarrassing but disastrous for those ulterior purposes. The Bill of Rights had a great healing effect, however; it did, as Mason originally proposed, "give great quiet" to people. The opposition to the Constitution, Jefferson informed Lafayette, "almost totally disappeared," as Antifederalist leaders lost "almost all their followers." The people of the United States had possessed the good sense, nourished by traditions of freedom, to support the Constitution and the Bill of Rights.

The traditions that gave shape and substance to the Bill of Rights had English roots; but a unique American experience colored that shape and substance. "We began with freedom," as Emerson wrote in "The Fortune of the Republic." The first charter of Virginia contained a provision that the colonists and their descendants "shall have and enjoy all Liberties, Franchises, and Immunities . . . as if they had been abiding and born, within this our Realm of England. . . ." Later charters of Virginia contained similar clauses, which extended to legal rights of land tenure and inheritance, trial by jury, and little else; but the vague language, which was repeated in numerous other charters for colonies from New England to the South, allowed Americans to believe they were entitled to all the rights of Englishmen, their constitutional system, and their common law. American experience with and interpretations of charters eased the way to written constitutions of fundamental law that contained bills of rights.

Freedom was mainly the product of New World conditions, of English legal inheritance, and of the new nation's having skipped a feudal stage. Because of America's postfeudal beginnings, it was unencumbered by oppressions associated with an ancien régime, a rigid clas system dominated by a reactionary and hereditary aristocracy, arbitrary government by despotic kings, and a single established church extirpating dissent. Americans were the freest people, therefore the first colonists to rebel. A free people, as Edmund Burke said, can sniff tyranny in a far-off breeze—even if nonexistent. American "radicals" actually believed that the Stamp Act reduced Americans to slavery. They resorted to arms in 1775, the Continental Congress declared, "not to establish new liberties, but to defend old ones." In fact they established many new liberties but convinced themselves that those liberties were old. That was an English custom: marching forward into the future facing backward to the past, while adapting old law to changing values. Thus Magna Carta had come to mean indictment by grand jury, trial by jury, and a cluster of related rights of the criminally accused, and Englishmen believed, or made believe, that it was ever so. That habit crossed the Atlantic.

So did the hyperbolic style of expression by a free people outraged by injustice. Thus, James Madison exclaimed that the "diabolical Hell conceived principle of persecution rages," because some Baptist ministers were briefly jailed for unlicensed preaching. By European standards, persecution hardly existed in America, not even in the seventeenth century except on a local and sporadic basis. America never experienced anything like the Inquisition, the fires of Smithfield, the St. Bartholomew's Day Massacre, or the deaths of over 5,000 nonconformist ministers in the jails of Restoration England. Draconian colonial statutes existed but were rarely enforced. Broad libertarian practices were the rule, not the exception.

On any comparative basis civil liberty flourished in America, a fact that intensified the notoriety of exceptional abridgments, such as the hanging of four Quakers in Massachusetts or the prosecution of John Peter Zenger in 1735 for seditious libel. Although a stunted concept of the meaning and scope of freedom of the press existed in America until the Jeffersonian reaction to the Sedition Act of 1798, an extraordinary degree of freedom of the press existed in practice in America as in England. Criticism of the government, especially of the popular assemblies, was dangerous. If Zenger, the printer of the *New-York Weekly Journal*, had attacked the assembly instead of the royal governor, he would have been summarily convicted at the bar of the house, jailed, and forgotten. But Zenger was an instrument of the popular party against a detested administration, and so the jury, stirred by an eloquent lawyer, returned a popular verdict of not guilty, against the instructions of the court. The law, as laid down by the court, incidentally, was correct and remained the law, despite the verdict. Zenger's case was one of only a very few prosecutions by "royal judges" for seditious libel and almost the last of its kind; prosecutions by governor and council or by the assemblies were a greater threat to a free press. When Alexander McDougall, a "Son of Liberty," assailed the New York assembly, it instigated a prosecution against him for seditious libel, jailed him when he refused to post excessive bail, and when the case again t him collapsed because of the death of the star witness for the prosecution, arrested and convicted him for libeling the house. Despite that 1770 case, the American press remained extraordinarily free except for the suppression of Tory opinion during the Revolution.

The predominance of the social compact theory in American thought reflected a condition of freedom and, like the experience with charters, contributed to the belief in written bills of rights. The social compact theory hypothesized a pre-political state of nature in which people were governed only by the laws of nature, free of human restraints. From the premise that man was born free, the deduction followed that he came into the world with God-given or natural rights. Born without the restraint of human laws, he had a right to possess liberty and to work for his own property. Born naked and stationless, he had a right to equality. Born with certain instincts and needs, he had a right to satisfy them—a right to the pursuit of happiness. These natural rights, as John Dickinson declared in 1766, "are created in us by the decrees of Providence, which establish the laws of our nature. They are born with us; exist with us; and cannot be taken from us by any human power without taking our lives." When people left the state of nature and compacted for government, the need to secure their rights motivated them. A half century before John Locke's *Second Treatise of Government*, Thomas Hooker of Connecticut expounded the social compact theory. Over a period of a century and a half, America became accustomed to the idea that government existed by consent of the governed, that the people created the government, that they did it by a written compact, that the compact reserved their natural rights, and that it constituted a fundamental law to which the government was subordinate. Constitutionalism, or the theory of limited government, was in part an outgrowth of the social compact.

In America, political theory and law, as well as religion, taught that government was limited. But Americans took their views on such matters from a highly selective and romanticized image of seventeenth-century England, and they perpetuated it in America even as that England changed. Seventeenth-century England was the England of the great struggle for constitutional liberty by the common law courts and Puritan parliaments against Stuart kings. Seventeenth-century England was the England of Edward Coke, John Lilburne, and John Locke. It was an England in which religion, law, and politics converged to produce limited monarchy and, ironically, parliamentary supremacy. To Americans, Parliament had irrevocably limited itself by reaffirmations of Magna Carta and passage of the Petition of Right of 1628, the Habeas Corpus Act of 1679, the Bill of Rights of 1689, and the Toleration Act of 1689. Americans learned that a free people are those who live under a government so constitutionally checked and controlled that its powers must be reasonably exercised without abridging individual rights.

In fact, Americans had progressed far beyond the English in securing their rights. The English constitutional documents limited only the crown and protected few rights. The Petition of Right reconfirmed Magna Carta's provision that no freeman could be imprisoned except by lawful judgment of his peers or "by the law of the land"; it also reconfirmed a 1354 version of the great charter that had first used the phrase "by due process of law" instead of "by the law of the land." The petition invigorated the liberty of the subject by condemning the military trial of civilians as well as imprisonment without cause or on mere executive authority. Other sections provided that no one could be taxed without Parliament's consent or be imprisoned or forced to incriminate himself by having to answer for refusing an exaction not authorized by Parliament. The Habeas Corpus Act safeguarded personal liberty, without which other liberties cannot be exercised. The act se⌐⌐ed an old right for the first time by making the writ of habeas corpus an effective remedy for illegal imprisonment. The only loophole in the act, the possibility of excessive bail, was plugged by the Bill of Rights ten years later. That enactment, its exalted name notwithstanding, had a narrow range of protections, including the freedoms of petition and assembly, free speech for members of Parliament, and, in language closely followed by the American Eighth Amendment, bans on excessive bail, excessive fines, and cruel and unusual punishments. As an antecedent of the American Bill of Rights, the English one was a skimpy affair, although important as a symbol of the rule of law and of fundamental law. The Toleration Act was actually "A Bill of Indulgence," exempting most nonconformists from the penalties of persecutory laws of the Restoration, leaving those laws in force but inapplicable to persons qualifying for indulgence. England maintained an establishment of the Anglican Church, merely tolerating the existence of non-Anglican trinitarians, who were still obligated to pay tithes and endure many civil disabilities.

In America, England promoted Anglicanism in New York and in the southern colonies but wisely prevented its establishments in America from obstructing religious peace, because immigrants were an economic asset, regardless of religion. England granted charters to colonial proprietors on a nondiscriminatory basis—to Cecil Calvert, a Roman Catholic, for Maryland; to Roger Williams, a Baptist, for Rhode Island; and to William Penn, a Quaker, for Pennsylvania and Delaware. The promise of life in America drew people from all of western Christendom and exposed them to a greater degree of liberty and religious differences than previously known. James Madison, whose practical achievements in the cause of freedom of religion were unsurpassed, said that it arose from "that multiplicity of sects which pervades America."

But a principled commitment to religious liberty came first in some colonies. Maryland's Toleration Act of 1649 was far more liberal than England's Toleration Act of forty years later. Until 1776 only Rhode Island, Pennsylvania, Delaware, and New Jersey guaranteed fuller freedom than Maryland by its act of 1649, which was the first to use the phrase "the free exercise of religion," later embodied in the First Amendment. The act also symbolized the extraordinary fact that for most of the seventeenth century in Maryland, Roman Catholics and Protestants openly worshiped as they chose and lived in peace, if not amity. The act applied to all trinitarian Christians but punished others as well as punishing the reproachful use of divisive terms such as heretic, puritan, papist, anabaptist, or antinomian. The Maryland act was a statute, but the Charter of Rhode Island, which remained its constitution until 1842, made the guarantee of religious liberty a part of the fundamental law. It secured for all inhabitants "the free exercise and enjoyment of their civil and religious rights" by providing that every peaceable person might "freely and fullye hav and enjoye his and theire owne judgments and consciences, in matters of religious concernments. . . ." Thus, the principle that the state has no legitimate authority over religion was institutionalized in some American colonies, including those under Quaker influence.

Massachusetts, the colony that least respected private judgment in religious matters, was the first to safeguard many other rights. Its Body of Liberties, adopted in 1641, was meant to limit the magistrates in whom all power had been concentrated. As John Winthrop observed, the objective was to frame limitations "in remarkable resemblance to Magna Charta, which . . . should be received for fundamental laws." The Body of Liberties was, in effect, a comprehensive bill of rights compared with which the later English Bill of Rights was rudimentary and the liberties of Englishmen few. Among the guarantees first protected in writing by Massachusetts were freedom of assembly and of speech at least in public meetings, the equal protection of the laws, just compensation for private property taken for public use, freedom to emigrate, the right to bail, the right to employ counsel, trial by jury in civil cases, the right to challenge jurors, restrictions on imprisonment for debt, speedy trial, no double jeopardy, and no cruel or excessive punishments. In addition to traditional liberties, like trial by jury in criminal cases, and Magna Carta's principle of the rule of law, the Body of Liberties also protected some rights of women: widows received a portion of the estate of husbands even if cut off by will; physical punishment of women by their husbands was prohibited; and daughters received a right to inherit if parents died intestate and without male heirs. Servants, slaves, foreigners, and even animals received humane consideration too.

The Body of Liberties was a statute, but the Charter or Fundamental Laws of West New Jersey (1677), the work probably of William Penn, functioned as a written constitution because it began with the provision that the "common law or fundamental rights" of the colony should be "the foundation of government, which is not to be altered by the Legislative authority . . . ." The liberty documents of England limited only the crown, not the legislature. The principle of limiting all governmental authority was written into Penn's Frame of Government for Pennsylvania in 1682, a document that extensively enumerated rights that were to last "for ever," including, for the first time, a ban on excessive fines, a guarantee of indictment by grand jury in capital cases, delivery to the accused of a copy of the charges against him, and assurance that a jury's verdict of not guilty was final. Penn's charter carefully particularized the rights of the criminally accused. Americans were learning that charters of liberty must assure fair and regularized procedures, without which there could be no liberty. Vicious and ad hoc procedures had been used to victimize religious and political minorities. A man's home could not be his castle or his property be his own, nor could his right to express his opinion or to worship his God be secure, if he could be searched, arrested, tried, and imprisoned in some arbitrary way.

The case of Sir Thomas Lawrence in 1693 is illustrative. Secretary of Maryland, a judge, and a member of the governor's council, Lawrence broke politically with the government and denounced it. Summoned by the council for examination, he was accused of having a treasonable letter. On his refusal to produce it, the council had him searched against his protests, found the letter, and convicted him of unspecified crimes, deprived him of his offices, and jailed him without bail. Lawrence appealed his conviction to the Assembly on the grounds of having been forced to incriminate himself by an illegal search, of having been convicted without trial by jury, without knowing the charges against him or the names of his accusers, and of having been denied bail and habeas corpus "which is the great security of the lives & Libertyes of every English Subject." The Assembly vindicated English liberties by supporting Lawrence on every point, found all the proceedings against him illegal, and freed and restored him.

The American colonial experience, climaxed by the controversy with England leading to the Revolution, honed American sensitivity to the need for written constitutions that protected rights grounded in "the immutable laws of nature" as well as in the British constitution and colonial charters. An English nobleman told Benjamin Franklin that Americans had the wrong ideas about the constitution. English and American ideas did differ radically because the Americans had a novel concept of "constitution." The word signified to them a supreme law creating government, limiting it, unalterable by it, and paramount to it. A town orator of Boston announced that independence offered the people a chance of reclaiming rights "attendant upon the original state of nature, with the opportunity of establishing a government for ourselves. . . ." "To secure these rights," Jefferson declared, "governments are instituted among men."

The Virginia constitution of 1776, the first permanent state constitution, began with a Declaration of Rights that restrained all branches of government. As the first such document it contained many constitutional "firsts," such as the statements that "all men" are equally free and have inherent rights that cannot be divested even by compact; that among these rights are the enjoyment of life, liberty, property, and the pursuit of happiness; and that all power derives from the people, who retain a right to change the government if it fails to secure its objectives. The declaration recognized "the free exercise of religion" and freedom of the press, and included clauses that were precursors, sometimes in rudimentary form, of the Fourth through the Eighth Amendments of the Constitution of the United States. Inexplicably the convention voted down a ban on bills of attainder and on ex post facto laws and omitted the freedom of speech, assembly, and petition, the right to the writ of habeas corpus, grand jury proceedings, the right to compulsory process to secure evidence in one's own behalf, the right to counsel, and freedom from double jeopardy. Although religious liberty was guaranteed, the ban on an establishment of religion awaited enactment of the Virginia Statute of Religious Freedom in 1786.

Pennsylvania's bill of rights was more comprehensive than Virginia's. Pennsylvania omitted bans on excessive fines and cruel punishments as well as the right to bail but added freedom of speech, assembly, and petition; separated church and state; recognized the right of conscientious objection; protected the right to counsel in all criminal cases; secured the right to keep arms; and guaranteed the right to travel or emigrate—all constitutional "firsts." Pennsylvania also recognized that "the people have a right to hold themselves, their houses, papers, and possessions free from search and seizure," in contrast to Virginia's prohibition of general warrants. Delaware's bill of rights was the first to ban ex post facto laws and the quartering of troops in homes during peacetime; Maryland added a prohibition on bills of attainder. Vermont's contribution was the first outlawing of slavery and the first constitutional provision for just compensation in cases of eminent domain. Connecticut and Rhode Island retained their charters as their constitutions, whereas New Jersey, Georgia, New York, and South Carolina protected some rights in their constitutional texts but had no separate bills of rights and no noteworthy innovations.

Massachusetts, the last of the original states to adopt a constitution (1780), contributed the most to the concept of a bill of rights. It had the most comprehensive bill of rights and was the first to secure citizens against "all unreasonable searches and seizures," the formulation closest to that of the later Fourth Amendment. Massachusetts was also the first state to replace the weak "ought not" found in all previous bills of rights—"the liberty of the press ought not be restrained"—with the injunction "shall not," which Madison later followed. Most important, Massachusetts was the first state to frame its fundamental law by a specially elected constitutional convention, which exercised no legislative authority and submitted the document for popular ratification. In every other state before 1780, legislatures, sometimes calling themselves conventions, wrote the fundamental law and promulgated it. Theoretically, a bill of rights framed by a legislature could be changed by ordinary legislation, a fact deplored by Jefferson as a capital defect in Virginia's model. The procedure first adopted by Massachusetts was copied by New Hampshire when it revised its constitution in 1784, with the first guarantee against double jeopardy; thereafter the Massachusetts procedure prevailed.

The framing of the first constitutions with bills of rights ranks among America's foremost achievements, the more remarkable because both unprecedented and realized during wartime. Nevertheless, the phrasing of various rights and the inclusion or omission of particular ones in any given state constitution seem careless. Why so few states protected the rights against double jeopardy and bills of attainder, and why so many omitted habeas corpus and freedom of speech, among others, is inexplicable except in terms of shoddy craftsmanship. Even so, the existence of eight state bills of rights with constitutional status invigorated Antifederalist arguments that a bill of rights should be appended to the Constitution of 1787. The state ratifying conventions produced about seventy-five recommendations for amendments, providing Madison with an invaluable list from which to create the proposals that he submitted to Congress.

Congress itself supplied a final precedent, the Northwest Ordinance of 1787, which planned the evolution of territories to statehood. The ordinance was the first federal document to contain a bill of rights. To extend "the fundamental principles of civil and religious liberty," Congress included articles that were to remain "forever . . . unalterable," guaranteeing to territorial inhabitants habeas corpus, trial by jury, representative government, judicial proceedings "according to the course of the common law," and, as an additional assurance of due process, an encapsulated provision from Magna Carta protecting liberty and property from being deprived except "by the judgment of . . . peers, or the law of the land." The ordinance also included articles protecting the right to bail except in capital cases, enjoined that all fines should be "moderate," and prohibited "cruel or unusual punishment." Another article provided a federal precedent for still another provision of the Bill of Rights, just compensation for property taken for public purposes. The ordinance also protected the sanctity of private contracts, outlawed sex discrimination in land ownership, banned slavery, and provided for religious liberty. Thus the federal as well as colonial and state experience with written instruments to safeguard rights enhanced the claim that a bill of rights should bridle the new national government.

The Bill of Rights did just that; it was a bill of restraints. The First Amendment begins with the clause, "Congress shall make no law respecting an establishment of religion." What is an establishment of religion? The debates of the Congress that proposed the amendment provide inadequate support for either a broad or narrow interpretation, although Congress rejected various phrasings that embraced the narrow one, namely, that Congress could not establish a state church or prefer one religion over others. Madison doubtessly believed that government aid to religion generally or on a nonpreferential basis to all religions constituted an establishment. But the "great object" of the Bill of Rights, he declared, was to "limit and qualify the powers of Government" by making certain that none of its granted powers could be used in forbidden fields, such as religion. A narrow interpretation of the clause leads to the impossible conclusion that the First Amendment added to Congress's powers. Congress was bereft of power to control or support religion even in the absence of the amendment. An express prohibition could not vest power to aid religion generally. Madison observed that the Bill of Rights was not framed "to imply powers not meant to be included in the enumeration." When Congress framed the First Amendment, six states maintained or authorized establishments. The amendment was meant to prevent congressional legislation concerning those establishments and to ensure that Congress could not do what those states were doing. In each of the six an establishment of religion was not restricted to a single state church or public support of one denomination; in all an establishment meant public support to all denominations and sects on a nonpreferential basis, not just public support of one over others. History explains the meaning of the text. Similarly the seemingly specific injunctions of the remainder of the Bill of Rights are not self-defining and do not necessarily exclude exceptions.

Freedom of speech and press may not be abridged, but what is an abridgment, and what is the "freedom of speech" that is protected? Libels, obscenity, and pornography, whatever they might mean, as well as direct and successful incitements to crime, were not intended to be constitutionally protected. The guarantee of freedom of religion is that it may not be "prohibited." But may it be abridged or regulated in some way short of a prohibition? The injunction against laws respecting an establishment of religion does not literally apply to speech or press. But can Congress pass laws respecting freedom of the press if not abridging it? What are the "arms" that may be kept and borne? When is the militia "well-regulated"? What is an "unreasonable" search or seizure? No warrants shall issue "but on probable cause." What is "a probable cause," and may there be searches without warrants? They existed in 1791. What is an "infamous" crime? What is the meaning of compulsion in the safeguard that no person shall be "compelled" to be a witness against himself in a criminal case? What is the process of law that is "due" to anyone who might be deprived of life, liberty, or property? What is "public use" or "just" compensation? Do the many rights of the Sixth Amendment really extend to "all" criminal prosecutions? Trial by jury did not extend to persons facing less than six months' imprisonment. When does a criminal prosecution or case begin, and does it include legislative or grand jury investigations? Does the "assistance of counsel" or the right not to be a witness against oneself apply to such investigations? What is a "speedy" trial or an "impartial" jury? Does trial by jury mean only a jury of twelve and a unanimous verdict? Does the ban against double jeopardy mean that an acquittal in federal court bars a state trial for the same act? What is "excessive" bail or a punishment that is "cruel and unusual"? There were probably no constitutional absolutes in 1791, and no guarantees that were clear and precise in meaning. Ambiguities cannot be strictly construed.

"Congress shall make no law . . . abridging the freedom of speech, or of the press" seems clear enough, in one sense. The intent was to prevent any congressional enactments regulating speech or press, as by means of a licensing act, a tax act, or a seditious libel act. The framers meant Congress to be totally without power to enact legislation respecting the press, although the First Amendment does not say so. At the time of its adoption, the English common law definition of freedom of the press was the only one known and no other definition existed in America: the press was free in the absence of previous restraints. One could speak or publish as one pleased without censorship, but one was not exempt from punishment for libelous utterances, whether scandalizing public morals, religion, or government. Jefferson, for example, when writing his great bill for religious liberty provided that "opinions in matters of religion" should never be punished unless they incited "overt acts against peace and good order." But he never applied the same principle to political opinions. When drafting a constitution for Virginia in 1776 he included a provision that religious freedom "shall not be held to justify any seditious preaching or conversation against the authority of the civil government." Everyone favored unrestricted public discussion of issues, but "unrestricted" meant merely the absence of censorship before publication; people were accountable under the criminal law for licentious use of freedom.

Before 1798 the avant-garde among American libertarians staked everything on the principles of the Zenger case, which they thought beyond improvement. They believed that no greater liberty could be conceived than a right to publish unrestricted, if only a person being prosecuted could plead truth as a defense and if a jury had authority to determine the criminality of his words. Libertarians never rejected the substance of the law of criminal libels, not until the Sedition Act of 1798 embodied Zengerian principles and the prosecutions revealed those principles to be virtually worthless. The Sedition Act of 1798 was unconstitutional not because it abridged the freedom of the press but because it was an exercise of power in a forbidden field; the First Amendment in that regard left prosecutions for criminal libel exclusively to the states. The Sedition Act would have been unconstitutional even in the absence of the First Amendment.

The Fourth Amendment consists of two parts, one embodying the rule that searches and seizures shall not be "unreasonable," the other requiring specific warrants. The principle of the rule originated in England, although the English limitations on the search process were few and slight. The English used general warrants on a massive basis in everyday law enforcement as well as to search for evidence of political crimes like seditious libel. Colonial governments also made widespread use of general warrants, but in Massachusetts the intense opposition to them led to their displacement by specific warrants, beginning in the 1750s. England's reliance on writs of assistance, a form of general warrant, to uproot colonial customs violations in the 1760s led to American arguments supporting specific warrants. In 1774 the Continental Congress censured general warrants as unreasonable violations of privacy, and eight of the early state constitutions repudiated them. The Massachusetts constitution of 1780 contained the model that Madison relied upon when writing what became the Fourth Amendment.

The Fifth Amendment, the most varied of all, guarantees grand jury proceedings before one can be put to trial for a serious offense; bans double jeopardy; safeguards against compulsory self-incrimination; requires due process of law before deprivation of life, liberty, or property; and assures just compensation for public takings of private property. The Sixth Amendment clusters many rights of the criminally accused. The Eighth proscribes excessive bail, fines, or punishment. Of these amendments, the self-incrimination and due process clauses of the Fifth pose special problems. The self-incrimination clause, although controversial, embodies a fundamental principle of liberty and justice that is inherent in the very idea of a free government. It protects a right, which developed before most others, to ward off inquisitions; it is the central feature of our accusatory system of criminal justice. Although the framers were committed to perpetuating a system that minimized the possibilities of convicting the innocent, they were not less concerned about the humanity that the supreme law should show even to offenders. Protection of the rights reflected their judgment that the determination of guilt or innocence by just procedures, in which the accused made no unwilling contribution to his conviction, was more important than punishing the guilty.

As for due process of law, which was to become the most influential concept in American constitutional law, it had developed as a rough equivalent to the more commonly used "law of the land" clause of Magna Carta. Due process had no single or fixed meaning in England or America. Still evolving in meaning, it then referred narrowly to specific common law writs, broadly to regularized courses of legal proceeding in civil and criminal cases, and still more broadly to the very concept of fundamental law. The first American constitution to include a due process clause was the federal Constitution, thanks to Madison's preference for that phrasing instead of "the law of the land." But the inclusion of the clause raised problems. Due process signified customary or appropriate procedures but also connoted protection of the substantive rights of life, liberty, and property. The same clause necessarily safeguarded both procedural and substantive rights but thereby invited confusion in interpretation. Moreover, the clause was redundant because every clause of the Constitution supposedly has an independent meaning. Due process was constitutional shorthand for many particular rights that other clauses of the Fifth and Sixth Amendments explicitly protected, most obviously grand jury proceedings and trial by jury. Inclusion of the clause showed conventional deference to Magna Carta and enhanced assurances that the new national government would treat citizens in accustomed ways, especially in matters of criminal justice.

By completing the Constitution with the Bill of Rights the framers sounded a tocsin against the dangers of government oppression of the individual. They were endorsing the principle that liberty of expression in matters of private conscience and public opinion is basic to a free society; so too, the rights of the criminally accused are legitimate defenses of the individual against government, because the enduring interests of that society require justice to be done as fairly as possible. The Bill of Rights symbolized a new system of public morality based on the premise that government is but an instrument of man, its sovereignty held in subordination to his rights. As amended, the Constitution became a permanent reminder of its framers' view that the citizen is the master of his government, not its subject. Americans understood that the individual may be free only if the government is not.

BIBLIOGRAPHY

Adair, Douglass. "The Tenth Federalist Revisited," *William and Mary Quarterly*, VIII (January 1951), 48–67.

Adams, Willie Paul. *The First American Constitution* (Chapel Hill, 1980).

Bancroft, George. *History of the Formation of the Constitution of the United States* (New York,, 1882, 2 vols.).

Beard, Charles A. *An Economic Interpretation of the Constitution of the United States* (New York, 1913).

—— *The Supreme Court and the Constitution* (New York, 1912).

Benson, Lee. *Turner and Beard: American Historical Writing Reconsidered* (Glencoe, Ill., 1960).

Blinkhoff, Maurice. "The Influence of Charles Beard on American Historiography," *University of Buffalo Studies*, XII (May 1936), 16–36.

Brant, Irving. *The Bill of Rights: Its Origin and Meaning* (Indianapolis, 1965).

Brown, Robert E. *Reinterpretation of the Formation of the American Constitution* (Boston, 1963).

—— *Charles Beard and the Constitution* (Princeton, N.J., 1956).

Commager, Henry S. "The Constitution: Was It an Economic Document?" *American Heritage*, X (December 1958), 58–61, 100–03.

Crosskey, William W. *Politics and the Constitution* (Chicago, 1953, 2 vols.).

Curtis, George Ticknor. *History of the Origin, Formation, and Adoption of the Constitution* (New York, 1854–56, 2 vols.).

Diamond, Martin. "Democracy and the Federalist: A Reconsideration of the Framers' Intent," *American Political Science Review*, LIII (March 1959), 52–68.

Dumbauld, Edward. *The Constitution of the United States* (Norman, Okla., 1965).

—— *The Bill of Rights and What It Means Today* (Norman, Okla., 1957).

Eidelberg. *The Philosophy of the American Constitution: A Reinterpretation of the Intentions of the Founding Fathers* (New York, 1968).

Elkins, Stanley M., and Eric McKitrick. "The Founding Fathers: Young Men of the Revolution," *Political Science Quarterly*, LXXVI (June 1961), 181–216.

Farrand, Max. *The Framing of the Constitution* (New Haven, Conn., 1913).

307

Ferguson, E. James. *The Power of the Purse: A History of American Public Finance, 1776–1790* (Chapel Hill, N.C., 1961).

Fiske, John. *The Critical Period of American History* (Boston, 1888).

Hofstadter, Richard. *The Progressive Historian: Turner, Beard, and Parrington* (New York, 1970).

—— "Beard and the Constitution: The History of an Idea," *American Quarterly*, II (Fall 1950), 195–213.

Jameson, John F., ed. *Essays in the Constitutional History of the United States in the Formative Period, 1775–1789* (Boston, 1889).

Jensen, Merrill. *The New Nation: A History of the United States During the Confederation, 1781–1789* (New York, 1950).

—— "The Idea of a National Government during the American Revolution," *Political Science Quarterly*, LVIII (September 1943), 356–79.

—— *The Articles of Confederation: An Interpretation of the Social-Constitutional History of the American Revolution* (Wisconsin, 1940).

Kelly, Alfred H., W. A. Harbison and H. Belz. *The American Constitution: Its Origins and Development* (New York, 1983, 6th ed.).

Kenyon, Cecelia. "An Economic Interpretation of the Constitution After Fifty Years," *The Centennial Review*, VII (Summer 1963), 327–52.

—— "Men of Little Faith: the Anti-Federalists on the Nature of Representative Government," *William and Mary Quarterly*, XII (1955), 3–43.

Levy, Leonard. *Judgments: Essays on American Constitutional History* (Chicago, 1972).

—— *Origins of the Fifth Amendment: The Right Against Self-Incrimination* (New York, 1968).

—— *Legacy of Suppression: Freedom of Speech and Press in Early American History* (Cambridge, Mass., 1960).

Levy, Leonard W., and Dennis J. Mahoney, eds. *The Constitution: Essays on Its Framing and Ratification* (New York, 1987).

McDonald, Forrest. *E Pluribus Unum: The Formation of the American Republic, 1776–1790* (Boston, 1965).

—— *We the People: The Economic Origins of the Constitution* (Chicago, 1958).

McLaughlin, Andrew C. *A Constitutional History of the United States* (New York, 1935).

—— *The Foundations of American Constitutionalism* (New York, 1932).

—— *The Confederation and the Constitution* (New York, 1905).

Main, Jackson T. *The Antifederalists: Critics of the Constitution, 1781–1788* (Chapel Hill, N.C., 1961).

—— "Charles A. Beard and the Constitution: A Critical Review of Forrest McDonald's *We the People*, with a Rebuttal by Forrest McDonald," *William and Mary Quarterly*, XVII (January 1960), 82–110.

Morris, Richard B. "The Confederation Period and the American Historian," *William and Mary Quarterly*, XIII (April 1956), 139–56.

Murphy, William P. *The Triumph of Nationalism: State Sovereignty, the Founding Fathers, and the Making of the Constitution* (Chicago, 1967).

Onuf, Peter S. *The Origins of the Federal Republic: Jurisdictional Controversies in the United States, 1775–1787* (Philadelphia, 1983).

Perry, Richard L., and John C. Cooper, eds. *Sources of Our Liberties: Documentary Origins of Individual Liberties in the United States Constitution and Bill of Rights* (Chicago, 1959).

Rakove, Jack N. *The Beginnings of National Politics: An Interpretive History of the Continental Congress* (New York, 1979).

Roche, John P. "The Founding Fathers: A Reform Caucus in Action," *American Political Science Review*, LV (December 1961), 799–816.

Rossiter, Clinton. *1787: The Grand Convention* (New York, 1965).

Rutland, Robert A. *The Ordeal of the Constitution: The Antifederalists and the Ratification Struggle of 1787–1788* (Norman, Okla., 1966).

—— *The Birth of the Bill of Rights, 1776–1791* (Chapel Hill, N.C., 1955).

Schuyler, Robert L. *The Constitution of the United States* (New York, 1923).

Schwartz, Bernard. *The Bill of Rights: A Documentary History* (New York, 1971, 2 vols.).

Thomas, Robert E. "A Re-appraisal of Charles A. Beard's 'An Economic Interpretation of the Constitution of the United States'." *American Historical Review*, LVII (January 1952), 370–75.

Van Doren, Carl. *The Great Rehearsal: The Story of the Making and Ratifying of the Constitution of the United States* (New York, 1948).

Warren, Charles. *The Making of the Constitution* (Boston, 1928).

Wright, Benjamin F. *Consensus and Continuity, 1776–1787* (Boston, 1958).